ACROSS AN ANGRY SEA

LIEUTENANT GENERAL SIR CEDRIC DELVES

Across an Angry Sea

The SAS in the Falklands War

HURST & COMPANY, LONDON

First published in the United Kingdom in 2018 by
C. Hurst & Co. (Publishers) Ltd.,
41 Great Russell Street, London, WC1B 3PL
© Cedric Delves, 2018
Foreword © Max Hastings, 2018
All rights reserved.
Printed in the United Kingdom by Bell & Bain Ltd, Glasgow

Distributed in the United States, Canada and Latin America by
Oxford University Press, 198 Madison Avenue, New York, NY 10016,
United States of America

The right of Cedric Delves to be identified as the author of
this publication is asserted by him in accordance with the
Copyright, Designs and Patents Act, 1988.

A Cataloguing-in-Publication data record for this book
is available from the British Library.

ISBN: 9781787381124

This book is printed using paper from registered sustainable
and managed sources.

www.hurstpublishers.com

'We are the Pilgrims, master; we shall go
Always a little further; it may be
Beyond that last blue mountain barred with snow
Across that angry or that glimmering sea.'

James Elroy Flecker

carl rhodes

Dedicated to the 'Merry Men' of D Squadron Group, 22 SAS, South Atlantic, 1982, and for all our loved ones.

Contents

Author's Note

The 1982 seizure of the Falkland Islands by Argentina, then governed by a military junta, came as a profound shock to virtually all Britons. The realisation that the United Kingdom had so diminished in another nation's estimation that even a pariah state, as Argentina was in those years, might use military force to seize one of her dependant territories and its people and think that they could get away with it, was almost too much to take in. But then the country did feel to be on its uppers, its citizens at odds with each other, in what felt like terminal economic decline, weak and uncertain of its place in the world. The resulting war seemed to arrest all that, to draw a line under one age and set the conditions for another to re-ignite our national optimism and self-belief.

Many historians and commentators have spoken and written about the nature of the Falklands conflict, its purpose and consequences. Chief among their views is the idea that we went to war to defend a profound principle, one bigger than just the matter of putting right a wrong, one more important than the Falklands or even the Falkland Islanders. They point out that we fought to uphold the right of all people, everywhere, to self-determination and the exercise of power to secure that end, particularly where the enjoyment of that right had been usurped by aggression. It was a cause near impossible to refute. They would add that it made the world sit up, and take us seriously once more, that it showed our spirits intact, that we understood strategic power and how to use it, all in an intensely-felt, commonly-held purpose.

Things were stacked against us. The war was to be conducted in the South Atlantic, at the very gateway to the Antarctic, deep in the Western Hemisphere. It is easy now to overlook that there were then those in the US Administration uncertain about supporting our venture, but very many more who could see clearly the principle and all else at stake, and the need to stand by a staunch friend. Weather, distance, the local balance of forces, all these suggested Argentina would win. The eventual success of our armed forces surprised most if not all informed observers, including many in uniform. It caused the Soviet Union to reassess their assumptions about western resolve and fighting capacity. Years later, President Gorbachev would admit that British actions in the South Atlantic played a part in convincing the Soviet leadership that the USSR was never likely to win the Cold War.

As for national decline, the same historians would offer that the Task Force demonstrated Britain to be as much a concept as a place: distinct, credible, and counting for more than a worn out imperial has-been. We could still distinguish right from wrong, what was important, what was not, and had the initiative and wherewithal to do something about it. The operation suggested that there remained much to us waiting yet to emerge, that we were ready to move on, to achieve another form of greatness.

In short, historians, commentators and many others have observed that during those austral, early winter months of 1982 we showed the world, and perhaps most importantly ourselves, that we still had what it took: the ability to achieve through common sense and practicality steered by principle. It had worked before, it worked still, it had achieved great things once, it could do so again.

To someone who fought in the war, who lived through the disheartening years immediately before, it can feel now that we have lost much of the unity, consensus and optimism that followed immediately upon our success in the South Atlantic. We look to be once more troubled and adrift.

This then is the story of those 100 days as experienced by D Squadron, 22 SAS. I believe we fought as well as we could, with decency, in a manner consistent with our shared, national values. I believe we helped to achieve success, did our bit to uphold the principles for which the country had to fight. In so doing perhaps we too helped to bring the United Kingdom to a good place after years of relative decline. It came at a cost that must never be forgotten.

I wish it had been possible to mention all members of the Squadron and its attached personnel. For one reason or another this has not been possible. Even so, this is the story of their part in an historic event as seen through my eyes. I hope this account goes at least some way to mark their achievements and nobility of spirit, bringing a degree of comfort and pride most particularly to our families and loved ones. And I trust the record can serve to reassure the British public in whose name, to whose values and with whose treasure we dared to do our best.

Foreword

I first met Major Cedric Delves, as he then was, on an early June night in 1982, when I landed by Sea King below the summit of Mount Kent on East Falkland with 22 SAS's commanding officer Michael Rose. Men of Cedric's D Squadron were in the midst of a firefight with Argentine troops, causing tracer rounds to slash open the darkness and to frighten the wits out of me. The SAS, of course, appeared wholly unfazed. As we flew towards that landing zone amid a waist-high welter of weapons, equipment and mortar rounds, I shouted to Mike above the engine racket: 'what happens if the Argies start shelling the LZ?' The doughty colonel shrugged and shouted nonchalantly back: 'Oh well, who dares wins!' Those men were, and their successors remain to this day, among the finest professional warriors in the world, of whom Cedric is an outstanding exemplar. No man saw more than he did at the sharp end of the 1982 action in the South Atlantic. He has now compiled an extraordinarily vivid narrative of his squadron's experiences. It tells me, as it will tell countless readers, all manner of details about the war, and about the remarkable contribution of the SAS to British victory, that have been hitherto unknown.

The Falklands campaign was a freak of history, an anachronism such as the world will never see again. I always regretted that I was not of an age to accompany Kitchener's 1898 expedition up the Nile to destroy the Dervishes. The next best thing was surely to accompany Margaret Thatcher, by proxy at least, down to the South Atlantic to defeat the Argentines. That crazy expedition gave Britain's armed forces an opportunity to display their skills at their very best before defence cuts and the coming of a new century removed both the means by which such things could be done, and the environment in which they could take place. Cedric describes how, on the brink of battle, he found himself summoning up memories of old war movies with which he, like me, had grown up: *The Cruel Sea, Sink The Bismarck!, Battle of The River Plate*. Down South, I was struck by the manner in which many officers and men seemed to compose their own scripts from a Second World War template, like the frigate captain whom I heard broadcast to his crew as an Argentine air attack approached San Carlos: 'Remember lads, when they come: give 'em hell!' And Jeremy Larken, captain of the command ship *Fearless*, observed to his bridge team after an Argentine bomb landed in the nearby briny: 'There's only one thing to be said for this business. When it's all over and they make the movie, there will be no part whatsoever for Robert Redford'. At this, his Canadian navigating officer piped up: 'what about me?!'

An outstanding element of this fine book is its honesty about the weaknesses and failures of the SAS, as well as their huge virtues and successes. The regiment is buoyed by an institutional confidence in its own powers, in 1982 reinforced by the recent storming of the Iranian Embassy in London, an achievement that made it world-famous. Cedric writes: 'The SAS can trigger an almost visceral dislike among certain military professionals stemming in part possibly from British cultural distrust of elitism, aggravated by a presumption that we were indulged'. This is true. The Regiment is sometimes accused, occasionally justly, of behaving like a private army, its operations having nothing to do with the rest of the campaign or forces deployed, and no proper business of their commanders. On passage to the South Atlantic Michael Rose, a relatively junior officer, made plain to all and sundry, including correspondents such as myself, his disapproval of Admiral Sandy Woodward, the naval task force commander, together with his belief that the Argentine army was a rabble that would crumble 'given one good push'.

Events proved Rose largely right, but Brigadier Julian Thompson, the admirably sensible officer commanding 3 Commando Brigade, often said to me: 'Mike wouldn't accept that we were a one-shot force—that we had to get each step of the assault on the islands right. If we tried something risky and failed, we could not just go back and try it again a month later, as in World War II'. The British forces that retook the Falklands performed superbly, but were also extraordinarily lucky. The author here recounts the near-horror story of the preliminary South Georgia operation, where SAS recce missions by helicopter and sea came close to wiping out his squadron, amid blizzards on the Fortuna Glacier and the almost black-comic setbacks of small-boat landings. Those disasters were retrieved when all the lost parties were miraculously retrieved, and the Argentine garrison surrendered. But as Cedric writes ruefully, the regiment's 'basic boating skills ... has been sorely tested in the Antarctic "deep end" and found to be wanting'.

He provides a superb narrative of his experience leading the subsequent night raid on the Argentine airfield on Pebble Island, in which eleven enemy aircraft were destroyed without the loss of a man, an operation as brilliant as any that the SAS executed in North Africa, in their early Second World War incarnation. With their counterparts of the Special Boat Service, Delves and his men acted in support of the main British landings at San Carlos on 21 May. Thereafter, he led the initial assault on the key strategic height of Mount Kent. He writes with the benefit of all these experiences, in a fashion common to all warriors in all conflicts 'war would remain nine parts the management of cock-ups'. In the Falklands the SAS benefited from possession of various revolutionary technologies. One of his men shot down an Argentine Pucara ground-attack aircraft in what was the first operational use of a US Stinger shoulder-fired missile. They also possessed UHF satellite radios, which he describes as 'a thing of wonder to us', contrasted against the clumsiness of Morse messaging. Thanks to the generosity of Michael Rose, I dictated a dispatch from ice-bound Mount Kent to SAS headquarters at Hereford on a voice link better than the average phone call from Newbury to London. My appearance on an SAS communications net enthralled me and my readers, but enraged the Ministry of Defence.

The last SAS operation of the war, an intended diversionary assault on a hill outside Port Stanley named Cortley, dissolved into shambles which caused Cedric to think then and write now: 'Fuck, fuck, fuck'. A seaborne assault troop found itself pinned down under heavy enemy fire. The author admits of the operation 'it was not executed as we would have wished'. In the memorable words of Arthur Tedder, the airman who was Eisenhower's 1944–45 deputy in North-West Europe, 'war is organised confusion'.

The SAS's twenty-first-century operations remain shrouded in official secrecy, on the whole for good reasons. It is welcome that Cedric Delves, an outstanding Special Forces officer of enormous experience, has been able to tell this remarkable tale of one of his regiment's finest hours, of which I was an enthralled and indeed sometimes awed spectator. His book represents a fine tribute to his comrades who perished in the South Atlantic, and a gripping narrative of an extraordinary campaign.

MAX HASTINGS
August 2018

Glossary

AAR	Air to Air Refuelling
AAWC	Anti-Air Warfare Control
AOA	Amphibious Operating Area
ASW	Anti-Submarine Warfare
AVTUR	Aviation Turbine Fuel
BAS	British Antarctic Survey
Bergen	Back-pack
C2	Command and Control
CAP	Combat Air Patrol
CASEVAC	Casualty Evacuation
CLFFI	Commander Land Forces Falkland Islands
CO	Commanding Officer
COA	Course of Action
COMAW	Commander Amphibious Warfare
COMCEN	Communications Centre
COMMS	Communications
CT	Counter-Terrorist
DA	Direct Action
DZ	Drop-Zone
ETA	Estimated Time of Arrival
FARP	Forward Arming and Refuelling Point
FCS	Flight Control System
FIGAS	Falkland Islands' Government Air Service
FLEET	Fleet Headquarters, Northwood
FLIR	Forward Looking Infra-red
FMA	Force Maintenance Area
FOB	Forward Operating Base

GLOSSARY

HE	High Explosive
IED	Improvised Explosive Device
ILLUM	Illumination
K	Kilometre
LAW	Light Anti-Tank Weapon
LPD	Landing Platform Dock
LS	Landing Site
LSL	Landing Ship Logistic
LUP	Lying Up Position
LZ	Landing Zone
MFC	Mortar Fire Controller
MHE	Mechanical Handling Equipment
MILAN	Anti-tank Missile
MPA	Maritime Patrol Aircraft
NBC	Nuclear Biological Chemical
NOTICAS	Notification of Casualties
NVG	Night Vision Goggles
OMG	Operational Manoeuvre Group
OP	Observation Post
ORBAT	Order of Battle
OTX	Overseas Training Exercise
PAX	Passengers
PTSD	Post Traumatic Stress Disorder
PW	Prisoner of War
QRF	Quick Reaction Force
R & R	Rest and Recuperation
RAS	Resupply at Sea
RFA	Royal Fleet Auxiliary
RHQ	Regimental Headquarters
ROE	Rules of Engagement
SACLOS	Semi-automatic Control to Line of Sight
SAS	Special Air Service
SBS	Special Boat Service

GLOSSARY

SEP	Surrendered Enemy Personnel
SF	Special Forces
SHAR	Sea Harrier
SHQ	Squadron Headquarters
SITREP	Situation Report
SLR	Self-Loading Rifle
SSM	Squadron Sergeant Major
SSN	Nuclear Powered Submarine
STOL	Short Take-off and Landing
STUFT	Ships Taken Up from Trade
TACSAT	Tactical Satellite [radio]
TEZ	Total Exclusion Zone
TFR	Terrain Following Radar
VERTREP	Vertical Replenishment
WETREP	Weather Report
WILCO	Will Comply

Acknowledgements

The idea of a book was first seeded by Suzy my beloved wife who died far too young. She had no time for fake and never much cared for mystique particularly when it was so obviously just overblown bull. The notion took form more recently after a conversation with General Sir Michael Rose my CO at the time of the war. We could see that Sir Lawrence Freedman's masterful, authorised history of the conflict had already exposed the Regiment's role, but that first-hand recollections building on his record should have their place. I register my debt to both: Suzy for the original thought and her common sense, Mike for his promotion of the project, and his insights and recollections that inform it. Similarly to dearest Anne without whose constancy and support little would have been achieved. And David Lyon, great friend, who on this and over many years provided wisdom and sage advice, gently exposing any lax thinking.

To set the scene to the book I draw on the views of many historians and commentators who have written and spoken about the war; notable among them would be Julian Lindsey-French, memorably expressive in his stimulating address at the 30th Anniversary Dinner, Pangbourne. Concerning the higher direction of the war, the narrative employs knowledge and impressions gained at the time, and conversations with Mike and numerous others since. Otherwise I have relied upon Sir Lawrence Freedman's *Official History of the Falklands Campaign, Vol. II* as the acknowledged, authoritative record.

Few of us kept a diary; that was to contravene our operational procedures. Hence the story relies mostly upon our fading memories; for South Georgia, where necessary I nudged mine by consulting Roger Perkins' exhaustively researched book *Operation Paraquat*, an invaluable record written soon after the events. Chris Parry provided more on the epic deeds of the fabled helicopter, 'Humphrey', including the Fortuna missions. In addition he kept me straight on a wide range of things Navy. I thank him also for inviting Danny West and me to the HMS *Antrim* Wardroom Survivors dinner, to meet up with old shipmates. I have taken the liberty to set down one or two of their tales.

Many members of the Squadron lent help. Chief among them was Danny West. He was always there to respond with advice not least on Regimental matters, and otherwise keep the show going—much as he did during the war. Geordie Woods gave unsparingly too, helping to map the book, employing his phenomenal powers of recall. Poor Geordie died before completion. Graham Collins, another member of the Squadron's 'head-shed', offered a typically under-stated account of his and Nobby Clark's part in maintaining our logistics. I apologise to both for my inadequate description of their Herculean efforts; it would take a book in itself. That incorrigible free spirit Carl Rhodes subjected me to a comprehensive explanation of the seemingly arcane firing sequence of the Stinger missile. I did not include it, but took unhesitatingly from his many other recollections and offers of help. Roy Fonseka gave a deeply moving view of the events surrounding his capture. Mercifully the Argentinians behaved with decency. Roy has met socially with some of his captors since, a shining example of reconciliation. To Roy and to all the 'Merry Men', everyone of them giving so readily and generously not just in respect of this book, but all else, I express my gratitude, words that go nowhere near capturing my admiration of their spirit and selfless sense of duty.

It was my great fortune to receive guidance and encouragement from Professor Michael Burleigh the distinguished academic and commentator, another free spirit. It was he who introduced me to Hurst Publishers. Michael Dwyer of Hurst took the book on, lending all manner of assistance. I cannot begin to thank him sufficiently for his confidence in the work and practical support in bringing it to maturity. And Sir Max Hastings, in a way another comrade-in-arms, we dared together in a good cause; I thank him for his most perceptive foreword. With all this help, if things don't work out there can be only one person to blame—I accept full responsibility.

Maps

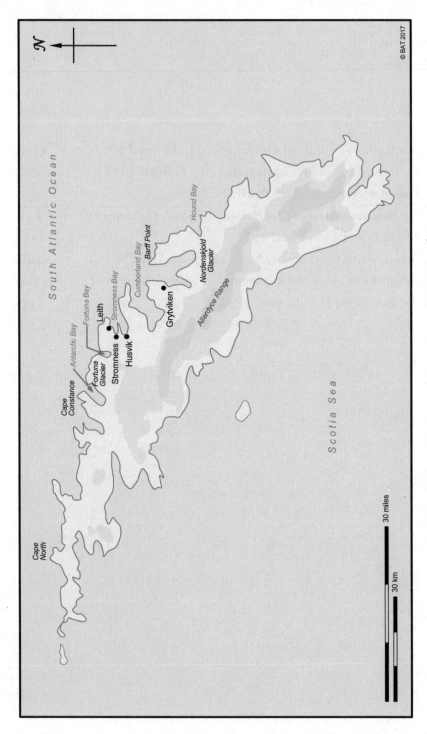

1: South Georgia, Area of Operations, 21–27 April 1982

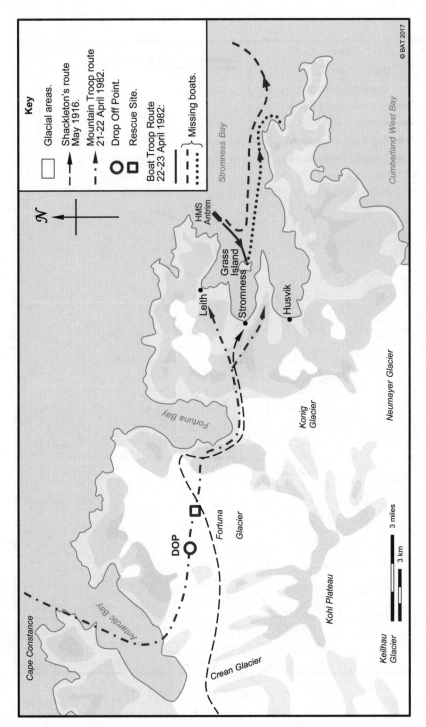

2: Reconnaissance of Stromess Bay, 21–25 April 1982

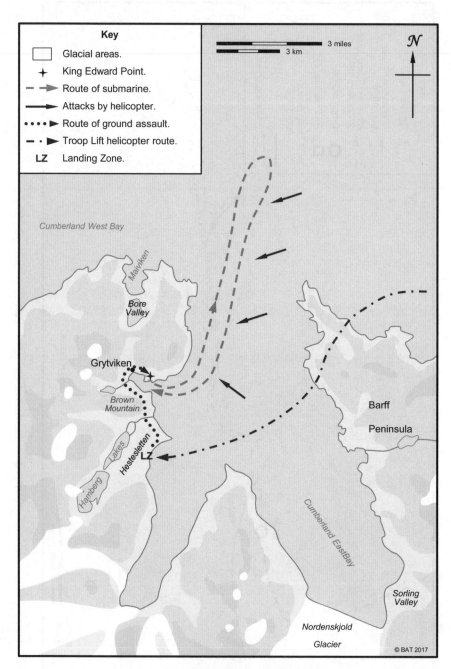

Key

Glacial areas.

✝ King Edward Point.

– ➔ Route of submarine.

━➤ Attacks by helicopter.

●●●●➤ Route of ground assault.

–·➤ Troop Lift helicopter route.

LZ Landing Zone.

3 miles

3 km

𝒩

Cumberland West Bay

Maiviken

Bore Valley

Grytviken

Brown Mountain

Lakes

Hamberg

Hestesletten

LZ

Barff Peninsula

Cumberland East Bay

Sorling Valley

Nordenskjold Glacier

© BAT 2017

3: Assault on Grytviken, 25 April 1982

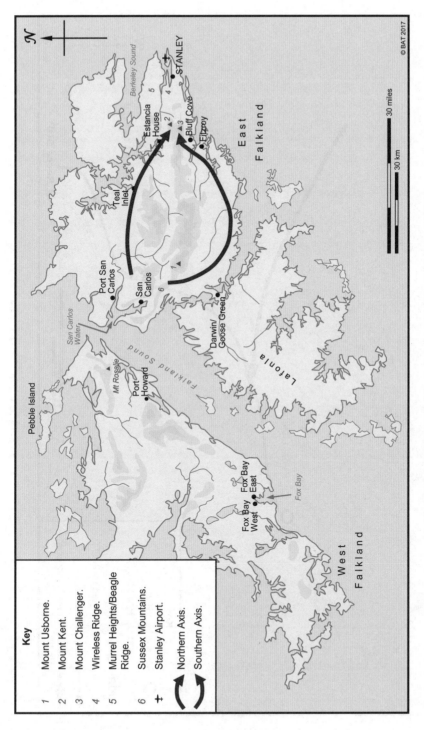

4: The Falklands Area of Operations, 11 May–15 June 1982

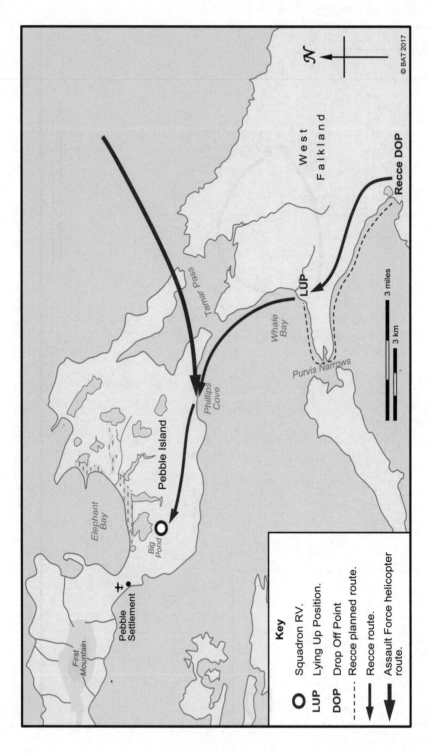

5: Pebble Island 11–15 May 1982

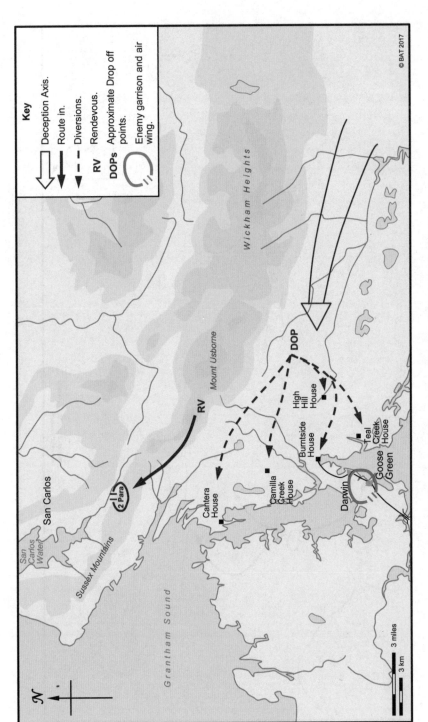

6: Diversionary Operations, Night of 20–21 May 1982

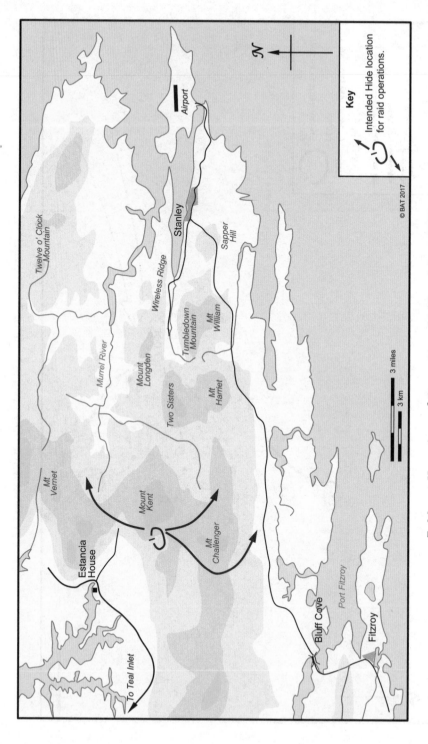

Key

Intended Hide location for raid operations.

Twelve o' Clock Mountain

Murrel River

Mt Vernet

Mount Kent

Mt Challenger

Estancia House

To Teal Inlet

Bluff Cove

Port Fitzroy

Fitzroy

Two Sisters

Mount Longden

Wireless Ridge

Tumbledown Mountain

Mt William

Mt Harriet

Sapper Hill

Stanley

Airport

3 km

3 miles

© BAT 2017

7: Mount Kent, Area of Operations, 24 May–3 June 1982

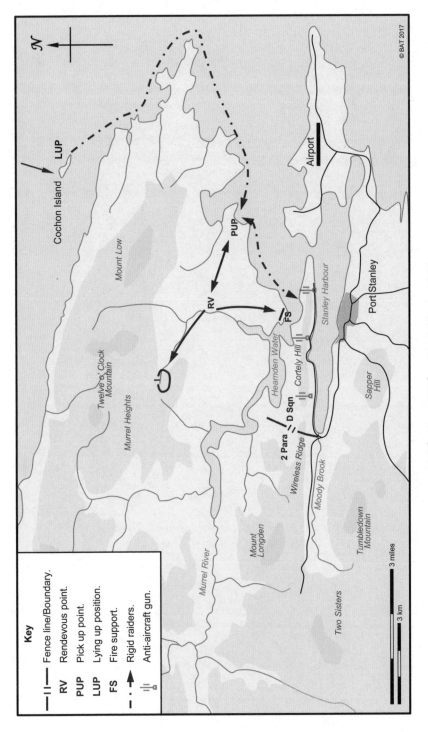

8: The Last Night, 14–15 June 1982

Key

—‖—	Fence line/Boundary.
RV	Rendevous point.
PUP	Pick up point.
LUP	Lying up position.
FS	Fire support.
·—·—	Rigid raiders.
⊨	Anti-aircraft gun.

Cochon Island

LUP

Mount Low

Twelve o' Clock Mountain

Murrel Heights

PUP

RV

FS

Airport

Stanley Harbour

Hearnden Water

Cortely Hill

Port Stanley

Sapper Hill

2 Para / D Sqn

Wireless Ridge

Moody Brook

Mount Longden

Murrel River

Tumbledown Mountain

Two Sisters

3 miles

3 km

N

Prologue

The light faded gradually, the grey turning to darkness as the aircraft carrier HMS *Hermes* made her move. Shouldering into mounting seas she and her two escort ships turned from the protection of the Task Force to make their dash through a known enemy submarine patrol area. They were heading for a point off the north coast of the Falklands.

It was 14 May 1982. A month earlier, in an unprovoked attack Argentina had seized Britain's South Atlantic dependencies. The United Kingdom responded by sending military forces to set free its people and take back its islands.

The SAS squadron that I commanded was aboard the carrier. Following the loss of HMS *Sheffield* to enemy air attack a few days previously, one of our reconnaissance parties had gone ashore to find eleven enemy aircraft at an airstrip on Pebble Island. The patrol provided us with all the information we needed to strike back. The carrier was repositioning to get our helicopters within range. It wasn't going to be easy to mount a raid. Weather alone threatened to exceed what men and machines might withstand.

The gale force winds had grown in intensity from the moment we set off, slowing the ships to a crawl. More time was lost as HMS *Broadsword*, one of the escorts, had had to slow still further to make repairs to her vital anti-aircraft system damaged by the mountainous waves.

Below decks we waited, grabbing a brew, having a smoke. I was on my third cigarette in an hour, feeling anxious and faintly off colour. Looking about me, I could detect the same tension in everyone else as they conversed in quiet tones or remained apart deep in their own thoughts. I was getting close to calling it off. The carefully calculated margins for error had been eroded bit by bit until scarcely anything was left; and we had yet to set foot ashore. Just then we all felt the ship slow down. The door opened, a naval officer stuck his head round, with a nod towards me, saying 'top side everyone, please.'

The Navy retained some faintly antiquated ways, the courteous 'please' noted and appreciated.

The cold was bitter, the night dense-black after the harsh lights below. The flight-deck heaved rhythmically up and down with a slight yaw, the wind howling across it, sucking air from our lungs, pushing determinedly as if to propel us over the nearby, open edge of the deck into the deadly sea beyond. The boundary between life and death appeared so absurdly fine.

We assembled in our pre-designated helicopter lifts as best we could, where the marshalling party directed us, roughly opposite an aircraft lashed to the deck. Wind, spray and driving rain blurred our vision. Howling gusts tore at the bergens on our backs. We wondered how the flight-deck crews could cope, with senses deadened by the brutality of the wind, rain, spray and intense cold.

Then, just as we were about to load, we were told to go back below; something to do with fuel. There was nothing for it. We did as we were told and made for the hatches. As we withdrew the helicopters started into life. They lifted and circled the carrier to dump fuel. The pilots and crews had been unable to prepare the airframes during the passage; the flight deck had been closed, too dangerous for use. Anyone stepping onto it might have been swept away.

Back down below we re-assembled with a mixture of resignation and disbelief. We could hardly credit it. This had to be it, time up, cancel. We did some more quick sums. It didn't look good. But perhaps it might still work, if all went smoothly from now on, no hold ups, no hiccups whatsoever. Shortly the call came to go back up. We did as invited, to face whatever the South Atlantic and the enemy might throw at us. We were probably out of time, but we had to give it a go.

PART I

SOUTH GEORGIA
With a Task Group: Feeling Our Way

1. Breaking Crisis

I had been in command of D Squadron 22 SAS for not much more than a year at the start of 1982. There was nothing to suggest that within a few months we would be at war, certainly not in the South Atlantic. So, as usual, with no war to fight the Squadron set about preparing for war. For most of the British Army at the time this meant getting ready to defend against the Soviet Union's Third Shock Army then threatening Central Europe. Not for us. Sure enough, we would have to cover the possibility of fighting alongside NATO allies should the Cold War go hot, but there was the greater likelihood of having to do other things else-where before that. We had no idea where or what. Hence our exercise in Kenya, knowing that whatever skills we honed there would need to be modified in the event for specific use elsewhere.

Lawrence Gallagher, D Squadron's Sergeant Major (SSM), and I had planned the training six months before. We took full account of the programme for the rest of the year—and the nature of the troops. They could be demanding, bordering upon awkward if not plain bloody-minded at times. This had much to do with the Regiment's 'unrelenting pursuit of excellence', the business of going 'always a little further'.[1] We would be forever striving for the heights, achieving one goal per-haps only to move straight onto the next. The troops were fully seized by the philosophy. And if that wasn't pressure enough, we placed no monopoly on a good idea. All were encouraged to contribute their thoughts, whatever their rank; any apparently questionable decision became open to challenge. Indeed, sometimes it could feel as though anything and everything would be contested as a matter of course, or

[1] Taken from *The Golden Road to Samarkand*, by James Elroy Flecker, and adopted by the post-war SAS to encapsulate its philosophy.

out of pure devilment. The troops wanted only the best, but compromise sat uneasily in the SAS. The relentless commitment kept all of us on our toes, particularly officers, the senior non-commissioned officers having additional, less formal ways of keeping dissent at comfortable levels. It helped, then, to have had Lawrence as SSM.

He had come to the Regiment fifteen years previously, from 9 Parachute Squadron Royal Engineers. This will mean something to anyone who knows the British Army, for 9 Squadron has form. Airborne Engineers, they are tough, hard, a bit of a handful to command, but plain inspiring on operations. Well, Lawrence was hard too, but in a gentle giant kind of way. A man of mild, sunny disposition he loved American country music, singing or humming it much of the time. He carried an air of quiet authority. Utterly fair-minded, he would always see the good in people, this deriving from his natural charm and optimism. Everyone held him in high regard. They liked him and accepted what he had to say, not because of his rank particularly. It never really worked like that in the SAS. They acted on what he said because it came from him, a man of stature in a wider, regimental sense. It was a great help to have his support. He much looked forward to the year, starting as it did in Kenya. He particularly liked that, getting a new year under way in a warm climate. Unfortunately, the exercise turned out to be neither as effective nor as much fun as we intended.

The Squadron had recently completed a spell on NATO commitments, moving to a period of 'stand-by' for operations world-wide. Towards the end of the year we would assume the highly stylised counter terrorist (CT) role. The terrorist threat tended to dominate. It took a determined effort to get our attention onto anything else. The Kenya Overseas Training Exercise (OTX) was designed to help by sharpening a range of skills that might be adapted as and when a crisis erupted and its specifics became known. Yet training was never going to be tidily compartmented. Operational skills bleed across from one area and discipline to another.

The four troops of the Squadron each specialised in a certain method of making entry into an operating area. They were named accordingly:

Air, Boat, Mountain, and Mobility (essentially, specialised vehicles). There was a degree of interoperability. For example, the Boat Troop would do an amount of rock climbing with Mountain Troop to enable them to scale cliffs. The Mobility Troop would maintain a few of Air Troop's skills, and vice versa. And tentatively related matters might fall to the troop with the assumed best or most relevant disposition: Air Troop had some expertise in anti-aircraft weapons for instance, Boat Troop a capacity for diving. Naturally, there were insertion skills common to all, including the much-disliked static-line parachuting.

The exercise would start with troop level specialisations, bringing these back up to good working levels. With that done, our handling of heavier, crew-served weapons would be refined before embarking upon advanced, live field-firing. The training would culminate in a gruelling two-sided exercise. The emphasis throughout was to be upon achieving a solid grounding in the basics without which it would be near impossible to adapt and extemporise in order to meet the demands of the unexpected.

It all went well enough until the final exercise. It was my decision that caused the problem. The exercise required the Squadron to insert up-country in two groups either side of a suspected guerrilla operating area; for this we had secured the use of a remote tribal area. It gave both groups a decent approach march of about twenty miles, followed by plenty of opportunity to exercise patrol and tracking skills. The error was to jump in using static-line parachutes, an insertion method we should maintain. But the drop-zones (DZs) lay at around 5,000–6,000 feet above sea level, the temperatures in the high 70s Fahrenheit.

Hot and high didn't mix well with the static-line parachutes then in use, not much better than those our founders jumped back in the 1940s. Even so, I felt obliged to go for parachuting, not least because the RAF had provided us a C130 for just that purpose. I could see Lawrence wasn't happy, but he too knew that we had to do it from time to time. The results were drastic, casualties excessive at 33 per cent. Fortunately, nothing life-changing, but nevertheless several injuries were grim, one soldier going into and then dragged out of a camel-thorn bush, the thorns two to three-inch steel-like spikes.

I managed to sustain some crush injury to both ankles. An x-ray years later showed fine sprays of bone. They were never quite the same. It kept me on my bum for about a week and hobbling through much of the early part of the coming war. None of us reported sick, preferring to stay available, not wanting to miss anything should it turn up during our spell on stand-by. Besides, we had plenty of patrol medics in the Squadron, most of them all too keen to practise their faintly suspect clinical skills, 'Tiger Balm' being one of their preferred cure-alls at the time, a surprisingly effective muscle pain relief ointment picked up in the Far East during the Regiment's Borneo days. If things did go really bad, there was the staff of the Regimental Medical Centre to fall back on. They knew the form, when to insist and when to let us self-mend.

As for fun, a constant tussle with the commander of the British training support staff based in Nairobi served to tarnish that. He didn't so much withhold assistance, as give it grudgingly. His people were willing, but he set an unhelpful tone, his animosity creating uncertainty among them. It proved difficult to identify his gripe. Perhaps he just came that way, a man with a chip on his shoulder. He certainly took an immediate dislike to us. It happens.

The SAS can trigger an almost visceral dislike among certain military professionals, possibly in part stemming from a British cultural distrust of elitism, aggravated by a perception that we were indulged, getting away with things others couldn't, given equipment they hadn't had and which they envied. There may have been some justification to their aversion, ironically resonating with our own sensibilities. Since coming to public attention two years previously at the Iranian Embassy siege[2] the Regiment had been subject to all manner of over-blown, fanciful glorification. This could be expected to play badly with colleagues, whose

[2] In May 1980 the SAS in support of the Metropolitan Police successfully stormed the Iranian embassy in London to free hostages seized by six armed terrorists.

own place and contribution might get overlooked, or reduced by comparison. Worse, the constant flummery stood to erode our own preferred humility, the publicity our need for a degree of obscurity.

One or two heads were turned, but wiser counsel within the Regiment continued to see that under ideal circumstances there should be no need for Special Forces; that conventional forces would have everything covered. But there were always gaps in coverage, such that the SAS was held to attend to those falling within its sphere. Notable among these would be the gathering of information; attacking in both physical and psychological 'depth'; and operating on the margins where conventional military capacities butt up to those of other regular and irregular security services.

Indeed, it could be said that one of the primary, unspecified responsibilities of the SAS concerned searching out and meeting gaps in our conventional capabilities. But hubris, real or perceived, could impair this objective, blinding ourselves to possibilities, and dissuading others from turning to us. It demanded constant vigilance, as even wholly respectable self-confidence and self-esteem were open to misinterpretation. For things to work well we should 'fit in', be tolerated if not embraced: no easy matter when the Regiment's *raison d'être* concerned challenging orthodoxy, seeking out what others might have missed or been unable to attend to themselves. Due humility helped.

It would always be difficult to predict future capability gaps. Accepting this and by extension the then hard reality that our continued existence depended upon an ability speedily to meet unexpected needs, the SAS was managed for change. By design or omission, at the time we were kept in a 'state of permanent impermanence', as I liked to think of it. The Regiment operated with considerable latitude. It then had a pretty clear field, with no other special operations force to its 'right', none to its 'left'. It was free to shift unfettered by organisational boundaries. Operating virtually alone within a broad arc of interest, it could track risks and threats, adjusting itself as needs arose.

Thus, one SAS generation might operate deep in the Malayan and Borneo jungles more or less independently; another in Dhofar working closely with the Sultan of Oman's tribal-based irregular forces, with its emphasis on civil affairs; and the 1980s generation on counter-terrorism, much of it in support of the police and other civil powers. Naturally commitments were more layered than that, especially given our Alliance obligations. The SAS could respond so fast to change as to appear at times to have got out in front. This demanded a certain opportunism on the part of Special Forces and required the active support of a High Command able to resource, tolerate, and even encourage the necessary and often uncomfortable departures from the norm. It was uncertainty by design, the promotion of genuine originality, true non-conformity, far removed from contrariness. The best SAS operators were those grounded in the disciplines of regular soldiering or those of the other Armed Services, able to gauge when, where and how to depart standard practice. The Regiment's leadership needed to be able to read the bigger, strategic and operational picture, seeing how Special Forces might adapt in order to extend the power of the conventional.

As the coming war unfolded, this requisite opportunism and attendant ease with extemporisation would generate friction. It sat uncomfortably with a certain type of soldier and marine, which was probably inevitable. Marines are naturally suspicious of 'loose cannons'. They are brought up to see that 'untidiness' had no place aboard Her Majesty's Ships. This may in part account for their deep-rooted discipline, patience and phenomenal steadiness. By contrast our constant, urgent shifting—to get out and about—to seek yet other ways to contribute must have been profoundly disturbing to some of them, all too easy to view as self-absorbed ill-discipline. Ironically, it didn't seem to bother the Navy, the very service that over hundreds of years had a hand in conditioning the Marines. The Navy simply accepted us for what we were, notably the submariners. They appeared altogether comfortable with responsible 'privateers' alongside, assisting the wider effort.

All that is as maybe. More assuredly, we never discovered what vexed the commander of the training staff in Nairobi. He was no submariner; and he certainly had no clue about Special Forces. But he knew he didn't like us; it might have been me. I had once asked whether he felt alright, not going mad, hadn't been in the 'sun' too long. This on the memorable occasion when he lurched towards me over his desk, clutching his head, snarling that that was the Army's problem: 'disobedience', before going on to explain that we should all be more like the Imperial Japanese Army of the 1930s/1940s, 'obedient to the last command'. Well, the common Japanese imperial soldier might have been fearsomely brave, but I didn't want to be pigeon-holed with their command ethos, and told him as much—politely. Besides, I wasn't aware that I had failed to deliver on any *banzai*-fuelled order of his.

Perhaps he wasn't keen on the British Army's then relatively recent interest in 'Mission Command' which involved telling someone not how to do a task, but what to achieve, leaving them to work out the 'how' with the wherewithal provided. It proceeded on the basis that war is untidy, that things rarely go to plan, and ultimately it depends upon individuals and groups on the spot exercising their own initiative to resolve matters. In effect, 'Mission Command', or *Auftragstaktik* (the technique had been central to the German way of war since the nineteenth century), sought to encourage initiative as an institutional approach to 'chaos', harnessing it in deliberate fashion in pursuit of higher designs. The method demands people be prepared to accept, even seek out, responsibility, to sort things for themselves if necessary and always to a common goal. There would be a lot of *Auftragstaktik* on display over the coming months.

When first broadcast on 19 March, along with most other people we didn't really appreciate the significance of Argentinian scrap-metal men landing on South Georgia without licence. To an extent, the diplomatic niceties and legal implications passed us by. It came over as so much ado about little. We paid it scant attention, turning our minds instead to the approaching tour on counter-terrorism. The invasion of the Falklands on 2 April was a different matter altogether. That truly hit hard. Along with most of the country, we were incensed by the images coming from Stanley. The sight of Royal Marines, lying on the ground, stood over by what we took to be Argentine Special Forces, was almost unbearable.

We couldn't help but notice that the Argentinians had some handy look-ing kit. But despite the odd bit of dispassionate professional interest, the strongest reaction had been outrage. We might be on our national uppers, but this was too much.

Back in Hereford, Ian Crooke, or 'Crooky', the Regimental Operations Officer and I stood in steady, drizzling rain discussing the situation and our possible place in it all. We didn't think to get out of the wet. We had thoughts only for how we might contribute to the fightback that must surely come. The Commanding Officer was doing what he could, but not much by way of direction was getting down to our base at Hereford. What to do? To sit on our hands didn't seem right. So, we started doing what anybody on stand-by for operations would do in a breaking crisis. We started reaching for the right maps and air photo-graphs, sorting kit and filling any gapped posts in our numbers, our Order of Battle (ORBAT).[3] It included getting Danny West back into the Squadron. There were a good many members of D Squadron on detach-ment, a normal situation, with the Reserve for instance, or NATO, or on long career courses. They all wanted to return. Several did get a place as we brought our four Troops fully up to strength. But, if I had anything to do with it, Danny was always coming as the Squadron's second-in-com-mand, to take over from me if that became necessary.

Danny was wise, sensible, notably quick-witted, a seriously accom-plished SAS officer with bags of operational experience. Born and bred in Glasgow, he had started his SAS career serving in 264 (SAS) Signals Squadron before transferring to D Squadron where he made his mark as a first-rate Arabist. He not only mastered Arabic, but also the local Dhofari dialect. It was where I first met him, eight years previously in Dhofar, the southernmost province of Oman, bordering Yemen. We were fighting a war there against Communist insurgents. Operation STORM was the SAS contribution to what came to be regarded as a model coun-ter-insurgency. Our role involved working with the Sultan's irregular

[3] Pronounced 'or bat', it refers to the essential organisation of any particular fighting force, manpower and hence equipment holdings.

forces. Many of them had fought previously on the enemy's side. Surrendered Enemy Personnel (SEPs), we knew them as the *firquat*, each group based in its own tribal area. We got on well, the SAS and the *fir-quat*, sharing deeply held character traits. They were tough, brave, independently-minded, tricky to handle on occasions, but faithful to us, and utterly loyal to the Sultan, whom we all recognised as 'the Boss'.

Danny had always known how to get the best out of his *firquat*. He admired them for their nobility of spirit. They reciprocated, respecting his openness, integrity and evident commitment to them. He would defuse any situation with wisdom and good humour. I sensed that we could be getting into another hard fight with the potential to get ugly. There were many with the necessary combat-skills, but Danny had more. He had that spiritual extra that makes the difference: a fine-tuned moral compass. Besides, he and Lawrence were close, the three of us friends. Add in Graham Collins to take care of our logistics, another friend; and Geordie Woods, to cover communications, another; and the Squadron 'head-shed' had a rock solid feel to it.

Meanwhile Crooky had been getting on with things too. As far as we were aware he had taken it upon himself to order and arrange our early move forward to Ascension Island, an obvious staging-point half-way down the Atlantic. Mike Rose, our Commanding Officer, had yet to secure us a specific role, spending much of his time on the road, cutting around such places as Plymouth, visiting 3 Commando Brigade, to ensure we didn't get overlooked as the Task Force was put together. But it was evident to everyone that if there was to be a war the SAS should be there, to serve as 'force multipliers', as NATO Americans then liked to refer to Special Forces. It was a useful expression, an altogether suitable way of viewing our place on major operations. It served to empha-sise that the 'supported' conventional forces were expected to win wars short of all-out nuclear conflict, but that the judicious use of 'support-ing' SF could help. We understood and wholly accepted the implication that our function was to supplement, extend the capacities of others.

Thus, Ian was probably more right than wrong to get us away as soon as he did. For, whatever the eventual, higher-level plan it must surely involve some form of SF advance-force effort. And other things were bound to come along, as the campaign got under way, revealing 'gaps' in conventional force coverage. The immediate priority seemed clear: get as far forward as possible, as soon as possible, to help prepare the way.

Nonetheless, a touch less haste might have led to a different war for the Squadron. G Squadron would be formally committed shortly after our move out, following a more measured, exhaustive force-generation and planning process than ours. G regularly trained in Norway over the winter months, their NATO role taking them into those northern regions alongside the Royal Marines. They were Arctic, cold-weather mountain experts and familiar with the workings of 3 Commando Brigade. D Squadron's NATO orientation was to the Mediterranean, the Southern Flank, an altogether different proposition.

D might have to cope with mountains and cold weather. And we had our mountain experts, among them Lofty Arthy, recently returned from a successful trip to Everest. There were others, including graduates of the renowned German mountain guides' course. Overall though, of the available SAS Squadrons, G was probably better prepared than D for the approaching challenges in close proximity to the Antarctic. But fate can turn on impulse and so it proved for us.

I did manage to catch Mike Rose before our departure, moments before the coaches were due to leave for RAF Brize Norton. He was in his office, on the phone. Things couldn't have been going well for us, not at all. Something was afoot, something had him agitated. He eventually finished his call. It had been his wife Angela; it concerned the Officers' Mess. He soon had me fully up to speed on an interior designer from an obscure, central department of public works who was insisting on an 'inappropriate carpet' for the place. He and Angela were right. The carpet eventually went into the Mess, proving to be truly horrid, a garish, busy pattern intended to disguise the marks of heavy foot-traffic—which it did with terrible efficiency. It was laid during the course of the war, because once certain institutional gears are in motion there is no stopping them. There it remained, in all its arresting, visual vigour for many, many years; indeed, until 22 SAS moved on, across town to another site, leaving it behind.

I eventually managed to cut in, explaining that I had to be off if we were to make our flight out of Brize, down to Ascension.

'Oh, yes. Of course, away you go then.' I got as far as the door, not far.

'Wait. I better tell you what to do, what to look out for.'

This wasn't going to be as straightforward as it might sound for as far as I was aware there were no developed or rehearsed higher-level plans for this eventuality. Large-scale, national contingency planning was focused on NATO, keeping open the North Atlantic lines of communication and fighting alongside allies on the Central Front. Our tri-service preparations reflected this long-standing strategic posture. The coming campaign was going to put our defence assumptions under severe pressure: the Army optimised for continental, armoured warfare, the Navy for keeping the North Atlantic sea lanes open, the Air Force for operations from hardened, fixed bases, all of us in close proximity to the national supply lines. Instead, at every level the three Services would be wrestling with the uncertainties attendant upon projecting force 8,000 miles down the Atlantic, through a harsh southern winter, only to launch an attack from the sea upon an enemy on land in fully prepared positions.

If all that were not challenging enough, there was also little or no retained institutional memory of major amphibious landing operations to draw upon either. Things once known had faded, been lost or neglected. But we all clung to one certainty: the need to demonstrate national resolve. At that moment we may not have been physically or conceptually fully up to speed, but morale was right where it needed to be. We were fighting mad, raring to go. Yes, I was aware of the significance of the moment, intrigued and excited by what might be coming. There truly was a sense of history, of being on the threshold of momentous events.

'Got a notebook?'

'Yep'.

'And pencil?' I nodded.

He started with, 'Direct Action'. I even wrote it down.

It happened to be the first of our three generic roles. The words appeared at the top of the first vu-foil slide of the Regimental brief, used to explain 22 SAS to visitors. It concerned the range of destructive activity that the Regiment might undertake, sabotage, demolitions, raiding, that kind of thing. Below that came 'Information Reporting', it might have been the other way round: covert surveillance and observation and such like. Sure enough, I got that. I didn't write it down. What next?

I knew the third, standard role would be a challenge, for it then involved operations with indigenous and irregular forces, partisans, the sort of work we had done in Dhofar with the *firqat*. There couldn't be much if any scope for that in our South Atlantic dependencies, populated by about 3,000 hardy people all under occupation, and countless, wholly impartial penguins, at liberty and mostly back out at sea for the winter. But there was no stopping Mike in full flow. My pencil poised in keen anticipation. This must be the one, the unique, defining 'force multiplier' thingy this time round. The contribution we would be remembered for, perhaps celebrated for. There was the very slightest suggestion of hesitation before it came:

'Specialist assistance to amphibious operations', delivered with a flourish and a broad 'gotcha-there' grin.

And with that the Squadron went to war, me supressing all lingering thoughts of the officers' Mess carpet, the Squadron steered by mission command in its purest form. Who could ask for more?

The nine-hour flight down to Ascension by VC10 proved uneventful, but it gave time to take stock. We were at full strength, mostly fit, save for the odd injury from Kenya. The lack of operational clarity held no particular concern. These were early days. We had enough to be getting on with. Something would turn up. The CO was working on that at his level. And we should look out for opportunities at ours. We had been given virtually free access to weapons and war stock: all the customary and familiar fire-arms and equipment, a handful that were not, including

MILAN anti-tank missiles. I made a note to ensure that we found time to practice on the less familiar items, preferably while on Ascension before embarking. In addition to our own Service gear and munitions, our American Special Forces friends, prominent among them that maverick Bucky Burruss, had already provided some seriously up-to-date stuff, most notably four or five Tactical Satellite radios (TACSAT).

UHF TACSAT was a thing of wonder to us; not to the Navy, more of a worry to them when they learnt we had it. They knew how easy UHF sets could be to pinpoint when transmitting. And they also appreciated that it could interfere with a ship's weapon and sensor systems. Unsurprisingly they set sensible conditions on its use. TACSAT enabled us to talk in real time over thousands of miles, the conversation secured as one spoke. This was a near unfathomable advance on our standard patrol communications that relied upon off-line encryption of messages transmitted over a HF link using hand keyed Morse. We would have to continue with HF through the war, having too few TACSAT for other than our principal command nodes. But it heralded the future.

The ability to converse from one part of the globe to another using a handheld device has become so commonplace as to excite only irritation when reception might fall off. Back then we had to learn to use the development with utmost care, to avoid circumventing the Navy's formal chain-of-command, for instance, which we could readily outpace. There would come moments when Hereford and our headquarters in London knew of the loss of a ship many hours before the Commander-in-Chief Fleet himself. Often we would sit on such information. Similarly, it enabled higher commanders to reach forward to subordinates, threatening to impair initiative at lower levels. We learnt to mitigate those risks too.

Over the course of the war, I would try to be unavailable for many of the more routine TACSAT calls. The Commanding Officer, based on HMS *Fearless* for much of the time, and the Operations Officer back in Hereford did most of the talking anyway. They discussed matters of considerable interest, but of no direct relevance to us. Since I was likely to go ashore behind enemy lines, thus prone to capture, I thought the less I knew the better. It's difficult to reveal what you don't know. I don't think they noticed my absences. They never mentioned it.

We assumed the Americans had to be listening-in on our TACSAT conferences. Access to Special Forces traffic was likely to yield insight into the UK's campaign-level thinking and activities. We did what we could to guard our conversations, cloaking them in veiled speech. As the war progressed, and the US showed increasingly open support, so we became correspondingly less concerned, never unwary.

As we taxied onto the ramp at Ascension, a Canadian voice came over the plane's address system, the captain of the VC10. He wished us all well, success and a safe return. It was a surprisingly moving moment. It made us aware that we were not alone. All good people must be with us. A terrible thing had been done and it needed to be put right. This certainty would be disturbed a little as the United States went through its diplomatic efforts. Some people erroneously saw parallels with Suez, when the US had understandably come down against us. But we all knew that this had to be different, the cause wholly noble. The US administration of President Ronald Reagan probably had to be seen to exhaust all avenues before openly supporting our use of force.

Eventually, all manner of good kit came out of the US arsenal, some of it shipped through Hereford for us courtesy of our close and dear friends in Special Forces. This had the top-level approval of the Secretary of Defence himself, Caspar Weinberger. A year or more later I had an opportunity to brief him on our experiences. The US Armed forces were then embarking upon a comprehensive programme of 'revitalization'—their term. This included their Special Operations Forces, and they were keen to learn from our experiences. I took advantage of the occasion to thank him at the end of the briefing. He gave me one of his wry, faintly shy smiles, making light of the matter. He was a true gentleman, a staunch friend of the United Kingdom.

2. Getting Forward

Ascension was hot, sunny and harshly bright. It had that back-water feeling to it. A heavy silence was relieved by the faintest whisper of a steady yet perfectly gentle breeze, weighted with warm dampness from the surrounding deep blue ocean. The muffled sound of a vehicle or item of airfield machinery occasionally carried through the heat-haze, across the shimmering airfield ramp. Little moved. It wasn't exactly what we had expected, but then we hadn't really known what to expect. Crooky had told us to get to the island to await, then embark the *Fort Austin*, a type of naval ship called an 'RFA'. We soon learnt to appreciate the Royal Fleet Auxiliary and its ships. They made things possible in that unheralded way of the best logistical organisations. They were indispensable, seemingly always in the right place at the right time with their vital support: fuel, food, munitions; things without which operations would grind to a halt.

Danny and I were directed towards a hangar to the side of the ramp. There we found a Royal Navy lieutenant commander sitting at that essential piece of British military expeditionary equipment, the six-foot, collapsible table. It looked as though it would collapse at any moment despite holding little more than a near-empty tray hosting a couple of sheets of paper weighed down by a lump of local lava rock. This was it, the most forward element of our military response to Argentina's vile act of aggression, the very tip of our avenging forces lancing out of the UK: a folding table placed carefully as to get the sun, though not too much, some breeze, but out of the worst of any wind.

We explained ourselves to the placid, engaging naval officer apparently logging people in, some out, by hand, with pen and ink into a ledger. We mentioned that we needed to get onto an RFA vessel called

Fort Austin. He listened patiently in a kindly, indulgent sort of way, seeing that we were wrestling with matters unfamiliar. He explained that *Fort Austin* was at sea, a number of days away he believed, before talking about fur traps. No, she was definitely not in harbour. Ascension had no harbour. This seemed to get him back onto the subject of fur traps. Danny and I were struggling, before long pretty perplexed. He could see it and offered that it might be best for us to go and find somewhere to stay, then drop by from time to time for news. Why didn't we try a place called Two Boats?

'Up there,' he replied, pointing towards a steep, greenish hill emerging out of the otherwise brown landscape, shimmering in the heat. 'There's a school, probably still empty. You're the first people I've mentioned it to'. It sounded like good advice. We took it.

As we withdrew I asked Danny about the fur-trapping thing. 'Not a clue,' he confessed. 'Didn't like to ask.'

We learnt that VERTREP meant vertical replenishment, Navy jargon, shorthand for lifting people and stuff from one ship to another, or elsewhere, by helicopter. Over the next weeks it became all-too-familiar, as we embarked and disembarked seven ships in total, always by helicopter.

Two Boats proved a good move. There was indeed an empty school. We settled in. Graham took the opportunity to sort through our fifteen metric tons of stores. It could have been more—it felt like it—surely not less. Our approach to logistics was basic. Above all we aimed for self-sufficiency, keeping our specialist equipment holdings and reserves of materiel and ammunition with us wherever we went. Graham intended to manage everything centrally, with the exception of personal items, including small arms. When needed, each man would be issued precisely what he required for any given mission. Otherwise, we would scrounge more general consumables from whoever might be hosting us at any given moment.

To my knowledge, we received no comprehensive instructions concerning replenishment, or the shipboard handling and control of munitions; but essential autarky worked for us, albeit demanding a truly

heroic effort by Graham and his co-opted helpers. During the operation, taking account of the number of moves between ships, they would
lift equipment and stores equal to 150 metric tons. Much of it was
packaged in oversize wicker hampers. All items were man handled onto
and off the helicopters, into and out of the bowels of ships, down narrow corridors, through hatches, without the benefit of mechanical
equipment to ease the task. It included boats, outboard motors, canoes,
mountain equipment, anti-tank missiles, air-defence missiles, mortar
ammunition, everything a squadron might need. Graham had considered all eventualities. We wanted for nothing in his gift.

Indeed, about the only things drawn from the ships on a regular basis
were fresh food, tobacco, nutty bars and such fancy goods, including
beer. Thank goodness we didn't fight dry; the odd beer did wonders for
morale, and at one point probably saved my life.

While Graham sorted through our logistics, the rest of us checked
our personal equipment. We set up a range to zero our weapons, taking
the opportunity to acquaint ourselves with the MILAN missile and
other recently acquired weapons and items. I had never much liked the
standard issue Self-Loading Rifle (SLR), which I found large and
unwieldy, its ammunition heavy. It could fire only one-at-a-time: one
trigger pull, one shot. I preferred something lighter to handle, with
more weight-efficient ammunition, a weapon that could be fired on
automatic in a tight spot. The American M16 would have been the
answer. We didn't have any of those; but we had some early models of
the type, AR15 Armalites dating from the Borneo Confrontation of the
1960s. I had managed to get myself one. It seemed to work; but on
cleaning it after test firing, I found that over the decades much of the
rifling had been shot away, leaving little in the first third of the barrel.
But never mind, at one hundred yards it had sent the beer cans spinning.
Besides, if I was doing things right, I shouldn't need to fire. My job
involved getting the troops to the point of contact, for them to do the
clever, sharp-end stuff. If it ever required me to do any shooting, we
would be in trouble, the likely ranges short, my barrel-wear wholly
irrelevant to the outcome.

After a couple of days RFA *Fort Austin* turned up. The ever-helpful Naval Officer, who by then had two six-foot tables, arranged the necessary 'fur-trapping'. And before too long there we were, all of us afloat, almost immediately underway to RAS[1] (Resupply At Sea) the ice patrol ship HMS *Endurance* at that moment approaching Ascension from the South, having successfully evaded the invading Argentine forces down at South Georgia.

At the time, the *Fort Austin* was the flag-ship of the Royal Fleet Auxiliary and it showed in her handsome proportions and impeccable turn out. Her commander Commodore Sam Dunlop and his crew made us most welcome, the food coming as a singular treat after Graham's entirely respectable, perfectly understood best efforts back at Two Boats. We took the opportunity to sort out equipment, managing to test our boats with worrying results. The outboard motors proved temperamental. 16 Troop even managed to get in some free fall parachuting, as much to get 'South Atlantic' into their log books, I suspected, as to prepare for war. We all managed some fitness training, running miles around *Fort Austin's* decks. Physical Exercise (PE) would become a problem as the war went on, there being limited deck space on a warship, precious little space of any description. Further south, the seas would make the decks unsafe. And in closer proximity to the enemy we needed to keep out of the way, to allow the Navy to fight the ships. In the tropics, aboard *Fort Austin* there were no such complications, save for one thing.

We had been embarked a couple of days, making steady, comfortable passage south down the balmy waters of the mid Atlantic, soaking up the sun when Sam Dunlop called for me to join him in his day cabin. I was ushered into a delightfully airy and spacious, sunlit room. Warm,

---

[1] As a piece of Navy speak, RAS appeared to have wide utility, apparently referring to any form of acquisition, authorised or otherwise. For instance, our helpful naval officer may have RASed his six foot tables from the RAF's air-movers, who always seemed to have plenty, being an indispensible part of their notorious 'processing' methods when conducted under austere conditions.

moist tropical air wafted in through the open, generously proportioned windows. The tasteful, chintzy loose covers and matching curtains complimented the varnished glow of the woodwork adding to the sense of calm, comfortable refinement. He offered me a cup of tea, inviting me to take a chair. I accepted, sinking into a surprisingly, deep armchair, somehow managing to avoid spilling my tea with its biscuit nestled in the saucer. 'I'll come straight to it', he said, a disarming twinkle in his eye. 'Feel free to exercise on the decks, by all means, but could you get your people to cover up, wear a singlet or something in addition to just boots and shorts?' I must have looked a bit puzzled for he went on to explain. 'It's unsettling the crew. Well, a number of them'. Now I was puzzled. 'Passions have been aroused,' he added, 'it's caused arguments and an amount of upset'. The penny dropped. I got Lawrence onto it straight away.

We looked forward to our RV with HMS *Endurance*. She and her pugnacious commander, Captain Nick Barker, had gained quite a reputation. Ordered to put up a token resistance to the invading Argentinians, her small detachment of Royal Marines had managed to cripple an enemy frigate and shoot down a helicopter. Not a bad effort for a red hulled research vessel that must have departed the UK for the Antarctic never expecting to go to war. She and her ship's company served as a shining example to us all, something of a disturbing portent perhaps to our enemy. We hoped to add to her achievements, but had yet to receive word of any tasking for ourselves.

The answer came soon enough. We learnt that a task group of warships with a marine company and a small team of SBS-embarked had been despatched to take back South Georgia. It did momentarily cross our minds that this was off the main effort.[2] However, on further thought it made political sense to demonstrate resolve with an early,

[2] Main Effort has specific military meaning, referring to the physical elements or action(s) considered most critical to overall mission success. As such it should get the available resources it needs, as and when required. Its designation concentrates effort.

elegant riposte. A timely success should assist our diplomacy. But strategy belonged to others, not for us to lose sleep over, even though it always helps to have a credible target to steer towards. We were simply itching for a fight, looking for an opportunity to hit back—and, yes, to prove ourselves. We were young, fit and full of vim and vigour. If the High Command wanted to recover South Georgia, that was more than good enough for us.

I received instructions to reinforce the Task Group with Mountain Troop. They were to embark *Endurance*. She too would be joining the Group to lend her expertise, turning south as soon as she completed her RAS. Disappointingly there was nothing for the rest of us. We were to stay put on *Fort Austin*.

I reacted badly. We knew that G Squadron had been mobilised. They were still in the UK within reach of the national and campaign level planners; by virtue of this, they were probably well placed to pick up advance force reconnaissance requirements as these emerged from the planning. This should leave D Squadron to take on other things, Direct Action, raids and such. It could involve us operating at squadron strength. This division of labour did eventually emerge, perhaps less by design, more as a consequence of our quick getaway. But one way or another, right then it didn't seem an entirely good idea to be spreading the Squadron across too many RFAs, warships and task groups, any one of which could sail off to yet another part of this vast ocean, fragmenting my command.

With things in their nascent state, I felt that as far as practicable the Squadron should stay together, ready to meet the higher level SF tasking that was bound eventually to come down to us and probably at scale. And I was starting to worry about *Fort Austin* herself: an ammunition ship rumoured to be carrying nuclear munitions. She didn't seem the type of vessel the Navy would push far forward—and yet forward and beyond was the place we should be making for, our natural habitat.[3]

[3] I couldn't have been more wrong, she did go forward, right into the Amphibious Operating area of San Carlos at the height of the Argentinian

Things were starting to feel messy. The immediate priority had to be unit integrity, getting back together. Beyond that? Frankly a diversion to South Georgia held out the seductive prospect of some early action, but eventually we must get to a platform or tight group of ships likely to get us all to the area of Main Effort. Certainly, cruising the tropics in mid-supply chain with the Squadron dispersed didn't feel right, whichever way one came at it.

Four days' sailing saw us at the RV with HMS *Endurance*. She did her RAS while we 'cross-decked' 19 (Mountain) Troop as ordered. Presently, bobbing and bouncing jauntily, the bright red *Endurance* turned back south soon fading from our wistful gaze with one quarter of my fighting strength, most of whom had to be feeling decidedly queasy after the sedate, stately progress of *Fort Austin*.

My misgivings intensified. Danny and I talked it over. Aside from 19 Troop's deployment, still nothing solid had come down from Hereford for the remainder of us. It seemed like the moment had come to start shaping our own destiny. The RFA was due to RAS the remainder of the South Georgia Task Group the following day. This offered us the opportunity to embark the rest of the Squadron. This should not only improve our ability to respond to subsequent tasking, getting back together, but it would further strengthen the South Georgia expedition, add to its resilience, surely a welcome thing.

There was a possibility that the South Georgia affair might become drawn-out, putting at risk our availability for other work, I supposed. That seemed unlikely, the whole basis of Operation Paraquet, as it was called, being founded upon getting at the enemy hard and fast where he appeared to be at his weakest. People were looking for a quick win. The risk felt acceptable, and it felt right to pitch in. We would try our luck.

---

air raids (21–25 May), carrying several hundred tons of ammunition. Sam Dunlop is quoted as saying to one of his junior officers, during a particularly heavy raid, 'you don't have to worry about going down with this ship, you'll only ever go up.'

There were two men to persuade: Captain Brian Young RN commanding HMS *Antrim*, the Task Group Commander, and Major Guy Sheridan, Royal Marines, his land-force commander. Clearly the two of them had their orders that included taking 19 Troop. This suggested that operational planners somewhere were starting to get a grip on things. Hence, this wasn't going to be a 'given', persuading the Task Group to take the rest of us without explicit higher authority. And I didn't want to compound our problems by encouraging another round of cherry picking, fragmenting the Squadron even more than it already was. It had to be all of us or nothing more. Tricky. But the Task Group would be in a hurry. And *Fort Austin* had orders to turn north directly after the RAS. Nobody would want to spend time faffing around. If I could get the pitch right, Young and Sheridan might simply exercise their initiative and take the offer, turning a Nelsonian blind eye to the matter of approvals, protocol and whatnot. With all the uncertainty, there had to be a fair chance of getting away with it. I would have to be wholly convincing, sounding more knowledgeable about the situation than was strictly the case, with authority to embark the Squadron, to do as I saw fit with my command.

The matter of regimental authority had to be more or less the case, given the instructions I had received in the CO's office and the spirit in which they were given. We had received nothing more specific since, save for the Mountain Troop instruction; nor did I feel any strong desire to seek greater clarity. I rarely did, throughout the war. I had enough direction. In this instance, the Operations Officer's instruction to board *Fort Austin* sounded a bit like expediency; there had been no indication as to why, aside from getting forward, nor for how long. When it came to seizing a fleeting chance Crooky had form; he would understand our move, surely support it, if necessary square it with the CO. And I knew that if Mike didn't have anything for us, he would expect us to find work for ourselves: South Georgia should do for a start.

In the event, the pitch to the Task Group went easier than expected. Brian Young was a very decent, modest man, placid in nature. Guy

Sheridan was similarly practical, measured and thoughtful. There was a sense of level-headed dependability about the two of them. This Task Group appeared to be in capable hands. They allowed me to make my pitch. I went at it brazenly as Danny and I had rehearsed the previous evening, intending to take and hold the initiative, to make an offer they really shouldn't refuse. I started by seeking their assurance. I asked them to tell me what they might have in mind for us before I embarked the Squadron, because I couldn't be expected to commit my entire unit without full justification. Aside from first unsettling them before offering them some certainty, I hoped they would infer from this that I had some conditional authority, even instruction to make available the whole 'enchilada'. It looked to be working, for they both appeared momentarily nonplussed, glancing across at one another, neither knowing quite how to respond. I drove on, offering to help them decide by outlining our capabilities. I laid it on thick: we were at full strength, fresh from work-up training with a range of weapons and skills; we had people just back from Everest, others skilled in small boat work and so on. We might do reconnaissance, or spearhead covert assaults and many other such things concurrently or sequentially. It was truly ladled on.

They were soon convinced, seeing that something powerfully useful was on offer that might enhance the Task Group's operational flexibility. But Young, being a careful and thorough man did consult with Northwood; persuasively as it turned out for shortly we were all invited aboard. I returned to *Fort Austin* with the warm, rosy feeling of having just blagged our way into an operation. Before long we had completed the VERTREP, most of us to HMS *Antrim*, the flagship, the remainder to HMS *Plymouth*, all of us now with a shared mission, in the same bit of ocean. Unorthodox in commission, our involvement turned out for the best, the additional troops proving instrumental when the decisive moment came.

HMS *Antrim* was a good-sized warship, a thoroughbred even to our untutored eyes. She had a twin gun turret where one should be; a bank of EXOCET missiles; a large flight deck complete with helicopter; and lots of other stuff hanging off her plentiful super-structure. She just looked and felt the part in a Grand Fleet kind of way: powerful, imposing, handsome, faintly imperial. We would develop a refined feel for ships. The moment we stepped onto[4] one, somehow we would know: happy, not that happy, welcoming, up for it, efficient, that sort of thing. As for a naval unit's maritime capabilities and function, those remained largely obscure to me. I never gained a sure grip on those aspects. I saw ships more in terms of whether or not they could support our operations: did it have a gun, how big was the flight deck and the like.

HMS *Antrim* came across as purposeful, dependable, highly professional yet friendly, at ease with herself. She had been built at Govan by the Upper Clyde ship-builders twenty or more years previously: a plaque above a central stairway testified to this. Fitted out as a potential flagship, she sported a sizeable admiral's quarters. With no admiral to occupy them, Captain Young made the space available to the embarked forces, the day cabin serving as a joint operations-room where we soon settled in to commence our planning.

Guy Sheridan and I were the same rank: major. I knew enough about the Royal Marines to know that they could view their majors as being the equivalent to the Army's lieutenant-colonels, an anomaly that one or two of them might draw upon occasionally should it suit. Guy never mentioned it. He didn't need to. He was the designated land-force Commander and Brian Young our Boss: both these things were indisputably clear.

There was never any confusion about the Task Group's chain of command. And mostly it functioned as it should, effectively and with civility. I experienced one notable spat, a minor tactical incident involving neither Guy nor the 'Boss'. To guard against issues such as inappropriate tasking, inadequate combat support, and similar difficulties, the Regiment maintained its own discrete chain of command in those days,

---

[4] The Royal Navy say that they are 'in' ships, rather than on, living and operating as a community.

enabling us to refer any issues up and down for resolution, if necessary co-opting higher authorities. This facility would be used sparingly, the preference being always to operate agreeably within the supported command structures. Thus we would always attempt to position our-selves alongside the highest levels of operational command in any situ-ation. In this case I believed that our principles had been adhered to: I was alongside the overall commander and his deputy, and my troops were under command of their own officers. Both Young and Sheridan understood and seemed okay with things. And I made certain that the Squadron knew where we all stood.

I was conscious of the cultural differences that could ruffle relations when working alongside or with conventional forces, our apparently casual regard for rank and the use of first names between ourselves being obvious, outward social manifestations. There were other things that would grate, chief among them in planning terms the 'Chinese parliament', which brought people together early in the assessment process to ensure that nobody's relevant thoughts got overlooked. If you had a suggestion to make, an idea, no matter your rank, we believed it should be heard. The parliament sought to harness the power of collective wisdom, simultaneously guarding against template solutions. We were aware of the dangers of 'group think'; the parlia-ment, comprising strong personalities, all capable of independent thought, was unlikely to commit that error. It could get out of hand, certainly look Bolshevik viewed from the outside. To work optimally, all involved had to exercise a degree of self-discipline, and the boss needed to know when to draw the strands together and to make the decision. Once the process had been completed, all must shut up and get on with whatever had been decided. If Guy found it odd, he never said; and Captain Young never got to see it in action.

More important were our respective philosophical approaches to the actual operation. The SAS, SBS and Marines were very much aligned, the Navy in another place, any differences being founded not so much on the contrasting disciplines of our operational environments as on the respective levels of operational experience at that initial stage in the conflict. The Navy had not been in all-out shooting action for some time. Guy, his people and ourselves had been at it one way or another for a while. We were certainly respectful of the enemy ashore, the Navy perhaps a touch less so.

The Regiment had been on operations almost continuously since the 1950s. We had learnt never to underestimate the human genius for violence. Perhaps that had made us a touch careful, inclined to circumspection. We were especially wary when entering into any new relationship with an enemy. From the outset, often one side or the other would enjoy an advantage. But as adversaries got the measure of one another, a see-sawing or leap-frogging dynamic might take hold as one of the adversaries moved ahead, only to be overtaken by the other and so on, on a rising trajectory of sophistication. The process is maintained until one or the other fails to keep up.[5] We had experienced this in Dhofar, where we came out on top. And the Army was feeling it in Northern Ireland at the time, the IRA proving an ingenious opponent.

Our relationship with Argentina's armed forces was well underway. Concerning operations in South Georgia, we all knew of Lieutenant Keith Mills' heroic performance at Grytviken (Map 1). He and his tiny detachment of Marines had inflicted substantial damage on the invading Argentine Task Group.[6] There were those who saw this as confirming

[5] My US Special Forces friend Pete Schoomaker took the theme further with me on one occasion, noting how it could be given an additional, often tense, frustrating twist when political leadership quite rightly sought to control any escalation, to impose limits on a conflict, particularly when the situation was deemed to be not nationally life-threatening. I believe he called it 'just enough'. He was always notably clear thinking and eventually came to head US Special Operations Forces before becoming Chief of Staff of the US Army.

[6] Lieutenant Keith Mills, Royal Marines, was landed by HMS *Endurance* with orders to put up a token resistance to the Argentine invasion of South Georgia. Over a two hour period he damaged a corvette, ARA *Guerrico*, that took no further part in the war, shot down a Puma helicopter and inflicted

our innate superiority; by contrast, we took the view that the Argentinians would probably have learnt from it. We were facing a clear reversal of role. This time round it would be a Royal Navy task group doing the seizing, the enemy the defending. Having been embarrassed on their offensive move, the Argentinians must surely know how to return the favour and more.

The enemy had spearheaded the opening round with a frigate, more than a match for *Endurance*, carrying sufficient troops to overwhelm her complement of embarked Marines. Had they reinforced since, knowing that we would return with at least one warship, probably more? How did they propose to deal with that if they couldn't outbid us in numbers of ships? The Navy must have an idea, but mines, submarines, armed helicopters and land-based anti-ship missiles sprang to our untutored minds. On land one could expect a defending force of anything from a platoon to a company group. We were certain that a British commander would very likely employ nothing less than a sub-unit, a company-group, for the conduct of such an important, independent and isolated task. We would be wise to work on the assumption that our enemy would do likewise, defend with at least a company group and that they would have ways to counter our warships and helicopters.

Conventional wisdom held that an attacker enjoys a three-to-one advantage to ensure success over an enemy in prepared defence; if they had a company-group, we should be attacking with a battle-group of three companies. We didn't have anything approaching the convention. We had one company-group of Royal Marines, the right type of troops for a fist-fight, and an SAS squadron more suited to covert operations, operating in small teams against enemy weakness, not strength. We would have to find a way round our assumed numerical deficit.

---

a number of casualties on the enemy. His team suffered one injured. They were repatriated to the United Kingdom, Mills receiving a well-earned Distinguished Service Cross in recognition of his and his men's superb example.

The apparent insufficiency did not unduly concern us; after all we had several powerful capabilities to tip things in our favour: two warships with guns and three armed helicopters for 'starters'. And in most respects, the Regiment's fighting ethos proceeded from assumed numerical inferiority, turning 'small' to advantage. Rather than scale, we sought to exploit other things to gain an edge, chief among them precision, surprise and daring. In the offence, this meant searching out an enemy's vulnerability, getting up on it by stealth before striking with overwhelming local, physical and psychological superiority. Preferably we would be hitting from an unexpected direction before the quarry could react. It was our way of doing mass-times-velocity, where small mass gets multiplied by high velocity, further emphasised by accuracy, vigour and fleeting application. This had been central to the Regiment's approach from inception, defined by our founder David Stirling, refined ever since. So, numerical disadvantage sat naturally, if that was what we were facing. We simply needed to know where, when and how to apply our mix of forces in suitably surprising 'high velocity' and probably unorthodox fashion.

The method can take time to apply, for almost always detailed information must be gathered by reconnaissance before striking a target. It takes patience. For those of big-mass persuasion the whole thing can seem tedious and unduly cautious. In this instance, and as time passed, the Navy inclined this way, having large platforms that were quick to move and big enough to shoulder resistance aside. But we would be the ones eventually going ashore to close with the enemy. We stuck to our preferred ways of doing things, giving our enemy the benefit of any doubt. The Navy accepted this.

Detailed planning started with a thorough evaluation of the mission as stated in a directive from Fleet Headquarters at Northwood. A sizeable document, it was nevertheless crystal clear in its purpose: the reoccupation of South Georgia with minimum loss of life and minimum damage to property. And we were equally clear of a need to keep the operation under wraps as best we could, for as long as possible, preferably right up to the moment we made our decisive move. Before going far with our planning, I emphasised that the Squadron could not be thought of as an eventual occupation force. We must help take back South Georgia. After that we would surely be required elsewhere, assuming a wider conflict. Everyone understood.

The directive's strictures on proportionality coloured much of our thinking, the two limitations in any case resonating with our instincts and practice. The UK was obviously keen to adopt a certain pattern of behaviour from the very outset. The South Georgia operation could very likely set the tone for any fighting to follow in the Falklands, respect for the conventions of war and civilised conduct carrying a premium. I liked to think this came naturally to all of us in the planning group irrespective of the Fleet's direction: the need to maintain moral authority by fighting hard, yet clean, without causing unnecessary harm. More prosaically, perhaps reflecting our counter terrorist instincts and the hostage barricade experience in us, we saw that unnecessary use of force could play badly in the Falklands where effectively we had three thousand of our own people held hostage by a military prone to the use of excessive and illegal force on their own citizens. Goodness knows what they might do to our people if provoked. Setting and maintaining a good example made sense in more ways than one.

As for secrecy, that would have been high in our thinking too, for tactical reasons alone. But as we were closing in on South Georgia, the shuttle diplomacy between London, Washington and New York was reaching a high pitch. Its purpose, to find a resolution to the crisis short of war, sat uncomfortably with our mission. Should news of our moves seep out prematurely there could be embarrassment. For this reason, apparently even the Foreign and Commonwealth Office was being kept somewhat in the dark by the War Cabinet over intentions for South Georgia.

I did not know how much Guy Sheridan and Brian Young were getting of the higher level picture, but we were gaining a fair insight over our TACSAT rear link. Aside from the politics, there were growing military reservations. Concern over South Georgia would mount over the coming days; at one stage Mike Rose memorably remarking that Op Paraquet (all too easily corrupted to paraquat, a notably toxic herbicide) needed to be killed off before it killed us off—by which he meant scupper the entire Falklands effort, Op Corporate itself.

Strategically, the operation had probably been mounted because it could be involving a relatively small number of warships and few troops. It held the prospect of an early win, this serving to strengthen the country's diplomacy.

On the other hand, it could be viewed as a distraction from the Main Effort, the Falklands and its population, diverting resources, presenting a range of unwanted and unnecessary risks. Setback stood to damage our morale, correspondingly raise that of our enemy. And the risks were severe. At times the difference between success and catastrophe hung upon the thinnest of margins. This would test nerves up to and including the highest levels. I met the Prime Minister, Margaret Thatcher, after the war. She quizzed me on South Georgia to the exclusion of everything else; clearly she had been seared by the close-run nature of it all.

If anything, the TACSAT conversations served to increase the pressure. I perhaps more than the others became distracted by 'secrecy', absolutely determined that the Squadron shouldn't be the cause of any early compromise of the operation. By comparison 'proportionality' weighed less heavily, coming almost as second nature to marine and soldier alike, brought up as we were on years of service in Northern Ireland where constraint and strict adherence to law were the commonplace. The Task Group would likely have been careful about both aspects in any event. Only the privileged information coming in on our SAS rear link coloured my thoughts, raising secrecy in particular to an uncommon pitch. I didn't feel able to share much of this information, not explicitly. It was awkward, resulting not so much in a difference of approach, as in contrasting emphases within a broadly agreed stratagem, the Navy impatient with anything coming across as undue caution.

Having analysed the mission, we took stock of the available information. We had maps, charts, a few old air-photographs, and good, but dated, militarily-sourced intelligence on the enemy from the initial contacts. And there was *Endurance*'s priceless local knowledge. Intelligence believed the Argentinians had yet to reinforce in any significant way, putting the enemy's all-up strength at about one hundred, having little to say about the quality of the defenders. We knew that it would be tough enough going up against conscripts in well-prepared positions, but if they were anything approaching the quality of our troops, Mills and his small band of determined Royal Marines, we could have quite a contest on our hands. It seemed important to get a feel for quality as much as quantity. Hereford trawled wider sources with no success. We would have to go and see for ourselves.

It didn't take long to come up with an outline Course of Action (COA). We started by dismissing the brute use of our naval power, that is sailing in to blast the Argentinian garrison to oblivion before landing troops to 'bin-bag' the remains. It didn't altogether square with Northwood's directions. And for much the same reasons we discounted its obvious subset, an amphibious assault landing, going over 'the beach' all guns blazing. Then a blockade was rejected for fear of it leading to a long and difficult stand-off during which Argentina could conduct diplomacy that might go against us, and bring down naval and air assets capable of inflicting loss, even defeat. We would have given up tactical surprise for uncertain gain.

Instead, we adopted a simple, two-phased COA. First, we would conduct reconnaissance to determine precisely what and where the enemy were. With that done, we would use the intelligence to put tailored forces up against the identified enemy weak points to defeat him. Simple, generic maybe, unimaginative perhaps, but this deliberate and measured approach should enable us to build subtlety and tactical surprises into the detail—where, as it turned out, there lurked a near-fatal amount of 'devil'.

Turning to the execution of the chosen course, we agreed that the SBS would recce Grytviken, the administrative centre of the territory and home of the British Antarctic Survey (BAS). There was never any dispute about this. Grytviken was likely to be the main enemy location, and it made sense to make this as far as practicable an all Royal Marine affair, reducing the uncertainties inherent in employing a mixed force unpractised in one another's ways. Furthermore, if it came to a pro-tracted fight on narrow frontages M Company had both the numbers and the necessary skills for the task. A Commando company is designed for mixing it, the reason why one was added to the Task Group in the first place. We would concentrate on the old whaling station at Leith, the last reported location of the scrap metal men, recceing for any other Argentinians in the wider Stromness Bay area (Map 2). We should be prepared to conduct any eventual assault.

Even though we set out with a likely division of labour, nothing was ruled out or in, save for the limitations within the directive. It wasn't going to be as clear-cut as it might have looked at first glance. If M Company were to take on the strongest location they would probably need support, almost certainly priority call on all available naval guns. And if the Squadron had reinforced M Company, the guns unavailable, how might that impact our ability to mount our own, simultaneous attack elsewhere? Would we have to conduct sequential attacks, thus forfeiting tactical surprise on whichever target was considered the lesser of the two? If indeed, there were only two.

There again, if the recces supported the idea of simultaneity, how exactly was that to be achieved over the likely distances involved, and against the demands of pre-positioning the separated forces preferably by stealth? Could we prevent the enemy locations from communicating with one another as the assaults went in, making tactical surprise that much less dependent upon achieving absolute concurrency? Did we actually have enough of anything to do more than one or two locations at once? So it went on, churning round and round, a seeming infinite combination of variables. We had to get 'eyes on' target urgently. Little would come clear until we did.

There is a primordial quality to South Georgia, its raw, harsh beauty compelling. Brutally hard, it is no place for superficiality, or the frivolous. Elemental, spiritual even, at one and the same time beguiling and unforgiving, it can mercilessly expose weakness. Stark mountains rise precipitously from the sea, their moods swinging in an instant. One moment there will be flat calm in the fiords, next, raging katabatic winds. One of the most ferocious, volatile environments on earth, we were about to discover that it didn't give up secrets readily, neither its own nor those of its residents.

We had two ways of getting onto the island: by small boat or helicopter. I didn't much care for the boating option and despite his keenness to lead off, nor did Ted Inshaw, the Boat Troop Commander. We maintained boating skills for insertion purposes, but at a relatively basic level compared to the SBS. The SBS on the planning team, notably experienced and mature operators, were advising extreme caution. Frankly, I wasn't inclined to put our seamanship to the test. South Georgia didn't come across as the best of places for that, particularly at the onset of an austral winter.

There was another, specific, more prosaic reason to avoid leading off with the Boat Troop and their Geminis: the outboard motors. Despite repeated efforts to modernise its holdings, the Regiment was still equipped with engines procured in the 1960s for use in the Far East. Twenty or more years on and the motors had become worn and unreliable, prone to fail under even the best conditions; and these were not the best conditions. They had failed repeatedly when we had put them over the side of *Fort Austin*, a few days back in the balmy warmth of the equatorial waters off Ascension. Ted thought he might be able to borrow an engine or two from the ships. But, one had simply to scan the threatening seas around us to know that boating around South Georgia in something little better than an elongated rubber dinghy was probably best avoided if offered a choice. It made more sense to go with the Mountain Troop and insert by helicopter. The Navy agreed on both counts: avoid boating and use helicopters. They had two Wessex Mk V troop-lift airframes aboard *Tidespring*, our accompanying RFA tanker, and a Wessex Mk III on *Antrim* for the purpose.

The Squadron's Mountain Troop had accomplished climbers, a number of them highly experienced mountaineers skilled in snow and ice work, some recently back from the Himalayas. In all respects it made sense to start ground operations with them. They were still over on *Endurance*. Although alongside those with the best local knowledge, the Troop was separate from the planning-cell on *Antrim*. The dispersion of ground forces across ships is perhaps an unavoidable feature of amphibious warfare and can severely complicate matters for any embarked forces. The eventual outcome of the operation may be determined on land, but until forces are put ashore naval imperatives are likely to predominate. Ships will move, fight, group and re-group over distances disconcerting to a soldier. At one moment an embarked force might be together, overnight dispersed, separated by scores, even hundreds, of miles. So it would prove with Op Paraquet.

To guard against the awkwardness that can result from such instability, I decided to group the mountaineers with Squadron Headquarters (SHQ) on *Antrim*. This would keep us together through the recce's planning and decision-making processes, the downside being separation of the mountaineers from the local knowledge available on *Endurance*. Denied face-to-face access, from then on we all had to draw upon *Endurance*'s knowledge by secure, voice radio and signal. It would be difficult to say how significant this separation proved to the events about to unfold. The fact remains, dispersion is a factor in maritime warfare that soldiers need to appreciate and take into account.

A VERTREP soon had us re-shuffled: the Mountain Troop embarked *Antrim*, the Air Troop to *Endurance*, the swapping of troops virtually man for man necessitated by pressures on accommodation.

With Mountain Troop alongside SHQ and the senior pilot and his team we could start addressing the tactics of the recce in earnest. While not underestimating the difficulties, the soldier in us knew that once ashore we should be able to make a go of things. Examining the problem from front to back, we thought it should be possible to do the job without getting close, using optics. It then became a matter of route-selection from a landing-site to the set back observation-points, noting that the Squadron would have to check all possible enemy locations in Stromness Bay: the old whaling stations of Leith, the enemy's last known location, Stromness and Husvik.

We should approach the target area with utmost caution, probably monitoring by day each major leg of the route for enemy activity before moving down it by night. This tactic alone pushed back the entry point, sufficient to allow the desired progression: one or maybe two nights, to get the troop into the bay area. Add in 'fudge factors', including the possible need for close-in recce, it could take four to five days to complete the task.

The entry-point would be determined mainly by the characteristics of the available helicopters. They were not equipped for covert, night operations and there was also the matter of their noise. Clearly we couldn't land within direct line-of-sight of the objective areas. We must mask the helicopter landing site(s) by use of ground, ruling out most if not all of Stromness Bay itself, certainly the shore-line and waterfront areas. This pushed us back, which was acceptable in terms of the steady progression we wished to conduct down any chosen approach, save that it took us into some seriously difficult terrain. We didn't care for the coast immediately north of Leith: overland routes from there looked both hazardous and relatively easy for an enemy to anticipate and so cover. Routes from south of Stromness Bay looked no better. The matter of noise compounded the difficulties, appearing to push us further out than even terrain masking required, into the surrounding mountains. At our request the aviators had produced a map overlay showing 'noise-safe' landing areas. There really wasn't much choice: no matter how hard we tried to see it otherwise the noise combined with going put us out to the east, up onto the Fortuna glacier.

Nobody liked this. But there were strong advantages. Aside from overcoming the matter of helicopter noise, the Fortuna lay out of sight from Stromness Bay and its whaling stations with a traversable mountain between. An approach from that direction should be unexpected, unlikely to be under observation. And the lie of the land should enable us to scrutinise each leg of the approach before going down it. It was simply that none of us welcomed the idea of crossing the Fortuna at that time of year, the onset of winter.

Guy, a hugely experienced mountaineer, advised us to avoid glaciers like the plague. *Endurance* expressed strong opposition, citing that the unpredictable weather loaded the dice against success. In the background and unknown to me, the British Antarctic Survey also briefed against going up onto glaciers, pointing out that even their experts were subject to tight safety-rules when venturing into South Georgia's mountains. The Fortuna route might have been rejected, but for the constantly nagging imperative to avoid early compromise of the mission. Besides, there didn't appear to be many other options for Mountain Troop and the helicopters. Thus we kept it under consideration.

The matter of crevasses and the practicality of crossing the glacier in a safe, timely fashion came up over and again. Ironically, it dominated the debate almost to the exclusion of all else including the weather. Where the Fortuna descended to the sea it was indeed a terrible mess of pressure-ridges and deep fissures; most definitely a place to be avoided. But on its top the going appeared altogether more benign. There was an amount of crevassing where we intended to come off the glacier towards Stromness Bay, but nothing impassable, a fairly forgiving transition from ice to bare rock.

Advice against the Fortuna came in general terms, that in favour referred to specifics. Back in Hereford, our successful Everest climbers, (Everest) Brummie Stokes and Bronco Lane, studied available imagery of the actual route proposed and drew upon other national sources. Provided we kept to the smooth, domed top, exactly as intended, they thought we should be okay. They sought confirmation, consulting others with first-hand experience of the very route. This included John Peacock who in 1964 had himself walked it when successfully re-tracing Ernest Shackleton's 1916 journey across South Georgia. 'Fortuna's a goer,' he said.

The example of Shackleton was ever-present. He had walked nearly the exact route when weak from hunger, and without the benefit of mountaineering equipment, save a rope. In fact he had taken thirty-six hours to cross South Georgia from its northern coast across to Stromness Bay, a distance of about thirty miles. We planned to take two to three days to walk five miles, only a couple of which would be on the ice.

I listened to the divergent views. I discussed them with John Hamilton, commander of Mountain Troop, and his people, the team that would have to do it. The Troop was content, concerned primarily about the weather. Ian Stanley, the senior pilot, and his team were consulted. They quizzed us keenly, mindful of the hazards involved in going 1000 feet up the Fortuna: icing, white out conditions, low cloud, high winds and wind shears. They too thought it workable given some half decent weather. Young, an aviator himself, and Sheridan, a mountaineer, confirmed that they would support whatever course we adopted. In the end only one person could make the decision: me. I decided to go with the Fortuna route.

3. To Stromness Bay

The day of the insertion came, 21 April, two weeks after our departure from Hereford, a week after joining the Task Group. Time raced by. The weather looked forbidding. Overnight the barometric pressure had fallen steeply. By first light we had a gale on our hands, with the prospect of things getting worse. The sea was building, its surface whipped with spindrift, the larger ships rolling about, *Endurance* positively bouncing. A solid sheeted, grey cloud base hung low at 400 feet, dark with the threat of snow; it needed to be well above that, the landing-site lying at around 1,000 feet. The bitter, damp cold carried the near certainty of icing on the airframes. Visibility wasn't too bad, though—two miles, thereabouts.

Unaware that we were experiencing the early signs of a gathering storm of staggering proportions, we pressed on, touchingly confident in our abilities, ignorant of the extent of our frailties, the Squadron comforted by the thought that things must be about normal for the Navy, seamen and aircrew alike taking things in their stride. Had we all known what was coming out of the Antarctic towards us, the whole operation would have been put on hold. Even by South Georgia's standards we were in for a phenomenal blow, a severe thrashing of pitiless ferocity.

Ian Stanley, his crew and their venerable Wessex III helicopter, affectionately named Humphrey,[1] were about to become the stuff of legend. Over the next days they would be called upon repeatedly, never once flinching.

[1] Royal Navy custom is to refer to a ship as 'she', a helicopter as 'he', this of course leading to ribald comment. Flight decks are sited towards the stern of most ships.

Ian needed all three available Wessex to lift the recce party. His own, a single engine 'dipper', was unsuitable for troop lifting, being under-powered and short on space. However, optimised for Anti-Submarine Warfare (ASW), the frame had capabilities the two troop-carrying Wessex Vs didn't. For a start it had a four man crew: two pilots, an observer and crewman. Chris Parry, the observer, was there to fight the airframe as part of the ship's weapons system, responsible for precise navigation, radar operation and control of other supporting helicopters. To aid him, he had a radar, offering a wide picture view and a limited collision avoidance capability; its efficiency though was severely reduced when among large topographical features such as mountains and gla-ciers. Chris also had use of something called a Flight Control System (FCS), a computerised device that helped the aircraft hold a particular position at a given height. These aids and functions, intended for use over the sea rather than land, would be employed to negotiate South Georgia's mountains in cloud, poor visibility and severe turbulence. The creative use of Humphrey's equipment, combined with his crew's peer-less team-work, would prove a game-saver.

The other two Wessex Vs were twin engine, utility helicopters. They had radio altimeters and stability equipment, but mainly they were flown by a single pilot, aided by an aircrewman observing from the door in the rear; there was no 'blind' flying equipment. The Wessex Vs would have to be guided by the Wessex III in anything other than good visibility.

After a postponement of about an hour, the weather showed faint signs of improvement. Ian was cleared to take a look at conditions ashore and atop the glacier. He lifted from *Antrim* to fly fast and low towards Possession Bay before coasting in at Cape Constance. From there he slowed, moving cautiously on the look-out for any Argentinians. Coming into Antarctic Bay, he gained his first glimpse of the Fortuna with its precipitous ice-falls, rock faces and the towering mountains looming above. He and his crew had been speaking to *Endurance*, but nothing had prepared them for the merciless, intimidating nature of this place crowd-ing in on them from all sides. There was grandeur, a forbidding, harsh, barren beauty. Brutally high winds swirled unpredictably, snatching at Humphrey as if to dash him into the sea or into the surrounding mountains. It made the crew feel small, intruding where they shouldn't, hemmed in by the wet, dripping, icy cliffs all around, the dark torn waters below, the grey swirling clouds above.

Ian made a careful circuit of the Bay: no enemy. He and Stewart Cooper, the co-pilot, noted a route up the glacier. On either side there were sheer rock faces and craggy outcrops, obscured intermittently by banks of tumbling cloud. It would be tight: little or no room for turning back once committed. From what they could see of the top, it looked more reassuring, opening out, offering space for manoeuvre. Satisfied that there was no enemy and the route viable, if challenging, Ian turned back for *Antrim* to collect the troops.

An hour or more later, the next sortie didn't go as well. Humphrey leading, he and the two Wessex Vs loaded with troops entered Possession Bay to be met by a wall of driving snow. Ian and Stewart knew where they were, but agreed that it would be foolish to press on. They turned back. Once aboard *Antrim* there followed an anxious consultation in the operations room. The day was passing with nothing much to show for it. Worse, the whole thing was starting to look impractical, a miscalculation.

Hiding my anxiety, I asked to be taken forward, with John Hamilton. I wanted the two of us to see what Ian had seen and experienced. Otherwise, Ian would find himself making the operation's go/no go decision—and that didn't seem altogether fair on him, or right. If the operation was to be abandoned, the Squadron should be part of the decision-making, a knowledgeable, fully-informed part.

We received permission to conduct another recce. Humphrey set off for his third trip ashore that day. Things went reasonably well. The weather had improved. Ian reached the foot of the Fortuna and from there hover-taxied his helicopter up the sheer slope in near-perfect visibility. The winds buffeted the airframe, not unduly, and at the top the dome of the glacier stretched out smoothly much as expected and wanted. Ian took the opportunity to fly around the dome, taking care not to expose the aircraft to possible observation from the Stromness area.

But something was eating John. I asked him what he thought. He hesitated. After a while, I again indicated through the din, over the intercom, that we had to decide there and then. We might be in a fair-weather window, but that could change at any moment. We couldn't hang around indefinitely. I wanted this to be the Troop's decision, for him to make the actual go/no go call. Unfortunately, because of a poor choice of words, over an imperfect, crackly intercom, I didn't come across as intended, but in a way open to an altogether different inter-pretation. Apparently I said, 'You've got to *get on*, John', meaning that he had to make up his mind immediately, one way or another.

It really was for him to decide, for even though drop off by helicop-ter looked feasible just then, he and his troop would have to do the rest. Hence, it should be his decision whether to proceed or not. But, John, understandably took me to be urging him to get onto the glacier, rather than getting on with a decision. I would have accepted 'no'. But on such careless phrasing events can turn, this being one of those. And thus we reached a decision, John agreeing to *get on* the glacier!

My otherwise unfortunate choice of words became a catch-phrase in *Antrim*, used repeatedly by Humphrey's crew and the ship's company over the next tumultuous days and weeks. When faced by a challenge they could probably have done without, they would buoy spirits and step forward once again with: 'You've got to get on John'.

We returned to the Task Group to mount the troops, John and his people eventually inserting onto the glacier in rapidly deteriorating flying conditions, the helicopters hit by a succession of driving snow and ice squalls. The pilots suffered periods of white-out. Humphrey, having two pilots in the 'cab' and an observer with FCS in the back, was able to avoid disorientation, leading the flight of helicopters safely up and down the Fortuna. Once back in *Antrim*, Ian and his crew expressed relief that it was all over and that they wouldn't have to go up there again.

It was almost as if South Georgia had been waiting for us, not that it hadn't served notice. From the moment the helicopters left, the weather worsened, hammering the troops. Humphrey had registered squalls of 80 knots when on the ground, 90 knots or more in the air, and yet the winds increased.[2] The troops started their move to get off the ice, as fast as they could. They had hoped to observe the route forward before cresting the dome, checking for any enemy beyond the glacier, covering the approaches into Stromness Bay. There was no visibility, perhaps a couple of yards. The wind drove ice-crystals into their faces, making vision near impossible even with goggles. They had to take a chance on the enemy, at that moment the least of their worries. Nobody would be out in such weather, surely? The situation had reduced to one of surviving the elements. South Georgia was asserting itself over our affairs, and how inconsequential they seemed right then.

There were crevasses. Disconcerting to start with, the troop quickly got their measure, hitting a rhythm that had to stop as the light failed. They had covered perhaps half a mile before nightfall, the hours spent on the insertion taking their toll. Almost across, they must nevertheless shelter as best they could, where they were on the exposed surface of the ice. They could not risk moving by dark, not against the full fury of these winds driving into them.

How different it could have been. But for the time lost they might have made it to the shelter of the rocks beyond as planned. The wind continued to rise in strength to an unimaginable degree; even the most seasoned among them had never before been subjected to winds of such seemingly pitiless, spiteful, malice. It felt personal and deadly. It was almost as though the shrieking, pounding winds were trying to hurl them bodily across the icy surface of the glacier, down the precipitous slopes not far distant, headlong towards the thrashed sea below. Breath was sucked from their lungs, exposed flesh lacerated by driving snow, sleet and ice crystals. Battered near senseless, they sheltered as best they could, huddled together. It was going to be a long night.

At sea, *Endurance* received approval to leave the Task Group until things blew over. She knew better than most of us what was happening

---

[2] Respectively: 92 mph and 103 mph.

and yet to come, where to find shelter along the coast; she was small enough to tuck into a bay. The rest of us had little option other than to lash down all that we could, close galleys, and try to keep station with one another, maintaining a heading into the rising seas. The wind and sea smashed into the ships with brutal strength. Waves grew mountainous and this on the sheltered side of South Georgia! The ships shrieked as the wind tore through their superstructure. Those of us in *Antrim*, struggling about the ship, if passing the Govan plaque, might glance up to read it once more, trusting that Scotland's riveters had done a good job for it sounded as though we were being torn apart. The seas pounded into the destroyer's 6,000 tons of steel, the hull booming with each blow. The barometer dived at dizzying speed, we were moving from gale to winds altogether more severe. In all their years at sea, few sailors had experienced anything like it. Captains remained on their bridges. Crews closed up. Young feared for the damage that might be done. There were no Royal Navy repair facilities south of Gibraltar.

On the flight deck of *Antrim* it had not been possible to get Humphrey into his hangar. A tricky enough operation in good weather, Ian told his people not to try. Any attempt would surely lead to injury, even loss of life. The helicopter would have to stay out. It was the same for one of the Wessex Vs on *Tidespring*, the standby airframe. He too must remain on deck to withstand the full might of the solid, water laden tempest. All that stood between their survival and destruction were the chains and webbing straps that tethered them to the wide open, flight decks. Stressed to the very limits, both airframes somehow came through to fight another day.

The winds rose without mercy, reaching above 100 mph according to some. We were reaching the top end of the Beaufort scale. A solid wall of spray ripped from the shredded waves. The ships shuddered, groaned and howled as if in agony. Captain Young invited his ship's company to the lower bridge, should they wish to view the seas, so that they might one day tell their grandchildren. I took up the offer. We saw mountainous, menacing seas. *Antrim* shivered and shook as the oncoming waves crashed repeatedly into her, at times stopping her dead in her tracks it felt, at others pitching her over as if never to return. The waves surged over her bows, burying her gun turret and all before. Each time, the ship must fight her way back. Valiantly, steadfastly, she shouldered from side to side, ridding herself of tons of deep green, grey, wind-thrashed water. Free, she would leap up only to plunge once more, sloping down as if into the very depths.

The seas all around were streaked with spindrift, the air dense with salt spray. As evening closed in, it had all taken on a faint, luminous grey-green glow, the fading light amplified by the white of the whirling spume. There came a point when it became necessary to turn the ship, to run with the sea, if we were to keep anywhere near station with our objective areas. The ship's company would be warned, the engines brought to full power before she launched always willingly into her turn, dashing to complete the move in a trough between waves. It was dangerous, bringing the ship side-on to such mountainous seas, a relief when it was done, the ship running on her reciprocal course. So, it went on all night, into the seas or running with the seas, each turnabout putting us at risk of broaching.

If conditions were severe down at sea-level, how must they be for Mountain Troop ashore, 1,000 feet up in the mountains, well above freezing level? Had they managed to find shelter, as the timetable intended? I hoped as much, but harboured doubts, as did others. Without being told, we all made our respective preparations for a following day of bad news.

The message came mid-morning. Somehow, the Troop had survived the night and for three or more hours after first light had battled the weather in another attempt to get off the glacier; but their clothes were soaked and much equipment had been lost, torn away during the night. Several of them were showing early signs of frostbite, some starting to go down with hypothermia. They saw no sensible alternative to calling it off, before they started taking mass, cold casualties; for once one went under others would surely follow, as is the way with environmental illness. John put through a request to come off, advising haste.

There was an unwritten rule in the SAS: the base accepts what comes from the patrol on the ground. Guy agreed with me. We should go with John's request. We must respect his on-the-spot assessment. It was what we had all been expecting. The helicopters were ready. They departed soon after the call. The storm had moderated a little. But snow-squalls continued to race out from the coast, momentarily cutting visibility to a few yards. Ian led them forward, Chris Parry down the back calling out information from Humphrey's FCS. They flew in loose formation, the trailing Wessex Vs keeping a very close eye on their leader. On reaching Cape Constance, Ian instructed the utility helicopters to land and wait as he went forward to take a closer look of the route up onto the glacier. Mike Tidd and Ian Georgeson, the pilots, acknowledged, setting down on a headland out of the worst of the wind.

The Fortuna was shut in by cloud just on or below the dome. Ian tried for thirty minutes. The winds tore at the airframe, hurling it first this way then that. At times he lost tail-rotor control. And the aircraft began to ice up, getting difficult to fly. His altimeter unwound and re-wound alarmingly as he crossed crevasses marking the glacier's precipitate fall to the sea. It was no place for Humphrey, let alone the utility cabs. He turned to run with the wind, collecting the other two helicopters as he was propelled back to the ships. They re-fuelled and waited for the weather to improve.

The second and fateful attempt started about an hour later. The weather had moderated a touch, becoming that less obviously dangerous. The cloud-base had lifted, the clouds thinning. There were even occasional, brief shafts of sunlight, their incongruous intensity serving to deepen the contrasting greyness of the sea and land beyond. They added to an aura of mysticism, for South Georgia even at its most tiresome never gave up its hold on one, its spirituality. Winds remained high, gusting unpredictably, but definitely reducing if only a little. The snow squalls were less frequent. We were tempted to give it a go. Humphrey lifted, gathered the other two, and made straight for the foot of the glacier to start a cautious ascent. The winds buffeted the air-frames, nothing that untoward, nothing that these seasoned naval aviators couldn't handle. Even so, the rock faces crowding in on either side had their attention.

John's troops couldn't believe their ears. They hadn't expected a second attempt. On hearing the helicopters approach, one of them set off a smoke grenade to mark a landing site. Stewart Cooper spotted it immediately. They were where the flight expected them to be. The three helicopters landed in turn. The troops immediately started to load, as the weather took a turn for the worse. It was a race to get away.

Mike Tidd was the first to complete loading. Glancing to his left he spotted a snow-squall advancing, about 800 yards away. He signalled Ian for permission to lift, to get ahead of it. He could see clearly to the series of slight ice ridges, about half a mile in front, marking the route down to the sea. 'Yes, go', came the prompt response.

All went well for Mike and his passengers—that is, until their helicopter was overtaken by another snow squall coming in from the side, yards short of the ridges and their descent to safety. White-out. Blinded, Mike lost all outside visual references. He knew they were in peril. He warned his crewman in the back; he too stared out of the aircraft, looking for anything that might help his pilot maintain level flight. Nothing. Mike knew that there was a rock face somewhere, about 700 feet to his left, and another, perhaps half a mile to the right. Immediately before the white-out he had flown over a rock outcrop. If he could find those rocks, they should give him the desperately needed reference points. One eye on instruments, one eye out the windscreen he suddenly noticed the altimeter unwind—very fast. He knew what must be coming. He pulled in the power to lift away. It softened the impact. His helicopter shuddered before falling reluctantly onto its side, then jerking and jumping as the rotors flailed into the ice of the glacier, the crash cushioned further by snow as they scudded into a gully. No casualties, thanks to Mike's lightning-fast reactions, his cool in emergency, and seasoned flying skills.

Ian Stanley and Ian Georgeson had witnessed the moment Mike had been engulfed by the snow squall. There had been no time to give a warning. He had been hit seconds from safety. Immediately, the pair hover-taxied across to pick up survivors, the air once again crystal clear, visibility a mile or more. I had accompanied Ian for no logical reason, in the back of Humphrey, glancing out the door as best I could. It was a grim, gut-wrenching moment. There would be other bad moments in this war, but this was the first made worse because there had been nothing to do but listen in on the unfolding drama.

A second bad moment fast approached. The surviving troops abandoned their heavy equipment before clambering aboard the rescue helicopters. Soon all were ready. Ian Stanley waited for good visibility as snow flurries again swept across the glacier's surface: he was after 800 yards of clear air. He soon had it and ordered lift off. Georgeson took up position behind and to port. Together they taxied carefully towards the ice ridges, the start of the route down. As Humphrey started to lift over the ridges, another squall hit. Immediately, Georgeson lost sight of his leader. Like Mike Tidd, Ian Georgeson was alone in his cab, having to look out as well as in. He tried to maintain level flight, slowing down. It was akin to peering through a glass of milk. His eyes shot down to his instruments, then back out. Instincts said one thing, senses something else, instruments another. And then his altimeter suddenly unwound; the first of the ice ridges. He pulled for height, trying to remain vertical. The first impact was soft. The aircraft shivered. He thought he had got away with it. But the Fortuna was in no mood to let up. The helicopter gently tipped. The rotors smashed into the glacier, thrashing until the frame eventually became still, lying on its starboard side. Stewart Cooper had seen the whole thing in Humphrey's rear view mirror.

'God, they've gone in,' he had blurted over the intercom.

It froze the blood in my veins. My mind went numb. No, it couldn't be happening. I felt physically sick. For a second or so nothing, then in measured tones Humphrey's crew took stock. They had no clear idea about survivors. The helicopter lay there on its side more or less intact. No fire. The impact had been gradual rather than catastrophically abrupt. Chris advised that they, 'go back to mum, boss'. They were overloaded as it was, with the weather shutting in the glacier as they spoke. Survivors started to emerge from the crash. Ian made his decision. They would return to 'mother' to deliver their load before returning as soon as possible. He passed this calmly and as a matter of fact. There was no drama, just reassuring certainty, everything stated in measured tones. This was leadership and team-work at its best, steady, resolute, free of emotion. For my part, the bystander who had set all this in motion, I felt seriously ill: punch-drunk, nauseous, and somewhat drained.

On reaching sea level, Chris Parry broke radio silence to pass a situation report (SITREP) to the ship 'we have lost our two chicks'. There came a pause before a stunned 'Roger', from mother, *Antrim*.

By the time Humphrey got back to the ship, the weather had worsened markedly; no longer simply gusting, the winds had picked up, rising once again to a full-on gale. The cloud-base had dropped, visibility coming in and out from a few feet back out to 800 yards. We loaded blankets and medical supplies. Ian sensed my near despair. He kept me in the cab; ostensibly to help with any decision-making, but mainly to keep me occupied, activity being effective therapy.

We were soon on our way. The weather had become savage, a pitiless, spiteful quality to it. The Fortuna had staked its claim, and showed no inclination to surrender what it had so mercilessly taken. We could all feel Ian fighting for control of the helicopter. How he managed to get to the top of the Fortuna once more, none of us shall ever know. But he did, clawing his way, Chris Parry doing what he could down the back with the FCS. Ian concentrated mainly on instruments, Stewart gazing out, passing visual information in a steady stream. The aircrewman and I did what we could, as best we could, observing through the open, rear door. On top it proved impossible to land, any attempt suicidal. Besides, we couldn't find the crash site, visibility mere yards in any direction. But Ian did make radio contact. Everyone had survived, no breaks, a few sprains. Ian told them to shelter as best they could; he would be back when the weather allowed, later that day he hoped.

Back in *Antrim*, in the quiet and warmth of the ops room, we took stock. Danny without saying a word rolled me a cigarette. A cigarette at the right moment helped. I found that it steadied the nerves, slowed things down, made time for thinking, brought comfort and a semblance of normality. Things were bad. We were experiencing dramatic and embarrassing failure. Thus far our efforts had cost the Task Group the loss of its assault helicopters. But neither then nor at any time during the operation did anyone openly criticise or blame us for complicating matters, even jeopardising success. It wouldn't have helped. It would simply have added pressure. It was unnecessary. It was time to get on (John), having learnt. Recrimination could wait if it were wanted or merited, was one's inclination.

We had recovered barely half the Troop. The sick bay reported everyone generally in decent health, one or two showing early signs of frostbite and hypothermia, but nothing that wouldn't mend. It was as well we went to their rescue when we did. The medics' report served to emphasise the urgency of the situation. Another night in the open and we would almost certainly have lost them to cold injury; we had to rescue the others within the next few hours.

We had lost most of our mountaineering gear, but need not have worried. *Endurance* stepped in, informing us that they had an amount of mountaineering kit belonging to a cancelled Tri-service Expedition; we could have it all, if that helped. The Navy was like that: generous and always looking for solutions. Nevertheless, the mountaineers were out of things for the moment. They should have a day or so to themselves to recover.

With troops still up on the glacier, thinking ahead was not proving easy; but somehow, between us, SHQ found the gumption to warn off Ted and his Boat Troop. They would probably be needed after all. For, whatever else might befall us over the next number of hours, the operation had to go on. I instructed him to get with the ship's navigator, to identify landing options and be prepared to go over his preferred COAs with the planning group later in the day, the moment we were free of the immediate crisis.

Meanwhile the weather had eased. There were seventeen men to be recovered from the Fortuna, including aircrew. Ian consulted his team. The four of them knew that the odds on their own survival must be shortening. They had used some of the waiting time to prepare themselves, each in his own way. Chris had written a letter to his wife, sealing his wedding ring in its envelope. Ian had run through things once more, taking stock, testing to confirm that all that could be done, had been done. He of all of them knew the risks they were running. His helicopter was elderly. The Mark III Wessex had a reputation for engine failure. He had experienced crash landings twice before, once into the sea. Humphrey had been up onto Fortuna eight times already. The airframe had been severely stressed; his engineers had expressed their concerns, doing all that they could to keep him flying. There could be time, with luck, to make two more flights before nightfall. They planned to rescue the survivors by repeating the earlier flight profile: keep low, hover-taxi to the top and back. They knew that it was going to be no picnic.

We all knew that Ian and his crew were pushing their luck. It could be seen in the way the flight-deck crew ushered Humphrey off from the deck; no hint of feigned nonchalance, just unspoken well wishes and people finding reassurance in performing familiar drills in the customary way. Everyone knew what was at stake, could feel the gravity of the situation.

The helicopter quickly faded into the gloom looking resolute, yet lonely as he battled forward once more. It was as though Humphrey carried the nation's fortunes just then, not only our destiny. On his shoulders rested the well-being of his crew; the survival of those still on the glacier; and perhaps the course of the entire Falklands enterprise. Were he to fail, the Task Force might make good the losses in tactical terms. But there was no telling what the wider, higher national consequences might be of such an inauspicious start to our campaign to recover the Islands. I felt pretty low, knowing the near crushing weight of responsibility in its widest sense. I remained up on the flight deck, keeping myself to myself.

On reaching the coast, Ian saw that the weather had worsened considerably since leaving the ship. A quick exchange over the intercom, and they all agreed a radical change of plan. Opting for Ian's idea, they chose to risk icing and ascend to 3,000 feet, to get on top of the cloud. This would put them 2,000 feet or so above the highest surface of the glacier, still with surrounding mountains looming all about. But, from there they might wait for a break in the clouds, locate the crash site, swoop to snatch some survivors. It was a courageous option, coolly calculated.

Humphrey responded eagerly to the pull on the collective, rising near-vertically to keep clear of the surrounding mountains, hidden from sight, out there in the swirling grey that enveloped them. After what felt like an age, the helicopter broke through into clear air, a world of blue sky, dazzling sunlight and snow-capped mountains. For a while they circled carefully above the solid mass of cloud below, noting how the westering sun was starting to bathe everything in a deep, golden glow. They would have to call it off soon, to get back down through the cloud and out to sea somehow. Then the clouds started to break up, shredded by the wind, wispily at first, then with distinct, sizeable gaps. Chris' navigation had been spot-on. Through a break in the cloud, Ian and Stewart simultaneously saw the crashed helicopter. They had made their luck. Humphrey dived, landing feet from the survivors.

Ian knew that it had to be the last flight of the day. In the steadily fading light, he ordered everyone aboard less kit. The troops did as they were told, without hesitation, retaining only their rifles. They couldn't give those up. Humphrey was rapidly loaded with twenty-one souls, including the four-man crew, arms and legs everywhere, some dangling out the door, Fitz Fitzgerald the aircrewman half in, half out, secured by his strap. Ian, with the full backing of his crew, was about to lift his helicopter, a single engine Wessex III, from a violently wind-swept glacier, down to a sea partly obscured by spindrift, across to a storm-tossed ship, all the while overloaded by upwards of 2,000 lbs. The blustering wind gave him the confidence to give it a go. Its strength should help Humphrey lift into the air.

He waited for a particularly strong, steady gust, about 80 knots, pulled in the collective, pedalled gently to take account of the opposing torque. The helicopter staggered, shook, as if surprised by what was being asked of him. Reluctantly at first, but up he came, barely, but gamely, the driving wind helping. Ian knew at once that Humphrey was incapable of hovering, the weight beyond anything that the aircraft had been designed to lift. He coaxed the machine up and into forward flight, gingerly, co-opting the wind, delicate pressures on the cyclic. He looked for additional power, but Humphrey had nothing more to give. Then, still making use of the wind, he carefully added pedal to slew the helicopter round, to make their run across to the edge of the glacier to sink down towards the sea. They picked up speed, the controls starting to feel less mushy, more responsive. The wind pushed and pulled as they made their run for it, propelling them out towards the waiting ship, and safety.

On approaching a ship a helicopter normally comes alongside from the stern, pauses in the hover, and then slides across to the flight deck. This ensures that, should anything go wrong, the aircraft has a chance of getting clear, with the ship left undamaged. It provides options.

I had been waiting at the back of the flight deck, in my anxiety and gloom still reluctant to take shelter. Perhaps if I stayed out sharing the conditions it might help in some way. Utter nonsense, obviously, but it showed how the mind could grasp at straws when under duress. Then, with no warning at all, Humphrey emerged from the fast-fading light. Something was up. He didn't look right. Heading straight for the stern, flying low with wipers thrashing, he started to rise.

Ian knew that the air was warmer down here at sea-level, giving him that much less lift, even finer margins to work with. And he knew he couldn't hover. He must come straight in over the port side in a shallow dive, somehow taking account of the rhythmically rising and falling deck. It would have to be done in one flowing motion, up, in, flair as best he could, down. Should it start to go wrong, his only fall back would be to go straight on through the transition and hope to give it another go having not lost critical airspeed in the attempt. Fail, and it would be a mess on the flight deck, more likely in the sea beyond. We could all see what Ian intended. The flight deck crew tensed.

Humphrey came on, looking small and strangely fragile, dwarfed by the green grey, gathering darkness, and the vastness of the heaving spray flecked sea. Then there he was, back with us, no ceremony, no marshalling: he came in, from no great height, over to one side of the stern, dropping onto the pitching, heaving deck, a bump, another, no harm done, then planted. The flight-deck crew burst into action, dashing forward with their strops to lash him down: done in seconds. Safely home. Then the survivors emerged, one at a time. The first man fell out onto the deck and gathered himself unsteadily. I counted them, everyone accounted for, alive and well. It didn't seem possible.

The aircrews, all of them, had performed with commitment and gallantry throughout the Fortuna episode, never once flinching. Humphrey had become legend, Ian Stanley and his crew rendering service outstanding even by Royal Navy standards. They had performed with exemplary skill and imagination. We had grown really fond of them. They had stepped forward repeatedly, each time displaying airmanship of the highest order along with quiet courage. They had done what they had to do without loss and without harm to their invaluable ASW helicopter. It was not the best of starts to the country's fight back, but Ian and his people had kept us in the game. And they had set us all an example difficult to match. For our part, the Squadron would press on; there would be no withdrawal by us, no turning in on ourselves, no feeling sorry. If anything, the experience had hardened our resolve to get onto the ground and into the fight.

That night John Hamilton and his Troop sought out Ian and his crew. Armed with a bottle of whisky, they gave their thanks. Meanwhile, the Squadron got down to the business of making another attempt to get on target.

It was not that easy to concentrate on the next planning session. Too much unhelpful noise kept pressing in. What if we had done this? What if we had that or the other? The trouble hadn't been the crevasses or the going. We had been right about that. It had been weather, unusual even by South Georgia's standards. Its violence had surprised most of us. There were things to learn about helicopter operations too. Unknown to us, the Navy was working on the matter at that very time, perfecting night-flying techniques as the main Task Force made passage south. In future covert SF helicopter operations would be flown at night employing NVG (Night Vision Goggles) capable, twin-engine Sea King helicopters, always with two pilots in the cab.

Having lost the troop lift helicopters, and with Mountain Troop out of things, the next attempt would have to be by boat. How exactly? Since receiving a warning order against the eventuality, Ted, the Boat Troop Commander, and his team had spent much of the time since thinking things through and otherwise preparing. Action in and around the target would be much the same as John Hamilton had envisaged; thank goodness we had brought the two most likely needed troops together on board the flag-ship, able to consult face to face. We concentrated our thinking on the insertion phase.

Ted went over his troop's assessment. It became immediately and uncomfortably apparent that he wanted to go straight in at the mouth of Stromness Bay, dropping off from *Antrim* behind a headland, just round from Leith the principal target. From there he proposed to make a two mile passage by Gemini to Grass Island lying offshore Leith and Stromness. From Grass Island the troop would be able to observe the mainland shore, checking it clear of enemy before making their landing.

I didn't much like it. Noise was no longer the problem, the boats much quieter than helicopters. No, the failed Fortuna option had offered an approach into the objective area from its most unlikely direction: South Georgia's hinterland. Wasn't it possible to achieve something comparable using the boats? Ted's proposal had us going straight up the most self-evident approach. Had he considered Fortuna Bay, to the rear, which would enable them to pick up John's original route?

He had considered and discounted Fortuna Bay because the charts showed it to be choked with kelp. Ice could prove an added difficulty, calving from the glaciers further up the coast it was likely to be accumulating in the bay. It threatened to puncture the boats. Kelp and ice combined made Fortuna Bay problematic in a way that the frontal approach didn't. Compelling. We ruled out Fortuna Bay. And that ruled in the entrance of Stromness Bay for there was no other small boat approach.

The whalers had sited stations on most of the accessible areas, all potential enemy locations ruling out overland approaches other than from the direction of Fortuna now rejected. There seemed nothing for it but to go straight in at the front 'door', making directly for Grass Island before crossing to the mainland having first established that the coast was clear. It seemed so disturbingly obvious, albeit simple and bold.

We went over the enemy's defences, in particular the possibility that they may have sited radar and heavy weapons on a headland to guard against the very thing we were proposing. It didn't look likely, the coastline being precipitous along most of its length. The ship's planners thought the risk acceptable, assuring us that the ship would be at action-stations, blacked-out and silent, able to slip in and out undetected in any event. I noted their high confidence.

The Navy undoubtedly favoured Boat Troop's proposal. I guessed they preferred its emphasis on seamanship, more familiar to them than the disciplines of mountaineering, a feature of the previous, Fortuna option. I continued to harbour reservations. Did it have to be the Geminis and their unreliable engines? None of us trusted the engines, Ted included. He had borrowed what he could from the Navy, but largely it would be our own kit. Couldn't we use the Klepper canoes? Rejected. They were likely to be pushed out to sea in any high winds, prone to capsize in little more than a heavy swell. Wasn't Grass Island rather obvious? Possibly, but what was the alternative, if they were to observe the mainland shore before making a landing? Only much later did we learn that Keith Mills had used Grass Island in defence of South Georgia just weeks before, only to be discovered by the Argentinians.

We went over the problem of the engines and other issues yet again. All precautions would be taken. *Antrim* would lend us one of her engines, the single spare available. We would warm the engines up in tanks of water before launching. Every aspect of the insertion was gone over repeatedly. The plan had to be as weather proof as possible. We had learnt that the hard way.

Eventually, we squared everything. We would go as Ted and the ship both wanted: in at the mouth of Stromness Bay, launching Geminis from *Antrim*, for the Boat Troop to move to the target areas via Grass Island. The distance from the drop off point to the island could not have been much more than a mile or so. Yet, still I worried. How much of that was scarring from Fortuna it would be difficult to say. I certainly didn't like going in the front. It ran counter to our earlier conclusions, let alone instincts. We made the decision within an hour of Humphrey's epic return from the glacier. Boat Troop would go in that night.

It was an improbably still evening as *Antrim* slipped into Stromness Bay. The sound and fury of the previous hours had been replaced by dead, flat calm. The storm had passed, spent itself. Water lapped against the ship's hull, the air still, only a faint breeze of the ship's making as she nosed gently into the Bay. The sheltered waters rippled softly with an oily slowness. The faint hum of machinery carried from below and every so often the muffled sounds of the outboard motors being warmed in the barrels of water. Surely that wouldn't carry to Leith, two miles round the headland? Countless, unfamiliar southern stars sparkled in the cloudless sky, stretching from the mountains across and down to the far horizon out at sea. No moon, the stars cast a gentle light. Not enough to betray *Antrim's* blacked-out presence to anyone on the shore just over there, surely.

We came to a gliding stop. The slightest of offshore breezes picked up, barely enough to start pushing *Antrim* almost imperceptibly towards shallow water. With troops over that side there wasn't a great deal the ship could do about it, but wait patiently for the waters to clear of small boats, before turning back to sea.

Ted and his people were quickly over the side, already one of the outboard engines playing up. The crew fought it hard, pulling over and over again on the starter chord. I could sense their mounting frustration. We were taking too long. The ship waited quietly, patiently, never once showing unease, slowly drifting towards the shallows. As ever with *Antrim*, there came no pressure. She knew we were doing our level best. We knew, though: time to 'Get on, John!' At last Ted told us to go.

He would manage. Yes, he was sure. By now two more outboards were faltering, but he would tow if necessary. Five boats should be enough for most if not all eventualities. With whispered 'good lucks' and 'take cares' they moved off, a shade uncertainly perhaps, at least one under tow, soon fading into the darkness. Immediately, silently, the destroyer turned for the sea. She was a pure-blooded, sea-going warship and despite her composure, creeping around at dead of night, close inshore, could not be coming naturally; nor to us. It was all a long way from Kenya. I decided to remain on deck: that illogical, sharing-conditions-with-the-troops thing again. The ship started to pick up forward motion, a fast walking pace, eagerly nosing her way free from the confines of the Bay.

It arrived as the merest, softest breeze caressing the nape of my neck; scarcely there, yet noticed immediately for it came from behind, from where it shouldn't, from where we had left the troops with at least one engine not working. Within minutes we were back to convulsed seas, spindrift, roaring winds—the whole bloody lot all over again! This time we had been hit by a katabatic wind, an onrush of cold, dense air accelerating down the mountains. It crashed into the Bay picking up ever greater speed as it funnelled out to sea, barrelling all before it. Spiteful, treacherous, unforgiving South Georgia was at it again. I knew it spelt trouble, no doubting it.

Ten minutes after departing the ship, before the wind struck, Boat Troop was struggling. Near simultaneously, three out of five engines stopped. Our fears concerning the age and reliability of the engines were playing out. The two boats with power took the others in tow. Then the wind struck. It smashed into them from in front. Flat calm to raging, shrieking, hammering in an instant, the air became dense with salt-laden spray. Eyes awash, stinging intensely, it became difficult to see in any direction. Waves grew remorselessly, reaching six or more feet. They combined with the wind to drive the boats back and out towards the open sea. Realisation burst upon the troops. This had become a fight for survival against nature and their physical strength felt wholly unequal to the challenge. They bent into the driving wind and waves, the boats lifting and twisting, threatening to capsize. Safety lay to the front. Somehow they must get forward.

Two of the boats reached their destination, one towing the other. Pausing only to ensure all was well with the team brought ashore, and sparing no thought for their own safety, Tommy Trenton and his crew went back out to help tow in the others. When their engine failed they too were propelled out towards the sea. Of the five Gemini that set out from *Antrim* that night, three would make it to Grass Island, two were swept away: Tommy's and the second commanded by Chippy Carpenter, Ted's deputy.

Ted reported the situation to *Antrim* first thing the following morning, after giving the missing boats time to make the objective. He passed on what little they knew: six men in two boats missing. The rest of Ted's SITREP indicated that he had Leith and Stromness under observation from Grass Island and that the enemy appeared unaware of their presence. Despite this last, spirits remained subdued. We all knew. The Geminis were probably out at sea, possibly capsized, the men drowned. We were facing the loss of six of our friends and colleagues lost under appalling circumstances. It didn't seem right. We expected to take hits. It was the way of things. But, like this? And, for what? What exactly had we achieved? What were we likely to achieve to justify such losses? Our earlier thrill at being on operations, the youthful enthusiasm and excitement had been replaced by an altogether more sombre mood. Over a twenty-four-hour period we had become seasoned South Atlantic soldiers, toughened by ordeal, informed by setbacks.

With undetected patrols ashore, Captain Young accepted the risk of mounting a search for the missing boats. The task fell to Humphrey.

Calculations put the boats well offshore and down the coast, almost certainly out of sight of the enemy's locations on land. The weather briefing gave scant encouragement: gale-force winds, sea-state rough to very rough, with a cloud-base of around 200 feet. In fact the cloud-base came down well below that, offering marginal visibility at best.

Ian lifted Humphrey with instructions to search for the missing men in an area off Busen Point about three miles up the coast from the mouth of Cumberland Bay. Staring out the rear door of the helicopter, with visibility obscured by dense spray and occasional squalls of driving sleet, Fitz gave it long odds. He knew that they could not use radar for fear of alerting the enemy to the Task Group's presence. It had to be 'Mark 1 Eyeball', in poor visibility only likely to worsen. Not at all promising. Chris Parry did his sums too. Employing the crew's own weather observations against the best guesses of the 'met' people, he advised Ian to head a distance down the coast beyond that given at the pre-flight briefing and further out than instructed. They box-searched for an hour or more, until their fuel ran low. On the last leg of their search, moments before heading back to the ship, Chris picked up the faint chirrup of a homing beacon.

Chippy and his crew had been catching the distant sound of a helicopter for some while. At first they thought it must be the enemy. But eventually, he and his patrol caught the briefest of glimpses as the aircraft emerged from a bank of mist in the far distance, at the very limits of their spray-blurred vision. Chippy checked with his team. Yes, they thought so too, pretty certain: a Wessex, the pilots' cab in its elevated position utterly distinctive. As far as they were aware the enemy had no Wessex. It had to be ours, Humphrey again. Confident in their assessment, that they had positively identified friend from foe, only then did Chippy seek help by opening up on his SARBE search and rescue beacon. Until that moment he had maintained radio-silence for fear of exposing the Task Group's presence to the enemy. Ian turned immediately towards the correct part of the ocean. Fitz spotted them first, a speck at the furthest point of visibility. Ian shot forward. Chippy immediately turned off his radio. Shortly after, he and his team were aboard Humphrey, the boat slashed and sunk.

Chippy and his patrol had been picked up a near incredible sixty-two miles offshore from where they had been dropped off the evening before. The position lay well distant from the entrances of both Stromness and Cumberland Bays. Visibility had been poor throughout. And aside from the one short burst on the SARBE, with its modest range, neither helicopter nor boat had made any other transmissions. The search had very likely passed undetected. Choosing to maintain radio silence as they did, Chippy and his crew had risked a certain and lonely death out in the vast emptiness of the South Atlantic. Their self-less dedication was almost too painful to contemplate. Of the other boat, there remained no news. We feared the worst.

During the time the Squadron had been making its attempts to get on target, the SBS had been experiencing similar frustration. Their selected route looked straightforward enough. They would launch from Endurance, their plan benefitting from the ship's detailed local knowl-edge. It displayed an elegant simplicity. Captain Barker and his navigator had encouraged the SBS to put ashore in Hound Bay using the ship's boat. They knew the chosen landing-site to be sheltered from the worst of the weather and most unlikely to be patrolled by the enemy. From there the recce team could move cautiously on foot through the Sorling Valley to Cumberland Bay East. Once they had proven the area clear of enemy, the patrol's boats would be brought forward by helicopter. If that went undetected, they would continue on, eventually taking to the waters of Cumberland Bay to get to their target area.

But for the ice, the insertion would most likely have worked. At a frequency impossible to predict, it calved from the Nordenskjold Glacier into Cumberland Bay in large, disintegrating chunks, many the size of a house, pushing out huge bow-waves. Even without the surges, the risk of ice puncturing the boats would have been acute. It formed a near-solid sheet of brash, choking the southern end of the Bay. Hit by one of the periodic 'tsunamis', rupture of any small craft would be a near certainty, swamping and capsizing even more likely. Survival in such cold water would be impossible, a matter of minutes. Yet the patrol made repeated, gallant attempts to make passage. Eventually, reluctantly, they had to accept the inevitable and call it off.

The SBS patrol's request for extraction came into *Antrim*'s ops room shortly after Chippy's rescue. It didn't go down well. There followed an amount of dissent from one or two of their planners. Too much, some of it strongly pitched. Was it really necessary? Shouldn't they stay on the ground a while longer, to give it another go?

It had little, if anything, to do with us, but neither Danny nor I liked this second-guessing. In the Regiment we went with the man on the spot. We had just, rather dramatically, demonstrated our approach. We stayed quiet, glancing across at Curtis Lee the SBS Liaison Officer who was arguing in favour of the patrol's request, silently indicating our sympathy as best we could. He was a highly experienced, mature operator, his judgement notably sound. He knew his people. If they said it couldn't be done, it couldn't be done. There was no point in wishing it otherwise. How could anyone in the rear gainsay that? The patrol on the ground would be as committed as any of us. It is not easy to 'call time', often morally easier to press on. They would have tried their utmost before 'calling it a day'.

I sensed there was something else in the arguments pitching back and forth. Danny and I seemed part of it, even though we were out of the specific tactical situation under discussion and keeping our own counsel. The issue seemed pregnant with things perhaps not being said openly about the Squadron's misfortunes: Fortuna most likely, not helped by those bloody outboard motors in Stromness Bay. There had always been healthy rivalry between SBS and SAS. Only, I was picking up an unattractive undercurrent at just that moment. Perhaps it reflected a determination by one or two of the SBS to avoid having their Service pigeon-holed along with us in Navy minds. That would be disappointing, but understandable given what we had all endured over the previous day or so.

Before long, good sense prevailed, Curtis won his case and instructions were issued for the recovery of the patrol. It had been an uncomfortable episode. I didn't much like the way Curtis had had to argue so forcefully in favour of the patrol's request. I liked it much less for what it might have been saying about our own efforts, including a possible falling-away of respect and confidence in me personally. Perhaps it was merely pressure starting to show, as our respective plans and theories got put to the test. But definitely, over the last twenty-four hours or more the light-hearted fellowship at the top of the embarked force had given way to a less easy state. There existed an undercurrent difficult to isolate, a certain tension that would persist.

Danny and I found a quiet corner. He scrambled his Rubik's cube and then as swiftly put it back into order. I never discovered how he did that. And he never showed me; and that was through no lack of asking! Neither of us felt particularly up-beat, Danny masking his concern better than me. I felt decidedly low. Along with everything else, my mind kept turning on Ted's missing patrol. I hoped my dank spirits didn't show too much. I tried my best to contain them. He tried to buck me up, sensing my dejection nevertheless. He was right. It could be worse. We could only do our best. And yes indeed, we did have troops on target. It helped. I got a grip. He re-spun his cube.

The following day started well enough, the missing patrol excepted. Overnight Ted had managed to get onto the 'mainland'. With tiresome predictability his outboard motors had played up. Struggling across the narrow stretch of water, they landed midway between Stromness and Leith to find a tangled mess of metal along the foreshore, debris from the whaling stations. Add in the slippery rocks and it had been no easy matter getting themselves and the rubber boats up the beach onto dry land without mishap. It took them an age, testing their patience to near breaking point. Although they had lost time they stuck with their plan, one party pushing on to Stromness, another to Leith, a third remaining to guard the hidden boats and stores.

Stromness proved to be clear of enemy, an eerie ghost-town constantly sighing and banging in the wind. In extremis, it might serve as somewhere to take shelter from the elements should that become necessary. The likelihood of being discovered among its many buildings had to be remote. The patrol filed the thought away, returning to the cached boats.

Ted and his patrol had made for Leith, taking up a position of observation in the area of Harbour Point. They could see lights below. There was a bit of movement, the odd glimpsed shape passing in front of a window. The steady *donk, donk,* of a diesel generator drifted on the wind. The engine stopped in the early hours as the Argentinians turned in for the night. It was late, two o'clock in the morning. Ted pondered that for a moment, putting it down to the fabled Latin preference for late nights before recalling that the Task Force, operated on ZULU (Greenwich Mean Time). This put us four hours ahead of local time.

The decision to place the entire Task Force on ZULU had been taken by Fleet's operational staff for the sensible if mundane purpose of keeping everyone on the same 'watch face' irrespective of international time-zone. This would simplify management for everyone: the coordination of meetings, scheduling of events, the annotation of papers, the logging of signals. Even body clocks would become aligned. Everybody and everything would be on a shared battle rhythm. It made a far-reaching contribution beyond managerial conveniences. The unforeseen, additional benefit was to put us at all times four hours ahead of our enemy. We would be up and breakfasted well before the start of their day, every day. The Argentinians never twigged.

Not everyone in Leith lay asleep. At one point a sentry let loose with a burst of automatic fire, spooked by a rock fall to his rear. The patrol looking down noted his position. At first light the entire garrison stood-to their defensive positions: all sixteen of them. An officer did his rounds, stopping at each trench to have a word. Conscientious maybe, but in so doing he pinpointed the exact location of each and every trench: the mortar, another machine-gun, and over there a radio, presumably the commander's trench.

Ted noted that the scheme laid before him covered the approaches from the sea to the near exclusion of all else—and not particularly skilfully at that. There was limited depth, rudimentary mutual support between trenches, and scant concealment. The mortar had been 'forward sloped', looking towards the sea and coastline more or less in plain sight of our presumed, most likely avenue of advance. Worse, actually better from our stand-point, the surrounding, higher ground had been left unattended. Yet, it overlooked everything. Provided the enemy stuck with what appeared to be their positional defence plan, it looked possible to snipe out more or less the entire garrison from where the patrol lay in watch.

This had to be the work of a poor tactician with minimal understanding of defence theory, a rank amateur. Nor did the troops come across as being particularly sharp. Ted soon had everything mapped out: each trench, shelter, other notable positions and the enemy's routine together with a recommended method of attack. He felt no need to push any further forward; simply keep the place under surveillance from where he was. Make note of any changes. He passed it all back to the *Antrim* ops room. We were hugely encouraged. The report clarified the situation. Boat Troop would require only modest reinforcement to defeat the enemy at Leith. We could concentrate the remainder of the Squadron's strength on Grytviken should that be necessary. Simultaneous, or near-simultaneous, assaults on Leith and Grytviken were feasible. The report helped reduce much of the hurt and disappointment of the previous days, underscoring the value of good, up-to-date target intelligence. It should have proved highly instrumental. It didn't, being rendered effectively redundant by all that was about to follow.

4. Search to Destruction

Eventually, the enemy started to play a more active role, a development from which they never recovered as we reacted one way and they failed to counteract effectively in another. On the morning of 23 April, shortly after Ted's report came into the operations' room, *Endurance* found what turned out to be one of two Argentine Hercules C130 aircraft in the area. Fortunately the ship escaped discovery. Not so lucky *Plymouth, Tidespring* and *Brambleleaf.* They were discovered well to the north-east of the Island conducting a much-needed refuelling. A third enemy aircraft also in the surveillance role, a Boeing 707, was later seen flying at low altitude down South Georgia's east coast. If the air activity wasn't worrying enough, *Endurance* then intercepted a radio transmission that could only have come from a submarine. All this activity had to be connected. It was. The developments chimed with highly classified intelligence from Northwood warning that the enemy intended to defeat us at sea, employing a submarine now in the area. The Navy kept much of this 'close-hold', thus for a while the embarked forces remaining blissfully unaware of the submarine menace.

Young must have felt the initiative passing to the enemy. Beyond all doubt he had lost the element of operational surprise. The Argentinians knew we were offshore. But Ted's efforts at Leith showed that it should still be possible to achieve tactical surprise at the local level, on land—in Stromness Bay at least. To add to the pressure, he and his deputy had recently been quizzed by their higher command on the lack of progress ashore and, it must be assumed, SF's shaky part in it all. It encouraged him and Guy to consider an early assault on Leith, employing the Squadron to exploit Ted's intelligence, leaving Grytviken for later. When asked my opinion, I offered that we could certainly do Leith if they

69

wanted, in the early hours of the following morning at the earliest, weather permitting. We would probably have to use the ship's boats to get ashore covertly, for we would want to get up onto our enemy by stealth, opening the assault at first light to catch them in their known positions.

In fact Leith looked bankable at any time provided it remained as Ted had found it. Its early loss to the enemy could be expected to dent spirits at Grytviken, their assumed main location. But there again, might a move against any lesser target be interpreted as a sign of our weakness rather than strength, a lack of confidence? Could it stiffen enemy resolve? And, what exactly would be achieved by taking Leith without Grytviken? We could suffer losses and reveal even more of our hand for little appreciable gain, because we must surely have to tackle Grytviken at some stage. Taking Leith early and alone didn't appear to add much. Eventually, it was decided that we should continue on land as we were: recce preceding an assault on Grytviken by the Marines as the main effort, Leith to be fitted in as best we could. As one might expect, a large part of me found the idea of the Squadron delivering an early result at modest risk hugely attractive, making up for some of the previous disappointments.

The Task Group commander with his wider responsibilities had felt compelled to address the developing maritime threat first, matters on land having to wait. This had to be right; a failure at sea threatened outright defeat. It was the wise call. Young made his decision, alerting his ships to prepare for a determined bout of anti-submarine warfare. Land forces he left to continue their recce efforts. This we did, most of us still unaware of the submarine at that juncture.

If Captain Young ever harboured doubts about his priorities, they would be dispelled the following morning when the BBC World Service passed on an Argentine report of the presence of two warships and a troop-carrying ship off South Georgia. The bulletin effectively confirmed that the enemy's Navy and Air Forces had located us, if not in whole, then certainly in part. By then *Tidespring*, our vital RFA oiler with her embarked Royal Marine company, had been removed to an area of safety 200 miles to the north east.

Endurance, carrying 16 Troop, kept close inshore where it should be difficult for any submarine to find, let alone engage her. Out at sea her noisy, non-military specification diesel engines would have been a booming give-away. Lurking among the fjords she remained a potent threat, poised to contribute with her WASP helicopters armed with air-to-surface missiles.

Antrim too pulled back from the immediate area to get herself into a better position from which to mount her ASW search. Naturally, SHQ and Mountain Troop had no other option than to go with her, to become wholly redundant bystanders. Such is the nature of naval warfare for embarked forces.

Northwood assessed the Task Group to be up against the *Santa Fe*, an ex US Navy ocean-going Guppy-class submarine of Second World War vintage. Her diesel-electric propulsion meant she could hover, remain still when submerged if needs be. It equipped her for delicate, close inshore work. Lying in ambush perhaps. And she was reasonably quiet. She would be tough to find. An antique, maybe, but armed with modern torpedoes, a veteran boat well up to the job. The odds were evenly matched.

The submarine had departed Mar del Plata ten days earlier. Fleet intelligence calculated that this should have her in and around South Georgia on or about 24–25 April. *Endurance*'s radio-intercept served to confirm the assessment. Taking all available information into account including what we knew of Leith, *Antrim*'s operational staff thought the submarine most likely to head for Grytviken, drop reinforcements and stores by night, before heading straight back out to sea to take us on. If they were right we could expect to find her coming out of Cumberland Bay early the following morning!

Northwood had kept the main Task Force commander, Rear Admiral Sandy Woodward, abreast of developments. A submariner himself, he understood the dangers confronting the Paraquet force. He saw that we could do with more helicopters, not just troop lift to make good the Fortuna losses, but ASW capable frames. He sent HMS *Brilliant*, a Type 22 frigate. Captained by John Coward, she proved not only brilliant in name, but brilliant by nature throughout the war, always there when needed.

Brilliant caught up with the Task Group in the nick of time. She brought two Lynx helicopters and another hull-mounted sonar comprising some of the Navy's most modern ASW equipment. It would be easy to overlook this, put this development down to good fortune. In fact, her timely arrival was the product of intelligence combined with professional forward thinking and the utterly determined implementation of a planned intervention. Captain Coward had raced to the scene pushing his ship to her limits knowing that he had little time to spare. Luck had little to do with it.

The Task Group commander's plan was straightforward. He had Leith under observation by Ted who would surely report the appearance of any submarine. Therefore, he would concentrate on Grytviken and Cumberland Bay as the intelligence suggested. To confuse matters though another report came in from a BAS field-station sited on Bird Island, at the very northern tip of South Georgia. Scientists there claimed to have seen two enemy warships and fast jet aircraft. Young viewed this with scepticism believing correctly that over the previous days they must have seen elements of the Task Group, mistaking these for Argentinians. Nevertheless, he factored into his arrangements the outside possibility of the report's accuracy. His warships would move in on the entrance to Cumberland Bay conducting ASW as they went. Given the distances involved, they would not arrive in time to catch any submarine coming out on the surface at first light the following morning. He would have to rely on his helicopters for that.

Young now had six aircraft available, but only his own, venerable Wessex III, the ubiquitous Humphrey, optimally equipped for anti-submarine operations. Thank goodness the helicopter and his crew had come through Fortuna. *Brilliant* could provide two, modern Lynx. These had limited ASW search capability, but came armed with homing torpedoes. Finally, *Endurance* and *Plymouth* could offer three WASP helicopters; these had no search capability beyond eyesight though they were armed with AS12 missiles. Crude by modern 'fire-and-forget' standards, an AS12 had to be manually guided to its target by its operator using a joystick. It took virtuosity under the best of conditions and heroic levels of steadiness on operations.

Once again fortunes would rest on the professional skills and capacities of the Fleet's Air Arm. Indeed, our lives, let alone operational success, lay in their hands. They knew it. Nothing was left to chance. Everything was double-checked: airframes, weapons, tactics, coordinating instructions. Nothing was overlooked. They fully understood the task and its dread gravity. It is not possible to do anything other than destroy an enemy submarine once found, one intending attack. Boarding is no option. Nor is it practical to call upon it to surrender. A hostile submarine must be found then killed—no ifs, no buts. The Navy had an expression for the work, unambiguous, stone-hearted, if faintly archaic: 'search to destruction'.

Ian Stanley and his crew would lead off and control the search by air. Launching from eighty miles offshore, they intended to enter Cumberland Bay at first light on 25 April armed with two depth-charges, a weapon of much the same vintage as the submarine they hoped to find. Concurrently, *Brilliant*'s two Lynx were to check the area of secondary importance off Possession Bay. They should be prepared to come to the aid of Humphrey if needed, bringing their homing torpedoes. The AS12 armed WASPs would remain on deck-alert ready to reinforce whichever search area came up with 'the goods'.

I became aware of the 'search to destruction' early that morning. I had first sensed it lying in my bunk. It had awakened me. Something was up. The ship was surging forward, purposefully, with conviction riding hard up and over the waves, with a slight yaw. There was eagerness in the pronounced, unceasing and rhythmic motion, a clear sense of determined commitment. Strange how machinery could take on personal qualities; at that moment the ship felt unusually eager, wholly concentrated on a matter of urgency. It got me out of bed. On the way to the wardroom to grab a brew, jostled by the motion, everyone I passed came across more animated than usual. The excitement was tangible. I grabbed a quick bacon sandwich and mug of tea before going off to learn more, the wardroom staff able to offer little beyond a submarine and Cumberland Bay.

Our ops room had the bare outlines. The Navy was certain: there was an enemy submarine out there somewhere. We were heading for Cumberland Bay, the most likely place to find it. Humphrey was up and Lynx from *Brilliant*. She had just arrived to reinforce us. Nothing found as yet. Instinctively, I made my way to the lower bridge to get a view. I had the place to myself. It should have been no surprise. There would be nothing to see. Besides, the ship's company would be at their action stations, manning their piece of the ship, now emphatically a single, complex machine of naval warfare bent on destructive purpose. Outside all looked as grim as ever: grey, windy, the waves flecked with spray, but a relatively easy swell for once, under the usual solid, low cloud, an occasional shaft of wintery sunlight relieving the gloom. Cumberland Bay lay seventy miles to our front, and we were well off-shore, out of sight of land.

After a short while, an off-duty, naval officer joined me. He should have been resting. But he too needed to see out. He confirmed what I already knew: we almost certainly had a submarine on our hands, prob-ably off Grytviken. We stood in comradely quiet, legs braced, enjoying *Antrim*'s surging, impatient progress, her bows methodically rising and lowering, spray flying up, whipped away by the wind. She was doing what she had been built to do: fight. And she was enjoying the thrill of it, the release, the sense of certainty that action brings, the sea for once letting her get on unimpeded.

Then Captain Young ordered the Battle Ensign to be broken out. I got the implication without need of telling, but my companion explained nevertheless: attack in progress. We had found an enemy and were closing in for the kill. The helicopters might have been leading the assault, beyond the ship's visual range, but they were ours, part of *Antrim*'s weapon system. By extension, the ship herself was engaged, fighting. We were going in. It was gripping, near intoxicating. I didn't know what to expect. Scenes from boyhood matinees sprung to mind: *The Cruel Sea, Sink the Bismarck, The Battle of the River Plate*. I could imagine Young played by Jack Hawkins, up there, steely, lantern-jawed, duffel-coated, binoculars round neck, wearing one of those dark peaked hats now disappointingly gone from the Navy's wardrobe for some reason, taking us to our rendezvous with fate, leaning into the driving spray. But of course *Antrim* had a closed bridge—even so!

Ian Stanley had coasted into Cumberland Bay on first light, the weather relatively quiet for South Georgia (Map 3). A brisk offshore wind blew broken patches of fog, visibility coming in and out and likely to improve as a weak sun came up. Chris controlled the ASW action. He had decided not to use his radar for fear of alerting any submarine. Instead, the entire flight crew employed 'Mark 1 Eyeball', Ian and Stewart observing out the front, Chris through his blister window and Fitz out the door. It wasn't going to work. They were seeking the small, dark speck of a submarine on the surface, one obscured by the gloom and drifting fog banks. Chris proposed to give it a single sweep of his radar, literally a one or two second burst. It could make the difference and escape the attention of any enemy listener.

By then Ian had flown well into the Bay, paralleling its eastern coast, keeping as far away from Grytviken as possible, camouflaging Humphrey against the grey land behind. Chris advised they return to the entrance for his burst of radar. It would give a view out to sea as well as into both arms of Cumberland Bay, East and West. Ian brought Humphrey round in a gentle turn. Dodging the odd fog bank, they soon reached the best position. Ian informed Chris who flicked his switches rapidly on, then off. Instantly blips appeared on his screen before slowly decaying. Icebergs. As expected. He had been monitoring their movements over the previous days, giving each its own designation. They were all where they should be, save for one small echo. He knew that he had something. It didn't fit, definitely in the wrong place. He alerted Ian with a bearing and distance.

Ian brought Humphrey gently round onto the suggested track. A minute or so later Ian announced to his crew in flat, calm tones, softly, with no hint of excitement, 'Submarine ahead'. He pulled back on his cyclic, easing down the collective to bring the helicopter's nose up, bleeding off speed, to hold him well back from the boat, Humphrey a predator now creeping up on his sighted prey. Ian and Chris rapidly conferred, sparse words over the intercom. They agreed, beyond all reasonable doubt that it had to be a Guppy-class submarine, exactly as predicted: the *Santa Fe* coming out of Cumberland Bay bang on time.

Ian slowed some more, coming into a near hover, keeping well astern to blend into the grey mist and backdrop of South Georgia's coastline. Chris quickly did his sums, calculating the release-point for their depth charges. He would say the maths was simple, but then he was clever like that, and would one day make admiral. He gave Ian a speed and height to travel, informing him that their depth charges would have to be released the instant they passed over the submarine's fin (conning tower) having come in over the stern. This allowed for the forward throw. Ian sank Humphrey to the height recommended, aligning him directly astern the target. The submarine continued its deliberate progress out to sea, oblivious of the menace.

With everything ready, Humphrey made his move, accelerating into his attack. Chris flipped up the safety cap of the weapon release toggle. They were now at precisely the calculated height and velocity. He could make out the dark sea passing rapidly below, between his legs, through a gap between the sonar housing and the airframe. He saw an easy swell, flecked with white spray, oddly familiar under the wholly unusual circumstances. Humphrey came on in a shallow dive: 100 knots exactly. And then there it was, one moment sea, next the black, sinister metal of a submarine hull passing below. Chris thumbed the release as Ian gave the order. The two available depth charges arced ahead. One grazed the fin as it hurtled by to splash in front of the boat, both sinking to thirty feet below the surface as the submarine passed.

The two explosions hit the submarine amidships, just as intended. The boat was tossed up and over to one side, stern fully out of the water, propellers momentarily thrashing. Down below, one moment orderly, hushed, the crew preparing to dive, responding to quietly passed orders for taking the war to us, the next turmoil: bodies sent flying, lights flickering, bulbs shattering, cables and cabinets sheared from bulkheads, sparks crackling, pipes bursting, jetting steam and scalding water, the smell and smoke of electrical fires. In an instant the reassuring business of going through well-practised drills had become a raw fight for survival. The tables had been turned.

Ian and his team knew that the boat must be hurt, almost certainly unable to dive safely. She careered to and fro, first in a struggle for control, then in a bid to get away from her unseen attackers. But her assailants were not to be thrown off. Nor could they show pity or compassion. That might come later. For now, the submarine must cease to be a threat. No doubts, no 'maybes', this had to end in the submarine's destruction. Ian withdrew 400 metres from the stricken submarine, for Fitz to engage the fin with his GPMG in an attempt to destroy sonars, masts and otherwise keep the enemy crew down below from where they would be unable to see clearly to navigate. He passed a situation report to *Antrim* and called for the other helicopters. It was then that the Battle Ensigns had cracked out across the Task Group.

First to arrive was one of *Brilliant*'s Lynx, piloted by Nick Butler and Barry Bryant. Humphrey handed them control of the engagement before withdrawing to *Antrim* to rearm. By now the *Santa Fe* had managed to turn. Slowly sinking by the stern and listing badly she was attempting to run for the relative safety of the fully alerted Argentinian garrison in Grytviken. Her commander, Captain Bicain, a wholly decent, mild-natured and cultured man we were to learn, saw the approaching Lynx through his periscope. He watched in dread as a torpedo dropped. He knew that it must be a Mark 46, capable of homing in on its target, tracking a submarine to a depth of 1,000 feet before exploding against the hull of its quarry. The weapon had a deadly reputation, rated to be among the best of its kind. He and his crew probably had minutes to live.

Bicain remained composed, keeping his knowledge and fears from his crew. There was not a lot he or they could do that they weren't already doing. Stay afloat. Get back to Grytviken. And trust that the boat would be too shallow in the water for torpedoes to get at them. His faith bore dividends. The torpedo set off eagerly enough, 'sniffing' for its prey, sweeping back and forth, at one point passing directly under the submarine's stern, before heading out somewhere beyond. No matter, Butler and Bryant were satisfied. They had expected it. But they had demonstrated the threat. It should keep the submarine on the surface for the AS12 equipped WASPs now on their way. They continued their attack using a door mounted GPMG, emulating Humphrey's efforts at destroying the submarine's sensors and other exposed ancillary equipment. Fire poured in and around the fin, rounds bouncing off the armoured casing.

Then the three WASPs arrived, all eager to get stuck in, the Navy in no mood for holding back as their 'search to destruction' neared its climax. The Lynx retained tactical control of the action, directing aircraft forward in turn. To the appalled Argentine onlookers ashore they appeared to swarm, the air thick with helicopters. The WASPs concentrated their aim at the junction of the fin with the hull below which lies the submarine's nerve centre. A few of the missiles failed to explode, passing through the light glass fibre of the fin, the material insufficiently hard to detonate the warhead. On it went, helicopter after helicopter, their crews firing off everything that came to hand once the missiles were expended: door-mounted GPMGs, rifles. At one stage a pilot even drew his pistol before having second thoughts and holstering it.

The *Santa Fe* did her heroic best to fight back. The fin took so much fire that the commander had to remain below to navigate using the periscope, just as his attackers intended. In desperation, a seaman was sent up to try to fight off the swarming helicopters with a machine-gun. Firing through a narrow aperture his futile, yet truly gallant resistance, was cut short when inevitably hit, losing a leg to an un-exploding AS12. The poor fellow fell back into the operations room adding to the sense of calamity.

At last the submarine limped its way to the jetty at King Edward Point, Grytviken. The helicopters started to receive ground-fire from the beleaguered garrison as troops frantically sought to help their comrades in the stricken boat. Ian Stanley returned with Humphrey, enabling Chris to take hold of the one-sided battle once again. He and Ian saw that the submarine was defeated, no longer a viable target. They called a halt.

5. Going In

A number of people might later claim to have recognised the decisive moment, the instant when the initiative passed emphatically to us, when the right response might lead to the defeat of our enemy. Perhaps they could all be right, for a military organisation is oddly organic, a thought or sentiment sometimes taking hold rapidly and almost unconsciously. However, I credit my naval companion with recognising it, certainly before I did.

The two of us still on the lower bridge staring out across the ship's bows could only sense the events unfolding to our front in full view of the Argentine garrison in Grytviken. Yet, turning to me he offered that it had to change everything. We had shown our hand, lost operational surprise. Why wait any longer to complete advance-force reconnaissance? Wouldn't the enemy be in a state of shock? Presumably they had been relying on the submarine to defeat us. Now they had no means of winning. They must see that the game was up. Surely, we need do little more than sail in and take the place back.

Perhaps a touch uncertain after our misfortunes, I responded that it would be good to know more about the defences at Grytviken before committing to an assault in broad daylight. Were there weapons on the headlands that could damage an approaching warship? Were there mines on land or at sea? I rehearsed the unfavourable relative strengths. The Marine company was hours away. And if we went with the Squadron alone, the enemy's numerical advantage would be even greater. There had always been an issue over relative strengths, hence our determination to achieve tactical surprise. And on I blathered, in a rather condescending way. And then it struck me too. To hell with Staff College thoroughness and any caution arising from recent misfortune if that was the problem. Get a grip. Don't hold back. This was a moment to go with instinct, fast and furious, to go with what the Germans would have termed *Fingerspitzengefühl*: finger-tip feeling, or intuition. My Navy companion had it spot-on. I told him so. No more fannying around. The situation had changed decisively. Opportunity beckoned. Seize it. I went off in search of Guy Sheridan knowing that only he would be able to get through to Captain Young at the height of the Navy's search-to-destruction.

I found Guy soon enough. Whether or not he had been having the same thoughts, I wouldn't like to say. But he too saw that the time had come. He would have to choose his moment to approach the Commander. He knew the Navy. They would be absorbed by the *Santa Fe*. He might get only the one opportunity to make his pitch. However, we decided to warn the troops for a possible rapid move.

By late morning the helicopters were all back aboard the ships, the crews deservedly flush with success. They had been magnificent, Humphrey peerless. They had found the threat and gone after it with absolute determination. We were proud of them, grateful too. In a stroke they had removed a mortal danger and brought us to the point of victory. One more push and the day should be ours. Job done!

But a seemingly interminable 'stock-take' started up as all were probed to establish the precise status of the submarine and the possible wider maritime picture. Even the aircrew grew impatient with it. Time passed. It proved difficult to get the land voice heard. Tempers frayed. Was the moment passing? Had it already passed?

It was a frustrating episode. Wholly free to concentrate on matters other than maritime, the embarked force had moved its thinking. We had ditched tactical surprise in near myopic favour of operational shock. Tactical surprise was lost, but we should cash in on the moral sway the Navy had just attained over the enemy. The Argentine garrison must be teetering upon psychological collapse, their hopes shattered, their defensive strategy in tatters. We needed to finish them off. They had just witnessed the loss of their forward and principal line of defence to a swarm of helicopters. Lord knows what they must think lay behind. We should feed their fears, get in before they could regain composure, threaten them with everything we could lay our hands on. Go, go, go, go, go!

The Navy most certainly shared the urge, being just that much more measured about it. Their care made sense. They needed to be sure that the submarine no longer constituted a threat, that there was no other nautical menace out there, that they could therefore lift their attention from the seaward approaches to focus wholly on Grytviken. Get it wrong, and the error could result in the loss of a ship, perhaps the defeat of our entire operation.

Maybe this spoke of a difference between the Navy's way of fighting from in and off platforms, from a soldier's more individually distributed form of warfare. A single misjudgement at sea and the consequences could be catastrophic, resulting in the loss of an entire unit and its crew in a flash. Tolerances were often fine, many risks apparently measurable. Land warfare carried its dangers, and tools and disciplines for their mitigation; but its physics appeared to offer greater opportunity to make good an error. It is simply not so easy to lose an entire unit of tactically dispersed individuals on land in one fell swoop, as it is at sea. This is not to say that maritime forces cannot nor will not go with instinct to run a risk. The Royal Navy could most certainly take calculated risks, with a brilliant history of doing just that. Only there are differences and at times of crisis, no matter how slight, these can rub uncomfortably, especially when and where the parties are unfamiliar with one another.

At length all came into balance, cost and gains calculated, maritime imperatives squared, land force needs and preferences similarly: Captain Young ordered an attack by air, sea and land to take back South Georgia that very afternoon.

Various options for the assault were considered. The 'gunners' simply envisaged sailing into Cumberland Bay to pulverise the enemy into submission. At one point Guy had advocated rushing the enemy, taking advantage of their assumed, thorough demoralisation. We, the Special Forces, didn't care for much of this, preferring to get on the ground in a place of relative safety before moving in to develop things according to how we found them, this to mitigate the Task Group's lack of target intelligence and loss of tactical surprise. The plan eventually accepted and approved by Captain Young exhibited the necessary degree of cir-cumspection, a reflection of his thorough and careful temperament.

The enemy probably had up to 100 men, in prepared defensive positions, employing a range of unpleasant devices: mines, wire, machine-guns on fixed lines, pre-ranged mortar targets and such like. We didn't know how they had deployed exactly, but their positions and localities should be mutually supporting, covering all likely approaches and sited as to be able to absorb an attack and defeat it. If they were worth their salt, they would have put out a screen to pick us up as we approached. They would use this to shape our attack, drawing us into their chosen killing areas. And we couldn't altogether discount the crew of the submarine either; at the very least they could thicken up the rear, fall back positions.

The Royal Marine company on RFA *Tidespring* was out of the match, 200 miles away. Otherwise, the land force had about seventy-five men immediately available from across the warships, significantly fewer than the enemy, only 25% of the number needed for the assault if working to the customary 3:1 attack ratio. Aside from being low on bayonet strength, ours would be a scratch force. Each ship had a small detach-ment of marines to offer, about a dozen in total. Otherwise, from his originally embarked force Guy could rustle up a single mortar team, a few recce troops, two Naval Gunfire Assistance (NGA) teams, and a section of SBS. Fortunately he had us too, a SAS squadron of three troops, Boat Troop being over at Leith. The assault force may have been ad hoc, its SAS core anything but. The Squadron came hardened, cohe-sive, and accustomed to extemporisation. We also had plenty of sup-port: missile-firing helicopters and two warships with rapid-firing 4.5 inch guns. Immense, raw power, it should be enough.

We crafted the assault in two parts, playing to our confidently assumed moral supremacy, and remaining true to Northwood's direction to avoid unnecessary loss of life and damage to property. The first comprised the 'foot soldiers', the second the 'combat fire support', the guns and armed helicopters. Normally, these would be viewed as two parts of a whole, fire support working to help the troops achieve their purpose. In a way this remained the case. But, on this occasion we found it helped to see a distinction, to regard the two as operating discretely in complementary fashion, certainly until it became necessary to combine them on a single tactical target.

So, the Squadron would get on the ground to squeeze in on the enemy, deliberately and methodically. Meanwhile the guns would be fired to one side, to demonstrate the threat of our overwhelming power. Only if the first ran into trouble would the two combine. Then, once any local resistance had been quashed, the process would resume. In effect we would show constraint bringing direct force to bear only as and when necessary, the level of escalation being theirs to choose more than ours to determine, geared to the degree to which they resisted; as they say, it takes two to tango. In this way we hoped to avoid a toe-to-toe, bare-knuckle fight, that our enemy would do the decent thing and surrender. We would certainly give them every opportunity.

It would be necessary to start the troops from a place well back and out of contact before advancing them to induce 'the squeeze'. At no point should our movements on the ground enable the enemy to regain the initiative. We mustn't get sucked into anything evenly matched, or worse. As for the fire plan, the guns would start with a heavy concentration at a short, but safe distance from King Edward Point, the enemy's main position. Otherwise they and the armed helicopters would be on priority call to support the advancing troops if called upon.

Given the press of time and all else, the concept never got articulated in quite this way within the Task Group's command team. Not that it really mattered. The Squadron would spearhead the assault on land. I knew how we would do it; and so did the Troops. As the only formed manoeuvre unit on the ground, we should determine the minor tactics and direct the close fire-support; or so I thought.

Map study showed a flat area, Hestesletten, about 2000 metres south of Grytviken. It looked to be free of prepared enemy positions, making it a likely Landing Zone (LZ) for the insertion. Between the possible LZ and Grytviken lay a sizeable obstacle, Brown Mountain with a ridge running off it down to the sea. The mountain screened the LZ from the enemy out at King Edward Point, but it also overlooked the LZ and the southern approaches to the settlement. Indeed, it commanded the entire area. We didn't like it, not at all, for whoever held the ridge, held that part of South Georgia. In military terms it was 'vital ground'.[1] Consequently, the enemy must surely hold it. And if they did, we could be in for a rough time.

We pored over the map, searching for other options. We consulted *Endurance*. There weren't any. Given the urgency of the situation, the need to get on top of a reeling enemy, we would have to go with what we had, landing as far south and distant from Brown Mountain as we could. To reduce risk further, the area of the LZ and overlooking slopes would be pounded with prophylactic fire immediately before our landing. That should get us ashore. However, there remained the ridge. We would still have to deal with it. But, once we got on top it should be pretty well 'game over' for the enemy. We would be looking down onto Grytviken and its surroundings. I really did not want to involve the Squadron in what could amount to a full frontal, conventional style company attack. But Brown Mountain held the key, and if that was what it took to win, that was what we would do—not before I had applied all the firepower available though, including the armed helicopters to snipe out all identifiable enemy trenches.

We planned to ferry troops ashore using *Brilliant*'s two Lynx and Humphrey, giving us a troop-lift of twenty-four men per sortie. The ships should be close inshore, three or four miles from the LZ, giving

[1] Vital Ground, a specific term referring to ground of such importance that it must be retained or controlled for the success of the mission.

a short turn-round time. Even so, it could take up to an hour to get the entire force ashore, more than enough time for an enemy to react. Rather than wait for everyone to arrive before moving from the LZ, I favoured boldness to move lickety-split with what we had on the first lift to make straight for the ridge. Only if we came up against a strong and composed enemy would we wait for everyone before unpicking the feature.

We may have had an outline concept of operations, but not much thought had been given to the 'what ifs'. There had been little or no time for that. What if we found mines on the LZ? What if they attempted to deny us the LZ with indirect fire? What if we failed to take Brown Mountain ridge? What if we didn't meet them until we got into the whaling station? What if they had mined the approaches to King Edward Point? What if they fought harder than expected, our premise concerning their morale wrong? What if the Navy had to withdraw to meet a maritime threat leaving us ashore unsupported?

In my verbal orders to the Squadron I explained how we would advance to within machine-gun range of the enemy, before sniping out individuals. If push came to shove, we would also bring to bear naval gunfire, mortar, and MILAN anti-tank and the WASPs' AS12 missiles. It might seem cautious, but should work. I stressed the importance of Brown Mountain, that we might have to storm it. As I finished, Danny asked if he could say a few words. He stepped forward to emphasise the need for restraint. He reminded us all that the enemy were soldiers, like us, they too would be following orders and have families. While they should be hit when necessary, there could be no place for gratuitous violence. Going in hard was one thing, unjustifiable killing quite another.

We eventually got under way at about 1430 hrs ZULU in perfect weather for the job. We didn't have a lot of daylight remaining, five or six hours perhaps. Mountain Troop would go first. They were fully recovered from Fortuna and raring to get stuck in. I decided to join them, taking a signaller. This could be the trickiest part of the whole thing; best to be on the spot from the outset. There could be one or two big, early decisions to be made. Danny would remain in *Antrim* to keep us linked to the Task Group Commander. Guy Sheridan and the Marine company commander intended to land too, making us anything but short of commanders for tactical control of my small body of 'storm-troopers'. I gave it no thought.

As the Squadron would be leading the 'charge', being the only available, customarily formed body of troops, we might have been designated the tactical main effort. We weren't. But then we were all feeling our way, unpractised in the arts of a joint battle. Indeed, very few of us had been involved before in anything quite like the operation unfolding: an assault by a Special Forces squadron masquerading as a rifle company, and some 'up-for-it' sundry others, delivered by helicopters optimised for naval warfare, onto an enemy-held coastline, mounted from warships themselves not specifically prepared for amphibious operations. Indeed, the Task Group's various, joint force elements had never operated together until that moment, the covert recce-insertions excepted. This was improvisation at its most extreme. We were going in unrehearsed, without the benefit of any shared grounding in even the basics of what we were attempting. What could possibly go wrong?

As we got underway, departing the ships, naval gunfire prepared the LZ for our arrival. It would switch to Brown Mountain minutes before our landing, the fire directed by Chris Brown from an aerial OP. When it actually came time to lift the fire onto the mountain Chris experienced difficulty with the narrowness of the ridge-line. If he got the fire very slightly off, the rounds slid past the ridge to explode harmlessly beyond or below. He gave it a few goes before proposing to move the fire to more profitable targets closer in towards the visible enemy out at King Edward Point. He advised me to deal with the ridge myself using the mortar in the first instance, assuring that he would bring naval gunfire back promptly if required. It sounded reasonable. I acknowledged the adjustment to the fire plan, noting that he was clearly on top of things, with a clear understanding of the tenets of the operation and its priorities.

We sped towards the shoreline, the Landing Zone lying yards beyond. Skimming feet above the sea at around 100 knots, the tension mounted; the customary thrill of knap-of–the-earth flying was lost on us. At that moment 'fast and low' had been reduced from fun to merely the safest thing to do, and the sooner over the better. We were stuffed in. Nobody much cared for this part of the operation, packaged and wholly dependent on the pilots. We were vulnerable, anxious to get out and get on with things in our own way. Part of me was questioning the sense of going into a potentially 'hot' LZ quite so brazenly and in full daylight! At least it was a shared decision this time, not mine alone. That helped. And besides, what alternative was there? That helped too. I cleared my mind, glancing round the cab from my position up against the back of the right hand pilot's seat. There they were, blank faces seen before on other, barely-comparable occasions, no emotion, their calm contrasting with the helicopters clamorous rush.

The shore-line raced towards us, strangely solid, oddly familiar after all those days at sea. I readied for the flare that would signal rapid deceleration, the transition, then touch-down. I looked down at my rifle, safety catch on. Ready to go. At that instant, we banked violently, unexpected 'g' forces crushed the breath from our lungs. We dashed back to sea. Like scalded cats, we hurtled away

'What the hell?' I blurted over the intercom, bewildered, not knowing what to think. Nobody hit. Not taking fire. Faces turned my way. Others craning out. 'What the hell is going on?'

Broken words crackled over my head-set, difficult to make out: something to do with running into our own fire. I hadn't seen any on the LZ. The pilot had seen nothing. Chris was directing the fire. I knew that he had it under control, his aerial OP giving him a clear view of everything. He would have lifted the guns from LZ to the new targets by now. Cock-up. Somebody was second-guessing us, trying to be helpful maybe, but meddling; a first indication of too many cooks at work? Something similar was about to follow.

Things were quickly sorted. We went back in, the pilot apologetic though blameless. No fire, nothing, anti-climax. We were ashore, back on 'dry land', once more in our element. It felt good. There was that familiar sensation of being cast adrift, those few seconds bordering upon reproach as the helicopters departed; then that faint, initial unease at the stillness after the commotion of the flight. The texture of the ground, vegetation, the smells, the sounds, all registered by senses heightened by the anticipation of a fight.

After the constant motion of the ships our feet planted unexpectedly, staying where placed. It took a few seconds to grow accustomed to the certainty of footfall. The troops shook out into a semblance of tactical order, moving quickly away from their landing spots. It was a vulnerable moment. A quick glance round showed John to be on top of things. His troops fanned out to check the LZ. Clear of enemy and obstacles. We reported back to Danny. The next lifts had a clear run; they would be coming into a secure LZ. We turned to face Brown Mountain, which towered before us, forbidding. We needed to get going.

The Marines' mortar had set up, controlled by its company commander right alongside. We could hear naval gunfire in the distance, a lot of it, not see it. I supposed it was falling around King Edward Point, as Chris had recommended, certainly nothing on the ridge. I called for the mortar to cover the ridge before we headed off. I wanted to know that we had high explosive on immediate call should we need it. This meant pre-registering a target, a known point on the hill from which we could adjust. I wasn't looking for preparatory fire for softening-up purposes, solely assurance that bombs would arrive the instant we required them. We would be exposed as we neared the foot of the hill, at risk of being cut to ribbons as we came within range of the plunging small arms fire of any enemy above. The mortar was the ideal weapon for the purpose, deadly, notably quick to come into action.

We didn't get the mortar, request denied, dismissed abruptly, busy with a target. We would have to wait. But how could that be? Who but us could have called for rounds. What target? We could see no enemy nor hear enemy fire. What was the mortar doing? What could be more important than the attack's Main Effort? Hell, we were it. There was no other

'Effort' on the ground. The whole thing was so absurd that I thought I must have misheard. I repeated the request. The Marine company commander came back explaining again that they were busy with a target, we would have to wait our turn. Refused! I told him not to be silly, robust words to that effect, and to get a particular kind of grip. Repeated refusals followed until a final abrupt and impertinent put-down telling me that I was clogging the air, to get off the frequency; and if that wasn't shocking enough, it was my own bloody squadron's frequency!

Apparently, as the mortar team set up they had seen movement where the ridge met the sea. Their company commander had taken control to direct fire onto a hapless group of elephant-seals, probably an old fellow and his harem. We had already noted them as harmless. They represented no risk to the mission, save perhaps in the self-inflicted way unfolding. But nothing would deflect the mortar's commander from his self-determined efforts. In fairness, things were hard on him. His company, that should have been leading the assault, was still hundreds of miles away on *Tidespring*. The disappointment would have been more than most could bear.

Whatever the ifs and buts, this second instance of dissonance caused me to snap. The red mist descended. Ad hoc assault force aside, if this had anything to do with the Squadron's performance to date, or my performance, or me personally, to hell with it. We would do this attack our way, and alone if it came to that—save for Chris, his guns and the armed helicopters. Anything coming with undue conditions attached could get lost. We couldn't afford any more hold ups, unnecessary complications or disputes. Like it or lump it, the Squadron was at the front of this assault. Anybody who couldn't see that and support us needed to get out of our way. I told John to get going, to get up onto the ridge as soon as he could. We had lost enough time. I checked to ensure Chris was on instant call with the Navy's guns and had the armed helicopters on call. He was and did. For good measure, I told him to take control of the mortar. It was not to engage any target unless cleared by him or me. I urged John on. He didn't need it.

I radioed Danny, instructing him to tell the rest of the Squadron to catch up as soon as they could. They must not wait around the LZ. 16 Troop should bring a couple of GPMG tripods; they might come in handy, to extend the machine guns' effective range. I then stormed off behind Mountain Troop as the second helicopter lift started to arrive, the mortar still doing for non-combatant seals.

Before long we reached the foot of the ridge, my fury subsiding as I took in the threatening hill above. None of us hung around. We all knew to get to the top as soon as we could. The next few minutes might determine the outcome, or at least its character. Speed was of the essence. Still no incoming fire, no 'crack and thump' from a hidden enemy. But we did catch sight of a worrying feature further up the mountain. It had the appearance of a prepared, defensive position, complete with a pole or antenna. It was silent, but in a bad place. I asked John to put a MILAN missile into it. Best play it safe. Besides, no harm in showing the enemy over at King Edward Point or Grytviken what we could do, snipe out their positions by missile from beyond small-arms ranges. The MILAN missile wobbled up the hill, crashing into the bunker with a satisfying crump. The remainder of us had meanwhile pushed on; almost there.

It was a steep climb. Nobby Clark was struggling. Normally he worked in the stores with Graham, who had allowed him ashore to carry a MILAN. Why not? After all, it was an all-hands-to-the-pumps occasion. Getting on in soldiering years, Nobby had a fine operational record having seen active service in Dhofar, Borneo and Kenya; Malaya too, we 'youngsters' wanted to believe. Fluent in Swahili and Malay, he had a reputation as a jungle fighter, accomplished then in environmental skills not that much in demand around the Antarctic. Ever-willing though, he had stepped forward, now shouldering his anti-tank missile, plodding manfully under the load, one painful step at a time up the slope, showing every year of his advancing age. He wasn't going to miss this outing, not for all the tea in China. I got to the crest ahead of him, not by much.

As we departed *Antrim*, the Navy had made it absolutely clear that they regarded the crippled submarine as unfinished business. If we got the opportunity, destroy the thing, do for it once and for all. An anti-tank missile into its operations room, where the fin met the hull, should do the trick they thought. I looked down the hill into Grytviken and there she lay, the *Santa Fe*, black, sinister, listing slightly at the jetty over at King Edward Point. And here came Nobby with the very thing we needed, a missile. He staggered up to the crest of the hill. I waved him over. He flopped down beside me, appreciating the soft, welcoming turf.

'Zifty boom wallah up the kapala, Boss'. None of us knew what it meant, a Nobby Clarkism. It probably meant in this instance that he was feeling knackered.

'Do you know how to use that thing' I asked, jerking my thumb at his MILAN.

'Sort of.'

'Quick, then. Soon as you can. Put it into that bloody submarine.'

He visibly perked up. Somebody must have given him a quick lesson—or maybe it was another of his hidden talents.

'Anywhere in particular?' That was impressive. He seemed to know what he was doing!

I told him, 'Where the conning tower meets the hull.'

There came an urgent tapping on my shoulder.

'Boss, Boss.'

'Not now,' I snapped, still a touch impatient of any hold up, no matter what from whom.

'We're busy?'

I checked to see how Nobby was doing. Sorting it, but not fast enough. I urged him on. We would continue our advance immediately after doing for the submarine. Must hurry.

'Come on, Nobby.'

'Boss, Boss listen to me.' It was Lofty Arthy. His voice had grown insistent, commanding, not to be fobbed off.

'What the hell is it?'

93

'They've surrendered!'

I looked up from Nobby and the submarine. Bloody hell, they had. White flags and sheets everywhere. How could I have missed it. I pushed Nobby away from his missile. He showed surprise, then disappointment.

'Zifty boom wallah.'

Thank goodness the troops had their wits about them, that at least one of us had taken it all in: the enemy to the front over at Grytviken, their white flags, the submarine, Nobby and his MILAN, and the Boss with his apparent submarine fixation. In Lofty's case he did more than just observe; he had the wit to act, and so prevented a potentially serious mishap.

What about the guns? I could hear nothing. Chris must have turned them off. A quick check confirmed that he had put the guns and mortar on hold five minutes earlier, as we were climbing the ridge, when he had spotted the white flags. So far, so good.

In theory, one should not go to a surrendering enemy. To do that is to expose oneself to harm. It should be the other way about. However, the most cursory of looks at the lie of this land showed that the theory would be difficult to apply. They were over on King Edward Point, round the cove and beyond Grytviken, a good two miles away, about 1,000 metres in a straight line across the water. If we went most the way round it might be possible to signal them to come out down the narrow track to meet us short of the whaling station. We could remain in cover of the buildings, they in the open. Even that seemed complicated though: communicating over the distance, down the track, and what about language. And even if we managed to find a way through all that, what then would we do with them? In fact they looked fine where they were, vulnerable and nicely contained. Perhaps on this occasion we should go to them.

I was not inclined to refer the matter upwards. The plan was working out better and faster than expected. I knew what had to be achieved, and had the best view of the situation on the ground. I felt no need for help in making what seemed the next tactical decision. How much the sentiment was fed by the frustrations of recent events, including the slight we had suffered on Hestesletten, it would be difficult to say. But we were enjoying our freedom to act and in no mood to stop before the job was wholly done.

Peering across the water to King Edward Point there wasn't much to see, the odd person out in the open, most of them keeping their heads down. They looked done in though, white cloth everywhere. Goodness knows how I could have missed it. I sensed they simply needed some means of formalising the end of open hostilities. There was probably no better way than going across to talk to them about it face to face. I decided to do just that. After all, the whole operation had been based upon exploiting an assumed moral ascendancy. So, get across there and exercise it.

I instructed John to deploy his people along the ridge-line, reinforcing his numbers with the others as they arrived from the LZ. He was to register all potential targets, allocating a means of destruction to each. Counter-intuitively, he should occasionally make one or two people visible, to convince the enemy that they did indeed face overwhelming strength, that they were overlooked, literally staring down the barrels of our guns. In effect, he was to reassure the enemy that surrender had to be the sensible option. This should help me in any negotiations.

If the enemy opened fire on us, breaking a putative truce, he was to respond to my orders. Should I be unable to communicate for any reason, he should engage and set about sniping his way methodically through the enemy garrison until they again threw in the towel. He must attempt to do this avoiding unnecessary damage to property, the BAS buildings in particular. I did not expect him to move forward, even to dig me out of a hole. That could lose us the initiative, get us embroiled in an incident probably irrelevant to mission achievement. He shouldn't forget the submarine. Why not start with it? Make a bloody great bang of it, to shock them back into surrender. Why damage our property when we could break theirs to get them back on track?

I then radioed Danny in *Antrim*, informing him of our intentions, asking him to pass them on to Captain Young and Guy. That done, and with John busily sorting his troops, we set off down the hill towards Grytviken,

We were a small group, each a volunteer: Geordie the Squadron's Yeoman of Signals, Stu another signaller, and Sid Davidson a thoroughly-amiable, mild-natured Mountain Troop man with a smattering of Spanish, or so he assured me. None of us had a clear idea as to how to proceed beyond finding a place on the far side of Grytviken from where we might call forward an enemy officer to parley. It seemed best though to keep the enemy out at King Edward Point where they were contained, out of the weather, and under our guns; but I should not involve the Squadron in guard duties. We had unfinished business over at Leith.

We harboured little doubt. The enemy appeared to be psychologically crushed. I glanced back. Yep, fine, we looked the part. I had no need to tell anyone. We all knew the theory, the folklore: that it was difficult to shoot a man wearing a smile. We should come across as confident, self-assured, unthreatening. We strode out, if not wearing a smile, at least looking amiable; well, perhaps not Geordie with his near perpetual scowl. I turned again, to smile at him, only to get a blank stare in return. Careful, he might think I was seeking reassurance. I increased the pace.

The old whaling-station moaned and sighed, a ghost-town. Rusted corrugated iron sheets clattered in the wind. We glanced through windows as we hastened by, at desks still loaded with papers, at workbenches complete with tools, as though everyone had simply left in an instant. The temptation to pause, to stop and explore proved almost irresistible. A small, white weather-boarded chapel stood back on a slight rise in dignified solitude, shining out from the surrounding grey. The *Petrel*, an old whaling vessel, lay drawn up on the beach, rusting but otherwise apparently ready, as if waiting to pick up from where she had left off. All the while there was that sense of Shackleton. He had been with us since before the Fortuna: never left. If we had time, we should visit his grave.

Through the whaling station, without pausing the four of us continued down the track to King Edward Point. There had been no conve-
niently located cover from which to call forward the enemy for parley.
Besides that didn't seem such a good idea any more, too timid under the
circumstances; and unnecessary, for John had just reported the garrison
formed up in the open, waiting for us presumably. We pressed on, strid-
ing fast and confidently as if owning the place, which in a way we did,
accepting that it was British, our small group representative of the
Crown. I dropped the smile. It felt too forced, implausible and stupid.
Besides, my face had started to ache. I carried my rifle at the trail instead,
trying to communicate trust in the enemy and their surrender. Sid lifted
his into the Northern Ireland style 'high port' to signal the same.

The submarine lay alongside the jetty, sinister, scarred yet still threatening in that dark, U-boat sort of way. And there stood our enemy as if
on parade. About 200 metres to go, we kept our pace, looking straight
ahead. We all knew to maintain an air of supreme confidence combined
with authority, avoiding any undue sense of superiority. I hoped to keep
this on a strict professional level, all emotion out of it. We had won,
they had lost, let's just talk the consequences. A machine-gun nest lay
off to the left, two Argentinians still standing in it, albeit with hands
raised. Sid waved them away to join the others formed up outside the
nearby buildings. They did. Good. Everything as it should be. At that
instant, with maybe 100 metres to go, probably less, certainly almost in
among them, Geordie called. Apparently Guy wanted us to stop.

'What? Why?'

'There are mines.'

We had been on the look-out for mines, finding no evidence of dis-
turbance on the track. We had registered the possible presence of
improvised, command detonated devices, to the side, now behind,
otherwise nothing.

'No there aren't.'

Yards to go, we could see the whites of their eyes. This was no time for
hesitation. In any case, we must be through any mine field. Sod it. I told

Geordie to ignore the call. We couldn't stop. Instead, we strode onto the Argentinians' makeshift parade ground and up to our enemy stood in formation. I told Geordie he could let Guy know that we were there.

'Thank him for the warning. And tell him, no mines on the track, as far as we can tell.'

Best not upset the boss; but back to the immediate business in hand.

The enemy looked in reasonable shape, formed up in three ranks, standing 'at ease'. Most of them gazed at us with studied curiosity. They looked disciplined and calm, well turned-out in those smart olive coloured, 1950s-style US Army cast-offs that Latin American armies favoured at the time, complete with GI helmets. Their weapons were obviously clean and well oiled. A major, I think, stepped forward. We exchanged salutes. He confirmed their wish to surrender, delivered in pretty fair English. I told him that it was very decent of him, and natu-rally we would accept his surrender, but he might prefer to offer it formally to my commander who should be with us very shortly. He made a good impression, a decent sort, proud but not haughty. He appeared to be finding the whole thing rather difficult, looking for some comfort in assumed procedure. I had no authority to discuss terms. That was for him or his commander and those above me. But I hoped by concentrating on the basics, showing consideration and due atten-tiveness he would find what he needed from me and together we might move things along. It was altogether a delicate business; and glancing around at the assembled mass of enemy soldiers, I was starting to feel outnumbered. I suggested that while we waited for Guy we begin by getting his men to stack their weapons, grenades, knives, all of them including crew-served weapons. Thankfully, he turned to do it. As he did, I noticed his holster. I called him back to offer that he and his offi-cers might keep their side-arms for the time being if they wished. I thought that would demonstrate our respect and trust in them. It wasn't altogether altruistic; it might make it easier for the officers to retain authority over their troops. Appreciating the gesture, if not the underly-ing point, he set about his instructions.

And somehow, for I hadn't called anyone forward, there was the great, looming, reassuring presence of Lawrence, over by the flagpole. With the aid of a couple of the enemy, for he could charm anyone, he was taking down the Argentine flag before running up the Union Jack. It snapped out in the stiff breeze, magnificent, its red, white and blue standing proud against the grey all around, proclaiming that things were as they should be once more in this elemental corner of the world. With that done, he waved at me, giving me one of his broad smiles and a thumbs up.

Guy arrived before too long bringing Marines. He seemed a bit distant, perhaps pissed off with me. I put it down to our liberal interpretation of mission command, and the Squadron's zip once unleashed. I decided to keep out of his way, being in no mood for another squabble; certainly not one with Guy. I liked him far too much for that. Throughout the episode, the Squadron had always known what to do, calculated the risks accurately, and been prepared to run them. The overpowering might of the Navy had in fact won the day. We had merely sealed things on shore. It didn't seem necessary to rake over events beyond that, not right then. Savour the moment. I left him and the Argentine commander to it. They had been introduced to one another. He could take things on from there with the Marines. Of course, we would help if needed. But my thoughts returned to Leith, and our missing patrol.

Meanwhile, Geordie had gone off with the submarine captain to retrieve codes from the *Santa Fe*. When asked where they were, the Argentinian had replied, 'over the side, what would you expect?'

'Nothing less,' Geordie growled with a broad, uncustomary grin.

They returned to the jetty in comradely silence, back out into the fresh, clean, damp air, Geordie clutching an armful of papers and documents that had taken his interest despite the Captain's charming assurance. They would be passed on to *Antrim's* communications officer, also a collector, who in turn would pass them and more back to Fleet Intelligence who did indeed find them all of interest.

The evening closed in, the light fading slowly, everything shaded in grey. I thought about a cigarette and ate a biscuit instead. A quick glance over to the buildings revealed Lawrence with a handful of the Squadron helping the Marines with the prisoners, sorting weapons, searching through equipment. Geordie was heading over to the radio-room to continue his search for intelligence goodies. Guy, flanked by Marines, appeared deep in conversation with a small group of Argentinian officers.

Everything looked to be under control. So, a handful of us, those with no pressing job, went back down the track to the cemetery, to pay our respects to Shackleton. It felt the right thing to do.

With Grytviken in our hands, that left the small Argentine garrison at Leith commanded by Captain Alfredo Astiz.[2] Later that evening, a brief, supervised radio conversation between him and Captain Bicain, the submarine captain, the assumed senior Argentinian on South Georgia, established that Astiz would not surrender. He would fight to the death. It didn't sound credible, so much bluster, but Guy Sheridan and Brian Young together devised a plan to oblige him.

It involved using those elements of the Squadron already aboard *Plymouth* and *Endurance*, the latter having sailed into Stromness Bay during the assault on Grytviken. The embarked troops would land early the following day, not a lot more to it than that. But Ted and his troop were already on the ground. They might employ the tactical plan sent in previously. It was notably sound. So, there would be more on offer than simply sailing in and perhaps landing to wing it. Captain Pentreath of *Plymouth* would command the operation. I had not met him face to face, though knew enough to trust him to use my people wisely. Never-

---

[2] Astiz was a bad man, wanted for questioning by a number of police forces for his part in some of Argentina's more excessive internal security activities involving the disappearance of foreign nationals as well as Argentine citizens. France and Sweden were both particularly keen to speak to him. In time he would be repatriated by the UK in strict compliance with the Geneva protocols.

theless, I arranged to join Ted with SHQ as soon as practicable, intending to arrive before the start of any assault.

I had bags of confidence in Ted; only, I felt I should be there to command any sizeable effort. Danny had already passed a warning-order advising that SHQ would be coming with additional troops, underscoring the by-now customary conditions concerning proportionality. The operation should be about persuasion rather than destruction, achieving the enemy's surrender. Ted had been advised on events in Grytviken, how the enemy had capitulated to the threat of violence. I envisaged achieving success without actually closing with the enemy, by sniping out his positions from the dominating ridgeline if necessary. Ted was advised not to attack or precipitate an assault at squadron level until I joined to control it. However, he had authority to proceed and command SAS forces at Leith in the event that I failed to join him in time, or the situation otherwise demanded, being so ordered by Captain Pentreath.

As things turned out, I got to Leith to find that Astiz had thrown in the towel almost immediately before my arrival, at the sight of *Plymouth* sailing into Stromness Bay to join *Endurance*. It was all over. And to cap it all, by late morning the Navy had recovered Tommy Trenton and his people, our missing patrol, from the area of Jason Point at the mouth of Stromness Bay. *Plymouth* had noted their position as she slipped into the Bay that morning. On seeing her, the patrol had flashed a distress signal; up to that moment Tommy and his team, like Chippy, had kept communication silence until sure that to do otherwise would not compromise the operation. Their fate had been weighing heavily on all of us. Certainly it had impacted my temperament. Spirits soared.

Thus we won without loss,[3] two helicopters and an amount of discomfort excepted. It truly wasn't a bad effort for a Task Group operating together for the first time in one of the most inhospitable environments on the planet. When the moment came we combined force well, employ-

---

[3] There was the one fatality, an Argentine submariner, Felix Artuso. The Navy buried him with full military honours in the whaler's cemetery, Grytviken.

ing it with decent levels of sophistication. The Task Group could take pleasure in its achievement.

Captain Young informed the country, and the world, by signal through his commander, Rear Admiral Sandy Woodward:

> Be pleased to inform Her Majesty that the White Ensign flies alongside the Union Flag in Grytviken, South Georgia. God save the Queen.

Old fashioned perhaps, Nelsonian maybe, its tone chimed; it reflected our sense of things. We had put matters right in South Georgia in a wholly British way: at times with muddle, mostly quiet professionalism, with flashes of brilliance, examples of heroism, and always with decency.

We found little or no time for celebration. RHQ wanted us back for operations on the strategic Main Effort, the recapture of the Falklands. We were ready to go. We all instinctively felt the need for tasking more in tune with our ways and means: less confined by the needs, interactions and necessary controls of the tactical level, when bound closely in time and space to conventional forces and their immediate objectives.

We were instructed to embark *Brilliant* and withdraw north to the Task Force, to get aboard Admiral Woodward's Flag Ship, the aircraft carrier HMS *Hermes*. At that very moment he and his carrier group were approaching the Falklands archipelago to impose a Total Exclusion Zone (TEZ), a device designed to demonstrate that the United Kingdom considered the Falklands, its waters and surrounding seas, a war zone. Ships and craft of any nation entering the zone were liable to be fired upon without warning. This did not preclude the UK from taking action outside the TEZ, consistent with the right of self-defence enshrined under United Nations Article 51; this held potential for some strategic-level tasking, an enticing prospect. We needed to get alongside the Force commander to see what he might have for us.

John Coward also came under pressure to make a quick getaway. The Task Force needed his ship back for close air-defence of *Hermes*, for *Brilliant* carried the Navy's most modern anti-aircraft missile, Sea Wolf.

Consequently, despite a challenging session of cross-decking, complicated by the relative shortage of helicopter-lift and the predictably spiteful weather, we were soon heading north.

The departure was tinged with regrets. We had made many new friends. We were sorry to be leaving them. Most of us had developed deep affection for our respective ships. We wished one another success, asking each to take care, promising to meet up somewhere, somehow, sometime. In particular, we found it a wrench to depart *Antrim*. We couldn't have been easy for her captain, her company and the Task Group as a whole. A source of anxiety for much of the time, but when the moment came, I liked to think that we had been there to cover the 'gap'. We had always been there doing all that we could, more than we should, a critic might say. But the troops kept at it, never flinching.

Once on board *Brilliant*, we took the opportunity to rest and enjoy a break from direct operational activity. It gave us time to reflect. I went over things with Danny, Lawrence, Geordie, Graham and the troop commanders to identify lessons learnt that might inform or modify our approach to whatever came next.

If there were things wholly new to us it would be war alongside the Navy, and under sub-Antarctic winter conditions. Hence, we turned our minds first to the sea and weather. Both had nearly done for us.

At the time we had very occasional contact with the SBS; we were part of the Army, and they a bijou specialist element of the Navy's Royal Marines. However, there existed a tacit understanding. The Regiment would maintain basic boating skills sufficient to enable us to come and go by sea or water. But when it came to operating in the water that would be for the SBS. Recent experience had shown this to be a fine distinction. We had always been respectful of the sea, or so we thought. We now knew that it demanded consideration beyond simple respect and a lot more than the occasional session of training off the Kenyan coast or in the swimming pool back at camp. Our 'basic' had been sorely tested in the Antarctic deep end and found to be wanting.

We concluded that the Regiment must reconsider its entire approach to water and that this should include its relationship with our counterparts in the Marines.[4] But much of that would have to wait. For the time being, we had a war to fight and must go with what and how we were. That said, we resolved to leave 'water' to the SBS for the rest of this war if possible. We would move by helicopter. If we had to cross water, we should aim to co-opt specialist help. We would certainly not be using our outboards again. If we really had to take to the water on our own, we would use the Klepper canoes and rely on muscle power. This meant sheltered water, nothing more. If faced with no alternative, and the task demanded, then it went without saying that we would get on the water.

As for the weather, we had been particularly unlucky. Both insertions had been conducted under exceptionally challenging conditions even by South Georgia's volatile and ferocious standards. We needed better forecasts. And nobody in D Squadron could overlook the importance of 'weather proofing' plans and all else to the maximum extent possible.

The enemy's ground forces seemed to have submitted to the weather whereas we had sought to work through it, if not exploit it for tactical advantage. Strikingly, they had orientated themselves to whatever seemed most obvious. At Leith they had spent most of their time indoors sheltering from the weather. And at both Leith and Grytviken their defences looked mainly out to sea. Defence theory appeared to be poorly understood. Individual positions were badly sited, affording little depth, limited mutual support and scant cover from view. Worse, they had made no attempt to protect their 'vital ground'.

Their 'air' and 'sea' forces were less easy to read. They clearly understood the need to work in combination, surveillance aircraft turning up at much the same moment as the submarine. But just how

[4] A number of years later the SAS and SBS would be brought together in a single command under a Director of Special Forces, an arrangement prompted by the 'Falklands generation' through a paper commissioned by the CO 22 SAS (Andy Massey), a legacy that stands to this day.

well these elements actually worked together it would be impossible to say. There was evidence of healthy innovation, the C130 and Boeing 707 having range and duration, neither designed specifically for maritime surveillance. And there was bravery, putting undefended aircraft up against the Royal Navy's missile systems; similarly, pitching a WW2 vintage submarine against one of the best-equipped, most practised ASW navies in NATO.

To summarise our initial view of the enemy, we saw serious defects in their land forces that displayed rudimentary levels of competence. Their arrangements were crude, stylised, and tactically defective. This suggested low levels of military education and training, possibly ruling out all but the most basic levels of all arms operation. This was not to underrate our enemy. They were sure to retain a capacity to surprise. Only, given the rudimentary competence of the troops, their senior commanders would be wise to keep things simple when it came to their design for battle on the Falklands.

We did note a rather puzzling, half-hearted quality to their efforts. We didn't want to read too much into it. Perhaps they had been told to put up only a token resistance; or maybe the submarine really had been it, once defeated all being lost. Things might be different on the Falklands, where Argentinians could be expected to be more spiritually committed. However, we wondered if the passivity signalled any deep-rooted sense of professional inferiority. If so, how much might it take to move an inferiority complex on to outright defeatism.

Astiz had laid an improvised explosive device (IED) underneath the Leith helicopter landing-site. No attacking force would land at such an obvious place. It must have been sited to catch the unwary, coming under conditions of parley for instance. We hoped that this was a 'one off', nothing other than the amateurish behaviour of a low and depraved man, not evidence of a wider Argentine ignorance or disregard for the rules and conventions of war. Noting how incendiary the matter could become, the Squadron's leadership was reminded to hold tightly to the Geneva Conventions, particularly if provoked, falling foul of enemy misbehaviour, wanton or otherwise.

Returning to their air and naval forces, much of their equipment may be obsolescent, but it looked as if they might use what they did have with imagination, determination and some flair. Indeed, any platform-based capabilities with high professional officer/senior non-commissioned officer staffing levels were likely to perform well enough, irrespective of service or arm of service. But how well they might combine for joint or all arms operations remained uncertain: not very, was the likelihood. However, we would continue to respect them all.

Captain Young was a careful commander who appreciated the benefits of having good target-intelligence before making an offensive move. We were with him on this, knowing that the better the target-intelligence, the greater the chances of success, confirming our faith in prior reconnaissance. Our preference to lead off with recce had not gone unchallenged however. So was advance-force, close target, recce conducted by Special Forces on the ground entirely appropriate under conditions of war, or something better suited to low intensity conflict? Did it indicate excessive caution? Had it prejudiced success? Was it a help or hindrance?

At first there had been an element of CT in our mentality, of reaching for the finest levels of target intelligence. Which way the doors opened at the British Antarctic Survey facilities in Grytviken was one early example of this, as if that could possibly matter. And the insertions had not gone smoothly. But despite the frustrations, we did get on target, the high value of the intelligence reduced only by the unexpected unfolding of events. Nor should the impromptu nature of the eventual assault refute the importance of advance force recce. The attack was a response to rapidly changing circumstances, a matter of seizing an apparently fleeting opportunity. The decision to go straight in had been based mainly upon calculation; yet there lurked a dose of instinct probably drawing upon impressions tucked away from Ted's observations of Leith. We concluded in favour, knowing that the Task Force's available surveillance and target acquisition technologies were a poor substitute for well conducted, manned recce, drawing out the wider factors as Ted had done so admirably at Leith.

In summary, we needed to refine our inter-operability with the Navy; stay close to the SBS; improve our coordination into the conventional battle space; bring everything up to the demands of the South Atlantic in winter; and continue to respect the enemy. And we would be sticking with recce as a *sine qua non*.

PART 2

THE FALKLANDS
With the Task Force: Soldiers of the Sea

6. The Task Force

Brilliant was in a hurry. Light and nimble, she skipped over the sea where *Antrim* had ploughed through it. But these seas were running in from behind, from half-left, causing the ship to lift and twist, plunge and bob. Hour after hour after hour the motion went, most of us put off our food, ship's company included.

We all liked *Brilliant*, taking to her captain from the moment he had shown up off South Georgia a few days previously. John Coward was soft spoken, with a disconcertingly steady, appraising stare. He had a submariner's brain: quick, coolly calculating, with that uncanny aware-ness for position and geometry. He simply knew where things were; how they ought to be; when it was right; when it was not. A noncon-formist in the very best sense, original, unorthodox, imaginative, a natural warrior, there was something of the pirate about him. His ship's company thought the world of him. We could see why. I think we saw a bit of ourselves in him and he a touch of himself in us. We certainly got on, right from the start.

His one regret appeared to be that his ship didn't have a gun turret, disqualifying him and his company from certain inshore operations, including slipping us ashore at dead of night, work he clearly wanted, along with anything else that had him taking the fight to the enemy.

He had a social device that I would commend to all commanders when in a tight spot, when those around might benefit from some reas-surance. When things got tough, events crowded in, he would start speaking softly. Those intended to hear would have to listen intently. It brought calm and quiet, speeding response, for noise and excitability mostly breed confusion.

As we approached the Task Force, he invited me up to the bridge. He pointed to the radar. I was no trained nor accomplished interpreter of a radar picture, but even I got this one. The screen displayed a shower of blips and echoes, each signifying a warship or helicopter. In a short while, we would see them with the naked eye spread widely across the sea from horizon to horizon. We moved steadily through the layered defences towards our destination, HMS *Hermes*, the flagship; each ship we passed purposeful, concentrated on war, heedless of all else, already stained and battered by the sea.

Here again was the nation's maritime power, the Fleet, assembled and steadily, relentlessly bearing down on an enemy. Aldis lamps blinked, flags snapped. The larger ships rode forward, their bows rising and falling rhythmically. Close escorts bounced busily, dashing from time to time to change station. The sheer weight of steel proclaimed deliberate, over-whelming, unstoppable force. It struck at primeval chords. The uncertain preoccupations of everyday life had little to no place; here everything fell to the single, great enterprise. We were as one.

Fortunately we were in the hands of a commander with his feet firmly planted: Admiral Sandy Woodward, another submariner, icily calm, coldly calculating, a masterful warrior. The 'Perisher' course seemed to produce them.[1]

We embarked *Hermes* at a significant moment. The diplomatic efforts to find a negotiated solution had yet to run their course, with frustration growing in parts of the United Kingdom over the time it was taking for the United States to come out unequivocally for us. After all, we were defending principles intensely shared, the US viewed as the clear leader and champion of those defining Free World values. On the other side, as news filtered out about the nature of their rather humiliating defeat in South Georgia, the Argentine military junta came under increasing pressure at home to act, to hit the approaching British fleet, to stop it in its tracks.

[1] The Submarine Commanders Course prepared officers for command of a submarine. Lasting four months, it was an intense, gruelling course with a high failure rate: 70%. It filtered out all but the very best. Those that failed could no longer serve in the submarine service, in any capacity. For both reasons, it became known as the 'Perisher Course'.

Within the Task Force we were unaware of the details of the diplomatic efforts, but many of us worried that the United States might eventually order a halt. We were keen to get on with things. The High Command also harboured acute operational concerns. We were pushing hard up against the limits of our national military capacities: operating over sea-lines of communication of around 8,000 miles from the home base, in winter, against an enemy with numerically-superior occupying and air forces. But at our level we never doubted the result. Once ashore there would be no stopping us. There might be hoops to jump through, conditions to be met, modalities to be respected, more as convention than as absolute necessity it would feel at times, but we were going to win.

G Squadron had been on board for a while, since *Hermes* had sailed from Ascension to impose the Exclusion Zone. They had been tasked to mount surveillance on all the likely Argentinian positions around the Falklands, including each of the main settlements (Map 4). The operational-level[2] staff needed the information to inform their campaign planning, that we simply assumed involved the full re-possession of the Falklands. We were unaware that options short of this goal were under consideration: one, for instance, envisaged the establishment of a toe-hold on West Falkland to serve as a bargaining chip. Had we known, I believe we would have been mystified, even outraged, at the implied defeatism. Fortunately we were not aware, and looked no further than a broadly logical military flow that would lead to our victory in and around Stanley presumably.

As part of this advance force effort, the SBS would recce the possible landing-sites, hugely sensitive work that demanded utmost care. The situation held parallels with the allied invasion of France in 1944; then,

---

[2] A term not much used by the British Military before the early 1980s, derived in part from study of the Soviet theory of 'Operational Art'. It concerns the level at which strategic goals are translated into actions, where campaigns are developed, and operations crafted to harness military forces to the higher end(s).

there had been only a few suitable landing-sites, both sides seeing the same, the Allies' selection guarded by secrecy and cloaked in deception, the choice of Normandy eventually coming as a surprise to the defenders. It was a comparable situation for us off the Falklands. There were relatively few sites that met the planners' criteria. Enemy attention must not be drawn to any particular one. The beach recce patrols must escape detection or put at risk the entire operation.

The gravity of the situation was not lost on any of us. For their part, G Squadron would ruthlessly minimise the frequency and number of helicopter insertions, viewing these as notably prone to detection by the enemy. As a consequence, to minimise movement most SAS patrols went ashore for protracted periods; conversely the SBS beach-recce patrols went in for relatively short spells, with what G considered almost alarming frequency. As one would expect the two operations differed markedly: G focused on longer term surveillance concerning the general disposition of the enemy's forces, and the SBS on the altogether more time-sensitive business of gaining detailed beach information to inform the invasion plan. There were only a handful of qualified SBS patrols for the work, far fewer than the number of beaches to be recced. And beach information couldn't be transmitted by Morse that easily. For both reasons the SBS had to come and go more often than they themselves would have wished.

Nevertheless, it became a source of irritation, G Squadron viewing SBS toing and froing as raising the risks for all patrols of the advance-force programme. In war small things can lead to major consequences. On this occasion friction arose out of an almost certainly necessary difference in tactics, compounded for the absence of a single, integrated special operations command that might have secured consensus, nailing concerns by issuing shared guidance and a clear set of priorities for all to follow. Instead, we relied upon a somewhat informal, amiable and comradely method of agreement to 'de-conflict' our separate missions, or otherwise work together as and when needed.

As for D Squadron, with reconnaissance covered by G and the SBS, we turned our minds to finding something suitably important to attack. Over the next few days a very specific, potent threat presented itself: the air-launched EXOCET anti-ship missile, carried to battle by Super Etendard aircraft of the Argentine navy operating from their mainland bases. These half-ton missiles, with a high-explosive warhead of 350 lbs, skimmed the sea's surface at a speed of 650 knots. Even if the war-head failed to explode on impact, its momentum would likely hit most ships for six, its still burning fuel adding to the damage. We could assuredly appreciate the danger they posed, being in an aircraft carrier, full of volatile material, one of the enemy's principal targets.

The EXOCET menace eventually grew acute. But an operation employing us to reduce the threat would have been pregnant with disproportionate risk, probably requiring a sizeable carrier task group to take forward the Squadron and its supporting helicopters, closing the Argentine mainland, bringing us all well within range of hundreds of enemy aircraft. And there could be no guarantee of nailing the objective, aircraft having a habit of moving. Nobody in his right mind would contemplate such a gamble. It was the sort of thing that could end in catastrophe and lose us the war. Thankfully, Admiral Woodward was well in control of his faculties. He chose to deal with the problem himself, using his air defence ships and Sea Harriers. This worked, but not without some cost. And so, ironically, there we were, with the Squadron too far forward in this instance to take on threats in strategic depth, any operation by us standing to endanger our 'Centre of Gravity',[3] the Task Force itself. We had become inextricably caught up in the forces imposing the TEZ. And there we would stay, at the theatre level, in unusually close, symbiotic relationship with our conventional counterparts.

So we concentrated on finding something to attack on the islands that might nevertheless confer value greater than the sum of its destroyed parts; most likely a target with psychological as well as material impact, with the greater emphasis on the first of these, a success that would move along our entire effort.

---

[3] In simple terms Centre of Gravity can be considered the source of strength. It enables one to do things; in military terms it confers 'freedom of action'.

Holding firm to the principle that SAS forces be commanded at the highest level, Euan Houstoun, G Squadron's commander, had established a notably good rapport with Admiral Woodward, enjoying ready access. We both assumed Woodward to be the overall, operational-level theatre commander. He was often encouraged by Fleet to think in those terms. Strictly though, he was not. He had responsibility for the carrier force imposing the TEZ and for setting the general conditions for a successful landing. The actual landings and responsibility for the subsequent land-campaign fell to others: respectively Commodore Clapp, commander of the amphibious force, and at first Brigadier Thompson, commander of 3 Commando Brigade. Eventually, the land campaign would become the responsibility of a major general, equivalent in rank to Woodward. In effect, FLEET held to itself command of the three major force elements: the carrier force, the amphibious force and the ground forces, there being no overall, in-theatre commander. This may sound fraught, effectively directing a theatre of war from the home base, at distance and so it proved.

But Euan and I believed that we were alongside the right man, in the right place, at the right time, the only senior commander in theatre at that moment. Issues involving the high command were for the CO rather than us. If or when the emphasis switched, we should be able to shift with it. In the meantime we got on with things. This meant leaving Euan to continue as Woodward's principal, day-to-day, SAS interlocutor. I saw no point in upsetting a perfectly effective, working arrangement, provided Euan and everyone else, including the Admiral, understood that only I could speak for the Squadron when it came to tasking.

The Joint Intelligence Committee back in London was warning that the Argentinians could be about to attack the Task Force. They saw that the enemy had deployed its surface units in three groups, declaring through diplomatic channels that they intended to strike at any British vessels coming within 200 miles of their shores, including the Falklands, an unambiguous area considerably bigger than the TEZ we had established.

Each enemy group posed a significant threat in their own right. Somewhere to the north lurked the *25 De Mayo*, an aircraft carrier capable of launching fighter-bombers. These might work in coordination with other aircraft from the mainland to distract or overwhelm our Sea Harriers (SHAR). This would greatly improve the enemy's chances of slipping one of their EXOCETs through our layered air defences. To the south the cruiser *Belgrano*, capable of out-gunning any of our ships, also EXOCET-equipped, positioned herself and her group to pick off any stragglers or survivors from the air strike against the carriers. A third group of frigates threatened similar from somewhere out to the east. Submarines added to the menace, as did the potential of fighter-bombers operating from the hard-surfaced, all-weather runway at Stanley.

It didn't look good. We were hemmed-in by a coordinated, still confident, well-equipped and numerous enemy. Yet, Woodward didn't seem unduly fussed, judging by his cool at the evening briefing sessions. He appeared to welcome the enemy's growing belligerence and willingness to engage. As he saw it, we must write down the enemy before attempting a landing and what better way to achieve that than by having a stand-up fight. Accordingly, he sought to provoke one on his terms, exploiting the situation presented.

He adopted a plan encouraging the enemy to think that we were an advance amphibious force come to make an initial landing. If the deception worked, they must respond vigorously. He would lure them in by concentrating his firepower on the airport at Stanley and any occupied, outlying auxiliary airstrips. As the Argentinians came forward to counter our attack, the *25 de Mayo* and *Belgrano* would be met by our nuclear-powered submarines, SSNs. Concurrently, he intended a vigorous ASW operation to neutralise the enemy's submarine threat. Not to be overlooked, screened by all this maritime activity, Woodward would start slipping his Special Forces ashore, using the night capable helicopters of 846 Naval Air Squadron. It was positive, nicely judged, confident, bearing all the hallmarks of Woodward's cool courage. It stood to knock Argentina's navy out of the war.

Seeing that Woodward had more than enough on his plate, we in D Squadron adopted a low profile, preferring to develop possible, complementary options quietly in the background, even though we were outside the immediate operational time-frame. The Admiral planned to trigger his plan on or about 1 May, just days after our arrival from South Georgia.

However, we might catch up and started looking for something to hit by trawling through the available intelligence files. It might not be anything sizeable, a tactical level facility most likely, but its harm or destruction should have a noticeable impact upon the enemy, Our minds turned instinctively to C2 (command and control) structures. The destruction of a well-chosen C2 node might temporarily paralyse the system, get noticed across their force. We even wondered if it might be possible to get at an enemy commander of suitable seniority. Either should get their attention.[4]

Dawn on 1 May, the day of Woodward's pre-emptive strikes, revealed a relatively calm sea, an easy swell under a grey, leaden sky. The ships had gone to action stations. When *Hermes* closed up, the Squadron and other embarked troops spread around the ship would don their anti-flash hoods and gloves along with everyone else, but otherwise try to keep out of the way, sitting or lying in the odd nook and cranny. I found it all a bit claustrophobic and unnerving, shrinking into an 'inaction station' below or on the water-line, waiting for goodness knows what. At times during an air raid alert *Hermes* would fire chaff decoys,[5] the crash of its discharge reverberating throughout the ship. We guessed that this meant that she had detected a missile close by, even possibly homing in on us. It came

[4] We were thinking back to the abduction by the SOE of General Kreipe, the German garrison commander on Crete on 26 April 1944. But not abduction in this instance, so much as an attack, something that might heighten the enemy's sense of vulnerability and isolation as the TEZ started to bite.

[5] Chaff is a radar counter measure. When discharged a cloud of aluminium, glass or plastic strips forms a cloud, confusing any search or weapon-homing radar.

across very much like a last-resort measure, doing little or nothing to ease the tension or improve one's confidence.

Instead of waiting for catastrophe below, and having no designated action-station or defensive task, I chose to exercise an assumed freedom to do what made sense to me. I found a piece of open deck above the bridge, a viewing-platform. From there I could look out. I fancied that if worse came to the worst, I might detect what was about to hit us and float off as we went down. Silly maybe, but it was a sentiment held in common with Michael Nicholson of ITV. We shared the same few square feet of deck for a couple of hours most days, both seeing it as a better option than remaining downstairs in the dark.

That was where we were the morning the Sea Harriers lifted from *Hermes* and *Invincible* to land the first blows that would lead to our eventual victory. The two flat-tops held steadily into the wind, within visual distance of one another, their close escorts darting busily to and fro, but keeping always on the most threatened flank. There was our trusted friend John Coward and *Brilliant*, guarding us. Goal-keeping, they called it. Reassuring to have John Coward and his people protecting *Hermes*: really heartening. Everyone had confidence in *Brilliant*, from the Admiral down. Much further out lay the other screening warships, most of them unseen or barely visible in the dull, grey light. A helicopter hovered alongside each carrier, ready to dash in to snatch aircrew from the sea should anything go wrong with their launch.

Sea Harriers crowded the flight decks as they queued to take their turn, inches between them. Marshalled forward, the pitch of their turbines rose and fell. One after another they came steadily to the launch position; the slightest of pauses; a near casual wave from the launch marshal, open hand inviting departure; and then, in an instant whine transformed to gut-vibrating roar. Each jet in turn leapt at the ramp in ecstatic release. The ship shook. For a moment each Harrier appeared to hang, hunched over the front of the bows as vectored-thrust louvres swivelled more fully to forward flight. Each, visibly loaded with bombs, climbed away to tuck in behind those that had gone before, circling around the fleet. Soon all were up.

They gathered into business-like formation, staggered loosely with airspace between, to allow independent manoeuvre if needed. One more circuit, then past the Flag Ship as if in salute, our aircraft headed steadily, purposefully out towards their targets at Stanley and Goose Green, their grey forms fast merging with the sombre, solid-sheeted clouds above.

Earlier, gun-equipped ships that could be spared from defence duties had set off for Stanley. They would follow up the air-strike with shell-fire. Unknown to most of us, the RAF had already landed the first punch, dropping 20,000 lbs of bombs from a single Vulcan bomber just before dawn. The bombs straddled the runway at Stanley, one of them hitting dead centre. The striking aircraft had required the support of ten tanker aircraft to complete its 8,000-mile round trip. This example of our strategic reach would not be lost on the junta's leadership in Buenos Aires.

The enemy saw the assault for what it wasn't: the opening moves of our landings. They could be forgiven. The scale of the deceptive lure and its careful orchestration was more than enough to suggest just that: something seriously big afoot.

The Argentinians activated their contingency plans, modifying their arrangements to take account of the newly realised strategic bomber threat. From then on they kept back aircraft for the defence of their mainland airfields. The adjustments confused things for a while, inflicting delays. Eventually they generated a counter attack of sixty sorties, only half making it into the target area to cause relatively light damage to our ships off Stanley. The Sea Harrier CAP intercepted and destroyed three attackers. However, when our ships withdrew, as intended, the enemy mistakenly believed that they had beaten off a determined effort to land ground forces, that they had inflicted substantial damage on several of our ships and downed a high percentage of our available air-defence aircraft.

Encouraged by their apparent success the Argentine naval units were ordered forward to spring their trap, to deliver the killer blow. The *25 de Mayo* with her air wing started in from the north west, the *Belgrano*, from the south. The orders instructing the moves were intercepted and instantly made known to Woodward. His design for battle was working, possibly even better than hoped.

Shortly before supper the following day we heard that *Belgrano* had been sunk, torpedoed by one of the SSNs, HMS *Conqueror*. Danny and I were snatching a quick beer when the announcement came over the address system, received by our shipmates in jubilation. She had been attacked outside the TEZ. The cheering didn't sound right. Danny clearly didn't much care for it. It jarred on me too, the thought of those sailors one moment in the warmth, the next cast into the bitterly cold, ferocious South Atlantic. It may have been a necessary, wholly justifiable act of war. It must surely have stopped the Argentine advance dead in its tracks. But the note of triumphalism grated. And it felt premature. However, what did we know of naval warfare? It seemed notably hard-edged. When things went wrong, they went badly wrong, calamitous for all involved regardless of station: abrupt, final with scant scope for recovery. Perhaps that was it, a spontaneous expression of relief from people more deeply aware than us.

In common with all embarked forces, we looked forward to getting ashore, regaining control of our destiny, being back once more in our own element. Relative inactivity, compounded by lack of control, heightened our sense of confinement. If anything, *Belgrano*'s sinking intensified feelings of vulnerability and impotence. It was becoming a nervy, tiresome matter, by-standing warships going about their business. The novelty was wearing thin.

The enemy suffered numerous blows over this period. *Belgrano*'s escort *Bouchard* had been damaged in the same incident when a torpedo hit her too, mercifully failing to explode. The following morning a patrol vessel was lost to Sea Skua missiles fired from a Lynx helicopter. And numerous aircraft were downed. It came as some comfort to hear later that we would not attack or otherwise interfere with enemy ships involved in rescue operations. The scale and frequency of it all caused the Argentine surface fleet to withdraw to the cover of their land-based air, where they stayed, driven back and effectively defeated.

But their losses drove them to revenge. They had suffered a bad start. The humiliation struck deep. They were determined to get back at us, to re-establish their theoretical advantage; for whichever way one came at it, things really should have been working more in their favour. We didn't have long to wait.

The next two days passed quietly enough with no sign of enemy retaliation. They had been trying. The intelligence community back in London became aware that the Argentinians had moved five of their French-built Super Étendard jets, EXOCET signature aircraft, to a forward operating base at Rio Gallegos. But our defence intelligence community took comfort in a belief that the contracted technicians were back in France, having failed to complete their work of converting Argentina's naval aircraft to EXOCET before the outbreak of hostilities. The forward deployment of the aircraft should have dispelled all such thinking. It suggested that the Argentinians with or without help had cracked any remaining software issues and that they were ready to hit back with a weapon capable of turning the tide of the war in an instant.

The weapon had been entrusted to selected aircrew of the 2nd Naval Fighter and Attack Squadron. Among Argentina's finest, they were being asked to fly at the very edge of operational limits, over ranges extended by air-to-air refuelling and at wave-top height when in close proximity of the Task Force. A sortie had turned back on 3 May when the attacking jets had failed to refuel from the slow-moving KC 130 tanker.

On 4 May another Vulcan bomber raid struck home. Again, the strike had been mounted to keep the enemy from using Stanley as a launch-point for their fast jets. No bombs hit the runway, but the raid had the desired effect, confining the enemy's 'fast-movers' to their mainland bases three hundred miles to the west. Admiral Woodward deployed his ships to take advantage of this, locating them at extreme range from the bases, off the south-east coast of the Falklands by day, moving them slowly back towards the Islands to insert G Squadron and SBS patrols by helicopter at night.

We were enjoying an unusually calm, bright day with visibility clear out to the horizon. Having done an amount of work in the ops room scrutinising intelligence reports for possible targets, and drawing up contingency plans, I had decided to take some fresh air up on the viewing platform. Michael Nicholson joined me after a while. We exchanged greetings, taking in Woodward's dispositions, but in no keenly developed way.

There were the goalkeepers, the two Type 22 frigates, *Brilliant* and *Broadsword*, tucked in on the up-threat side of the two aircraft-carriers. Actually the Type 22s were optimised for anti-submarine work, but in trials their Sea Wolf system had shown itself capable of hitting an artillery shell in flight. An EXOCET should be a piece of cake; hence the 22s for goal keeping.

Beyond the aircraft carriers and their two escorts, came the odd logistic ship. We guessed that they were there in part to take anything that managed to penetrate the defences that far; better one of them than one of the flat-tops. Everyone knew that the loss of one of the aircraft carriers probably spelt the end, curtains on any attempt to regain the Falklands by force of arms.

Beyond the capital ships lay a screen of anti-submarine and air-defence frigates. Further out still, on or over the horizon came the outer skin of our defences, the air defence pickets, on this fateful day Her Majesty's Ships *Coventry, Glasgow* and *Sheffield* armed with SEA DART missiles capable of firing out to about fifty miles and up to 30,000 feet.

Air-defence picket-duty was a lonely, risky business, at the very edge of the collective defences and first in the line of fire. The ships knew it. It meant being fully on top of one's game, utterly alert and ready to respond in an instant. Their crews knew that any enemy aircraft would come in low, beneath the ships' radars. Yet at a certain point the enemy would have to 'pop up' for a quick scan, as they neared, to switch on their target-locating radar. That should give any patrolling ship in the vicinity a fleeting warning and opportunity to defend itself. The aircraft might have to take a second look to achieve missile lock; after that it would be a matter of minutes, still time to get an air defence missile away and fire chaff. But tolerances were fine, with little margin for error.

On this day the attack would be flown by two of Argentina's finest, Lieutenant Commander Augusto Bedacarratz and Lieutenant Armando Mayora. Departing Rio Gallegos in thick fog shortly after dawn, they made for a rendezvous to the west of the Falklands to take fuel from a KC130 tanker. It went well. The two Super Etendards continued in close formation at high altitude for a while longer before dropping to wave-top height as they neared the target area. It became difficult to hold formation as they barrelled through fog and mist patches, occasionally losing sight of the sea just feet below.

Closing the position previously designated by a supporting maritime patrol aircraft, a venerable Neptune, and with visibility improving, Bedacarratz made a quick 'pop up'. Immediately, their radars saw targets: they had found the Task Force. Promptly, both pilots dropped back down to complete the firing sequence on their weapon systems. A few miles more and up they came once more to establish missile-lock. No particular target, no time for deliberation: up, lock, launch, down, make for home, trusting that they might escape the much-feared Sea Harriers. The time: 1402 ZULU, mid-morning local.

On this occasion, perhaps the time-difference had worked against us. All morning since breakfast the ships had been subject to false alarms. By afternoon (ZULU) scepticism had taken hold. The Task Force's principal Anti-Air Warfare Control (AAWC) on *Invincible* became reluctant to respond to any more warnings without confirmation. But *Glasgow* had seen it all, her timely observations passed to *Invincible*. In receipt of no second sourced report confirming the sighting the AAWC did not pass the alarm, keeping us all at the lowest alert state, Air Raid Warning White: no threat.

Glasgow tried repeatedly to raise *Sheffield*, not simply to warn her, but to get the needed confirmation back to the AAWC. *Sheffield* remained oblivious to all around her until hit at 1404 ZULU, two minutes after Bedacarratz and Mayora launched their missiles. The successful missile may have failed to explode. The other completed its run to disappear out at sea. But *Sheffield* had been mortally wounded, many of her company dead and injured. Set ablaze, listing and without power and pumps, she had to be abandoned some hours later. Repeated courageous attempts had failed to save her. A proud fighting ship had been brutally struck down in an instant.

The effect on the Task Force was immediate and salutary. The mood changed, all traces of any previous, overconfidence replaced by a wholly quieter, more thoughtful, measured determination. We remained assured, only that much more respectful of our enemy. The Navy showed what helped make it such a great institution, Woodward a striking example. Throughout the events of that day he remained icily cool, almost detached it seemed to those around him, giving instructions sufficient to ensure the integrity of the Task Force's defences, keeping it focused on the wider operation still to be conducted. He never lost sight of the bigger picture. Otherwise, he put trust in his captains, knowing that they would do all necessary and possible to contain the situation. They and their people in turn acted with studied calm after an initial, instinctive reaction to rush to *Sheffield*'s assistance.

There was bravery at all levels. Aboard the stricken ship the crew fought over and over, against the odds, going below to try to bring fires under control, to save something of the day. A number of them died or were terribly maimed. Rescue ships came alongside, helicopters too. At any moment the fires might have reached *Sheffield*'s magazines, taking all with her. At one point the ships were alerted to the possible presence of an enemy submarine come to exploit the situation. Counter measures were strengthened. The rescue and recovery ships held to their stations. The Squadron saw for itself that day what it meant, 'hearts of oak': cold, calculated steadiness under deadly duress.

The Navy also demonstrated its steely ruthlessness. Eventually *Sheffield* would be left to serve as bait to draw in any enemy submarine. No sentimentality there. And poor Captain Salt, commander of the ship, received not a lot of sympathy at the time. It went round that there might have been organisational and operational shortcomings. Ironically, people found some reassurance in that. I had come across the reaction before involving setbacks on other operations. When things go wrong, it can be less disturbing to find fault in one's own actions, than to acknowledge having been bested by the enemy. The first can be reduced to the relatively simple matter of putting right a momentary defect or error, thereby making it an issue with a solution pretty well within one's gift. The other is not altogether one's own to fix, holding the prospect of the enemy's actual superiority, an altogether more uncomfortable notion.

For our own part, over the next hours we helped as best we could. One of the dining areas on *Hermes* had been converted to a temporary casualty clearing station. Both Danny and Lawrence realised that the number of casualties coming in might exceed the ship's ability to cope. They immediately made available our twenty patrol medics, some with prior battlefield experience. The rest of us kept out of the way, to re-double our efforts at finding a way to get back at the enemy.

Paradoxically, events that day may have enhanced our potential. In the afternoon the Task Force had also lost a SHAR, to ground fire while attacking Goose Green. As a temporary measure, Woodward most sensibly stopped the SHAR ground attacks, keeping his aircraft back for air defence. We guessed that RAF GR7 fighter/bomber Harriers must be on the way down from the UK, with the amphibious forces, to prosecute the needed air-interdiction and other land support tasks. However, they could be days, perhaps weeks away. In the meantime, if the Task Force had to mount further precision strikes ashore perhaps we could help. There didn't appear to be many other options. And aside from that, we thought that we could all probably do with a lift after *Sheffield*. The enemy needed to be set back, their broken run of failures re-established. Surely then, it must be time for a raid ashore by special forces.

We considered it self-evident that a raid on foot, coming by stealth at dead of night, carried psychological impact that platform-based attack might struggle to match. The two can be equally destructive. But an

enemy hit from an aircraft or any other distant means involving his opponent's technological edge can find some solace if not strength in a sense
of offended fair play, even moral outrage. While similar can obtain with
'hand delivery', its inherent intimacy, the essential equalities of its man-
to-man character, serves to complicate. We needed to encourage the
Admiral and his ops staff to see it our way.

From the moment we stepped aboard *Hermes* we had been working
on our Direct Action (DA). We started by agreeing ground-rules
between the two squadrons and the SBS to ensure we didn't get in one
another's way. On the face of it this might seem straightforward. But
the three roles were very different, requiring careful 'de-confliction',
particularly as operational space around the Falklands was tight.

Surveillance demands patience and caution, more often than not
observation of a target over a protracted period. Besides gathering
detailed target-information, it can involve determining the established
pattern of life across an objective area. A patrol may have to make frequent, careful moves in order to cover all angles. Nothing should disturb or alert the enemy, or distract a patrol unduly, for a surveillance
team on the run evading is a call sign probably not reporting.

For G Squadron this meant putting patrols ashore for periods of up
to a month. They would go in by helicopter at night, patrols restricted
to two lifts, one in, one out. There would be no resupply or medical
evacuation unless absolutely necessary. They would land miles back
from their targets, beyond earshot and detection range of any surveillance devices. From their entry points, patrols would advance with
utmost caution to their targets. The vast acres of open grassland offered
long fields of vision. This enabled most to observe each major leg of
their route during daylight hours, ensuring it was clear of enemy or
obstacles, before patrolling down it the coming night. The process
might be repeated all the way into the target area, much as we had
intended in South Georgia.

Euan and his people had established close relationships with 846
Naval Air Squadron, our supporting helicopters. They found the aircrew

notably willing, recently in receipt of night vision goggles (NVG), but with little or no formal training in their use. Nor at first were the frames night adapted. But everyone had set to, learning on the job. Air and ground crews converted the cabs themselves with whatever came to hand, including wax crayon and duct-tape. Tactics and procedures were worked up over water during the passage south, everyone knowing that these would need further refinement for operations over land. Aside from NVG there were no other night-flying aids: no terrain following radar, no forward looking infra-red, no digital mapping. Each route had to be planned in exquisite detail and navigated with painstaking precision using paper maps and visual reference. But their efforts paid off, a signal contribution, going largely uncelebrated, yet another example of Navy 'can-do'.

Direct Action, an inherently robust activity, generally works to higher tolerances than surveillance; after all, at a certain point it should go 'noisy'. An attacking force might even break cover to complete its work on target and make good its withdrawal, exploiting the confusion that it helped create. One can also determine minima for success, reducing demands on the reconnaissance phase to basics such as finding a route in and out, what to hit: guard posts, other defences. Direct Action is more bounded and measurable than the open-ended nature of surveillance. It is important to avoid detection before initiating an attack, certainly during the reconnaissance phase. One doesn't want to reveal one's hand prematurely; and recce is rarely strong enough to mix it with an enemy, demanding commensurate caution.

Clearly, we should give G Squadron's operation a wide berth, keeping well away from both their targets and surrounding areas. Their information reporting activity must have priority. It was important to the planners above us. However, we should be prepared to respond to anything they found that justified a strike. And the same must obtain for the SBS and their advance force operations.

That narrowed down our options. G Squadron had put 'eyes' on every major settlement across the Falklands archipelago, namely all the obvious, most likely enemy locations. It didn't look promising for us, a matter of trawling through the areas left uncovered while remaining poised for anything that G and the SBS might be prepared to give us. We need not have worried. Almost immediately after coordinating our efforts, something did turn up, tucked away in an intelligence file: Pebble Island settlement off the north coast of West Falkland. All ours, neither G nor SBS with it on their dance cards.

7. Pebble Island

The intelligence referred to a small group of engineers and marines at Pebble Island settlement, little else. We had been searching for this sort of thing: an isolated enemy detachment to attack. We didn't mind what it was, exactly, provided its destruction or damage seized the imagination of the occupying force as a whole, precipitating anxiety. It shouldn't be too big. I had in mind an enemy facility of about sixty at most, a number· that we could overwhelm by the surprise and ferocity of our attack. The filed information suggested a small garrison of that size, up to no good, doing something interesting.

In a way we were branching off on our own again. I don't recall any hard and fast division of labour coming down to us, but with G and the SBS fully engaged on information-gathering, we simply assumed an offensive role. And within the TEZ, we were unaware of any force level, prioritised target list. There may have been something for the ships, and the Harriers before they were confined to air defence. If so, the list never got to us. And I never found out whether or not the carrier group's operational staff ever viewed us formally as a strike asset that they should be managing. It didn't seem to matter. We simply got on with things, the apparent informality not holding us back. And we rather liked it that way—the sense of freedom. We had enough guidance from the CO. We were alongside our admiral. We could read the situation in theatre. We reckoned it was time for a well-executed SAS raid.

It had taken South Georgia to open our eyes fully to the risk that we could pose to our own side. A dramatic failure coming hard on the heels of *Sheffield* would be awful. It might even damage national moral, erode the public's will to see things through. Yet part of the Regiment's purpose was to take on high risk for high gain, mitigating hazard by drawing upon our selection of people and privileged access to training resources and materiel. Recent events had thrown into sharp relief the efficacy of all that under the existing circumstances. The South Atlantic in winter was no picnic spot. It had exposed our limitations in a way that only a fool could ignore, and we were no fools. Its unbounded savagery had proved every bit as dangerous as the enemy, more difficult to contend with in many respects.

Thus, even though the time felt right for a spot of derring-do, and we were more than up for it, and might have found the appropriate objective to dare to win against, we weren't about to dive in head first. This was no over caution nor dissonant fall-out from South Georgia. Rather, it showed how far we had come since leaving Hereford a mere three weeks before. The next time we launched off one of Her Majesty's Ships, our actions were to be wholly informed by all that we had learnt to date.

With regard to Pebble Island, we consulted Roger Edwards, a pilot without a helicopter, who had become attached to the Squadron during our time on *Brilliant*. I never discovered exactly how he had come to join us, and never asked. I think Danny had a hand in it. Roger was married to Norma, a Falkland Islands girl then back in Britain with her young family. He had invaluable local knowledge of the Islands and helped us make the most of our limited information.

Roger first explained how the Islands worked in broad socio-economic terms. There was Stanley. And there was the 'Camp', the land outside Stanley, dotted with settlements, sheep farms mainly, operating more like ranches than farms in the sense understood back home. The settlements were isolated, but connected by radio, a few on East Falklands enjoying a telephone link into Stanley. There were farm tracks in and around the settlements, but no roads to speak of between settlements. Traversing the Camp by vehicle was laborious, demanding local know-how to avoid the many bogs, something of an art form. It might take the better part of a day to get from one settlement to its neighbour. People were correspondingly self-sufficient in farm and maintenance work. They were hardy, independently minded, yet with a strong sense of community.

The terrain might remind one of Dartmoor, though generally lower lying with open grassland and heather, the presence of the sea strongly felt. The weather was highly changeable. Near constant, often high winds brought cold and damp. We should be wary of stone-runs, miles of boulders, similar in appearance to glacial moraine. They were hazardous to negotiate on foot, virtually impossible by vehicle. Most common in East Falklands, they were a notable feature of the hills outside Stanley. Fences were also noteworthy, used as much to funnel sheep to the settlements' shearing-sheds during the annual round-up as to corral or delineate, their alignment being accurately marked on all local maps.

Heavy goods were transported by coastal vessel. Settlements and outlying farms were positioned for access to the sea, all having a substantial jetty capable of handling the tons of wool produced every year. Otherwise, the Falkland Island Government Air-Service (FIGAS) moved mail, smaller items and people by light aircraft, much like a taxi service. Each settlement had an airstrip, many of them fairly rudimentary, some limited in use to narrowly specific wind conditions. The strip at Darwin/ Goose Green had two crossing runways, on firm, well-draining soil, making it usable under a wide range of wind-directions and weather conditions. We knew that the enemy had stationed tactical aircraft there, creating a sizeable forward operating base. Roger thought the Pebble Island cross-strip to be similarly robust; furthermore, he understood the nearby beach had been registered as capable for use by heavier, short-take-off-landing (STOL) aircraft, up to the size of a C130 Hercules.

The Pebble airstrips had our attention. But before focusing on them we considered the island's other features. It lay close to the entrance of Falkand Sound. Roger pointed out that this made it an ideal radar site for looking out over the northern approaches to the archipelago, including the entrance to the Sound that ran north south, separating the main island of East Falkland from its counterpart, The West. It also covered the way in to San Carlos, but we were then unaware of the significance of that.

Radar started to feature prominently, possibly explaining why the enemy had located themselves in such an isolated spot distant from Stanley. And it made sense of the presence of engineers, there to help with life-support and other essential works: water-supply, shelter, defences, track and airstrip improvement and maintenance and so on. Their marines would be there for protection.

Meanwhile our thoughts turned mostly on the airstrip comprising two crossing runways. Although smaller than Darwin's, it was nevertheless sizeable by Falkland standards, fairly flat across its length and breadth, sloped at its edges. The level ground could be a mixed blessing, causing parts of the strip to waterlog during extended periods of wet weather. We were experiencing an unusually wet start to the winter. Roger reminded us all of the rudimentary nature of the settlements' strips, their sole purpose to support light STOL aircraft. We could rule out fast jets. There were currently no hangars at Pebble for instance, no all-weather runways, no hard standing, no fuel storage facilities, just grassland and a shed for the fire trailer.

Needless to say, we could all see that the enemy might make improvements. This took us back to the presence of those engineers. Perhaps the enemy had higher ambitions for the Pebble strip. The settlement could probably accommodate a hundred or more people at a squeeze. It would require pressing the sheep-shearing sheds into service, and it should be a straightforward matter to erect further, temporary accommodation. Winter rains were likely to ensure a plentiful supply of potable water, sufficient to support a sizeable garrison. It had a serviceable jetty, capable of receiving heavy engineering plant and materiel.

Stanley airfield had taken a pounding, frequently on the receiving end of naval gunfire, not to mention the occasional strategic bombing raid, and until recently SHAR strikes. Darwin had also received an amount of attention. Intelligence assessed that the Argentinians would maintain Stanley as their principal air-link to the mainland, Darwin a dispersal field for tactical air. But Darwin's central location offered further operational significance. Forces from there should be able to respond rapidly in all directions, across the Islands. We knew it had a large garrison. And we knew that the enemy had deployed Pucaras there. Could they all be part of an operational level reaction force, with Darwin its Forward Operting Base (FOB)? Pucaras could be a major component, fast to react, heavy hitting. They must take great care of the aircraft and their operational facilities. So was the enemy developing Pebble to serve as an auxiliary field of Darwin, to improve the air components' protection and resilience? Roger thought it a distinct possibility. So did the rest of us.

We went over what we knew about the Pucara: an Argentinian built ground-attack aircraft, intended ostensibly for Counter Insurgency Operations. It came armoured and engineered to take an amount of punishment from small arms fire. Its fixed armament comprised four 7.62mm Browning machine guns mounted two either side in the fuselage, in proximity to two 20mm cannon, also mounted in the fuselage. Three 'hard points', one under the fuselage, the others, one on each wing, enabled the carriage of a range of munitions, including dumb bombs and 2.75 inch rocket pods. It was a formidable weapon system, capable of inflicting serious harm on any troops caught out in the open or even in prepared defensive positions.

We started to view Pebble, and by extension the Pucaras, as having a significant place in the enemy's overall operational level plans for the defence of the 'Malvinas'. As was the case down at South Georgia, presumably their navy would constitute the first line of the enemy's defence, supported on this occasion by mainland based fast jets. Naval and air forces were probably meant to stop us in our tracks while still out at sea. But should we get ashore, doubtless air would continue to strike, supported by some form of response on the ground. And this must be where the air/land force at Darwin fitted in. It must surely be there for rapid response to pick up the counter-landing operations in the first instance, the Pucaras a notable element.

If we were right the enemy must take utmost care of the Darwin force, not least its air component. It would make sense to disperse the aircraft for their security as well as to improve their operational flexibility. We started to view Pebble as a target of high value: an auxiliary airfield albeit, but nevertheless a key component in Argentina's overall defence scheme.

We made a guess at its strength, basing our calculations on how we thought the RAF might do an auxiliary airfield. There would be the air-crew: not many. Then there would be aircraft engineers, ground-crew, a small operations staff, signallers, admin people: fifty or sixty? One had to add in the likelihood of a radar: six men? A troop of engineers: twenty to thirty? Finally, there would be airfield defenders, the marines: thirty, sixty or an entire company of ninety? We could be facing a garrison totalling 100–200; more than I had been looking for. However, it lay out on a limb, distant from immediate reinforcements. Given its composition, perhaps barely half the enemy force would amount to much in a close-quarter, knife-fight. The odds didn't seem too bad, not ideal, but probably workable. We should go take a look.

With only the one bit of hard, filed intelligence the rest supposition, we nevertheless set about developing a proposal for the Admiral. Having no detailed target information, the concept would have to be broad in outline, somewhat generic.

The operation must start with ground reconnaissance, to work out what the enemy might be doing, whether or not they did indeed constitute a suitable target. If the recce patrol found something worthwhile, it should go on to gather the tactical details necessary to support any subsequent raid, offering up a proposed method of attack based on pre-determined guidelines. Having done that, the recce must keep the target under observation, to pick up on any changes ahead of the attack going in. Given the size of the potential target and the range of advance-force tasks to be conducted, I would recommend that the recce be conducted at troop strength, about three patrols of a minimum of four men each.

As for the attack itself, we started by considering a covert method, employing sabotage techniques, the raiders emplacing explosive charges by stealth and making their withdrawal before the enemy became aware of anything untoward. Given our circumstances, I was not that keen on this. It would take a lot of time to accomplish on the night, involving getting around a probably large number of individual targets, of various sorts, spread across quite an area. Each category of target might require its own type of demolition device: a one pound standard charge of high explosive for an aircraft, perhaps a number for a radar complex, possibly something altogether different for a large accommodation block. Premature detection of any one element of the attack stood to compromise the whole effort, risking total failure.

And we must avoid civilian casualties if at all possible. Clearly explosives would be placed on military targets alone, but as initiation of the devices would or should occur long after our departure, there could be no way of preventing civilians from straying into the danger-areas. If that was not enough to rule out the covert method, there was also the matter of the time-pencils, or fuses.

Our time-pencils were simple devices of Second World War vintage. They comprised a spring-loaded plunger held back by a copper wire of varying thickness and a phial of acid, all contained in a tube about the length and width of a thick pencil. On crushing the tube, the acid would be released to eat through the plunger's retaining wire. The thickness of the wire determined the period between crimping and detonation: five minutes, thirty, an hour, twenty-four hours—a whole range of timings. We would need the lapsed times for getting round the targets and making good our escape. However, the pencils were notoriously unreliable, rarely going off at the precise moment intended, the odd one activating before, others after, a handful not at all. Even if they did work exactly as they should, it would be near impossible to synchronise so many detonations on so many targets, over such an area, involving so much covert movement.

Sneaking about at dead of night, in ones and twos, in and around enemy positions, may have held its romantic appeal, may even have been what an admiral might expect, but it wasn't for us. There were too many variables. Sabotage of an area target mounted from the sea against tight timelines seemed hardly an act of war.

We also discounted all methods of 'stand-off' attack, as it is known: for example, directing ship's gunfire or ground attack aircraft from a distance. Or perhaps sniping out targets using our own longer-range weapons: MILAN missiles, medium machine guns. It would be most difficult to achieve accuracy at night. Besides, the tactic lacked the intimacy that derives from getting in close, and hence the moral impact we were seeking just then.

That brought us round to an attack in strength: get into the objective area by stealth before going noisy, overwhelming the enemy by surprise, shock action and local weight of numbers. The sheer scale and ferocity should enable us to overcome all but the most tenacious resistance, making the raid less dependent upon precise target information, this in turn making it very much quicker to lay on and conduct. I strongly favoured this blunt option.

The ships had a lot on, fighting on the surface, sub-surface, in the air, in the airwaves. As far as possible they needed to be able to get on unimpeded by us or anyone else, free to move as and when they must. Any operation of ours should be conducted over as short a period as humanly possible, so as to avoid tying them down.

We would slant our proposal to protect the Navy's freedom of action as best we could (Map 5). Put us ashore in strength for a brief spell and we would push in and break stuff with as much precision as we could muster before getting out. If they had to push off to meet some unexpected and urgent nautical eventuality, or we got stuck for any reason, weather perhaps, being at strength we might be able to hold out until they could return. This reflected no lack of faith in the Navy. It did show that we were getting the measure of operating from the sea.

We would allow two to three days for the reconnaissance phase. Taking account of helicopter noise and radar signature, we planned to put ashore on the 'mainland' of West Falkland. If detected the patrol would have the entire 'West' in which to escape and evade. A helicopter insertion straight into the confines of Pebble struck us as altogether too risky. Putting in on the West would also enable the patrol to observe the route for a period checking it clear of enemy or obstacles before crossing by canoes to the island.

At one point during our preparations a naval officer had come across me examining this aspect on a one-inch Ordnance Survey style map. He introduced himself as a navigator before asking what I was doing. Accepting that he must be trustworthy, but cautioning him nevertheless, I explained that I was searching for places to cross from West Falkland to Pebble Island using canoes. The area of Phillip's Cove looked about right for a covert landing, the Tamar Pass or Inner Pass suitable waters, reasonably sheltered and no distance, less than a mile.

'Oh,' he said kindly, with a faint hint of indulgence, 'let's use this.' He exchanged my map for a chart.

'Where did you say?'

My finger prodded defiantly at his yellow map, with its rash of numbers, at the narrowest point between the mainland and Pebble.

'There, we shall cross there.'

'I see. But you do know that there's a rather strong rip tide running through there,' he responded softly, citing a seriously impressive number, a lot of knots.

'At slack water,' I retorted, quick as a flash, not knowing how that had come into my head, nor exactly what it meant. It sounded about right.

'Hmm.' There followed a quick nautical check of tide-tables and things. Before, 'lucky you, slack water, right in the middle of the night for the next week or so. It should do.'

The raid itself would need the lift of four or five Sea Kings, and in turn a ship with a large flight-deck. We would have to get relatively close in to the Falklands in order to achieve the turn-round distance given that the loads would be heavy in both directions, this impacting the helicopters' fuel load, hence duration. The only ships of the right size were the aircraft-carriers. I knew that this could be the sticking-point, a lot to ask of the Admiral, to stand one of his two vital flat-tops into harm's way for an SAS raid.

We put the plan to Woodward on 5 May, the day after the loss of *Sheffield*. I was right. The Admiral turned it down flat, politely, kindly even, but promptly and emphatically in that gimlet-eyed way of his. There were to be no SAS offensive operations for the time being.

I wanted to think that this solely reflected the current operational situation. The Force was facing multiple threats. It must have felt to the Admiral that things were crowding in on us. He should concentrate his forces on the maritime fight in hand. He could probably do without the distraction of a D Squadron raid just then, of running a lot of risk for uncertain gain. I hoped that was it and not fall out from South Georgia. I thought not. The chemistry between him and his Special Forces seemed sound. Woodward came across as someone who went at things objectively, coolly calculated. He could cut through 'noise', see things for what they were. He probably didn't think the time right; nothing more to it than that.

We alerted RHQ of our disappointment, asking whether they might help unstick things, get raiding back on the agenda. Not long after things did change. We didn't know why, but we were encouraged to start considering offensive tasks. I assumed Mike Rose must have had a word with someone with the necessary clout. For our part we had never stopped thinking about ways of getting at the enemy. We continued to cast around but found nothing to match Pebble's potential. Then a SHAR flying close to Pebble reported having been illuminated by a radar, possibly emitting from the island. I wasn't to know until years later that at much the same time, independent of the SHAR report, but fortuitously coincidental, Mike Rose fed into the *Hermes*' intelligence cell a snippet suggesting the presence of a surveillance radar on Pebble looking out to sea. He even specified a likely type, the detail of which he gathered from a reference book on Argentina's military radars. He had no hard evidence to support his conjecture, but it did the trick, for there then appeared to be two independent sources pointing to the possible presence of enemy radar located in a particularly awkward place. It changed everything.

Few people other than Woodward knew that the planners embarked on *Fearless*, which included Mike Rose, were strongly favouring San Carlos as the eventual landing-site. The prospect of a radar on Pebble covering the approaches to San Carlos was most unwelcome. Consequently, on 10 May Woodward called a meeting to discuss the issue. I didn't attend, thinking it a routine gathering, unaware that the meeting involved targeting. I left it to Euan as normal. The assembled operational staff concluded that the radar on Pebble Island posed a most significant threat. It must be pinpointed and destroyed. They considered their options. The option selected should not only remove the immediate danger but serve also to dissuade the enemy from any thought of reactivating it.

The staff discussed the obvious methods: naval gunfire or SHAR strike. For one reason or another nothing really appealed until Euan offered our assistance. The Admiral showed immediate interest. He saw that the enemy expected us to come at them using planes or ships. We had been doing that very thing over at Stanley and Darwin/Goose Green. They were showing commendable resilience, learning how to work through the attacks. But a visit by Special Forces, getting in and among them, had to be an altogether different proposition. Aside from the intimacy thing, high precision and moral impact, it should also serve to bring home to the enemy how vulnerable they were occupying any remote place other than in strength. It might discourage them from continuing at Pebble. It might spur them to draw in other detachments. A Special Forces raid had the potential to disrupt the enemy's operational infrastructure across the Islands.

Woodward saw all this without need of elaboration, asking how quickly it could be done. Influenced by the exhaustive, deliberate nature of his own Squadron's surveillance mission and experiences to date, Euan hesitated before responding with an estimate in the region of a week or more. The Admiral needed a solution within hours or days, not weeks. D Squadron was mentally in a wholly different place to G at that moment. We were thoroughly accustomed to seizing opportunity, responding near-instantaneously if required and remotely feasible. It was one of the things we had learnt down at South Georgia: the speed at which a situation can change at sea, how quick one had to be to keep up with the Navy when they got going.

'No good,' came Woodward's taut return.

He never wasted words. All submariners seemed alike: quick, direct and logical. They spent very little or no time on irrelevance, nor did they waste time on things beyond their immediate influence. There was an economy to it. We were out of the frame. Normally that would be it. Done. Move on. But unusually, perhaps out of a fondness for Euan, or because he had difficulty believing the timings offered, or he really was short of better options, the Admiral gave Euan another chance, an opportunity to think it over.

When I got to hear, I was mortified, upset with Euan, who looked crestfallen. But he got us both straight back in to brief the Admiral. I fixed hard on Woodward as to appear right on top of my brief. He had a pretty penetrating counter-gaze. I stated that we were ready. I reminded him that we had been thinking about Pebble for a while. We had a plan. The recce might go in the following night, rather than immediately, if acceptable. We should give the recce party a day or two on the 'ground'. I explained the need to move in carefully from the 'mainland' by canoe. As for the raid itself, I again recommended we go in heavy with the entire squadron because it would make things robust: essentially, go in and smash stuff. He agreed, getting the concept straight off. There were few questions. He stated that he wanted it done by absolutely no later than four nights hence, what he called his 'drop-dead time'. We had to get the radar. He stressed the radar.

'Okay?'

'Okay' I acknowledged.

'Well, make it so, then': a faintly anachronistic, strangely attractive and apt turn of phrase the Navy will use at chosen moments, when talking stops and action begins.

He said it with a faint nod, a slight smile and a definite twinkle in his eyes. I think the prospect of a Special Forces raid appealed to his submariner's instincts, stirring sentiments perhaps shared, lying deep within: the buccaneer in him, the hooligan in us.[1]

The process started more formally at the coordinating meeting that evening, when the Admiral and ship took stock of that day's operations and considered activities for the coming period, its purpose to harmonise efforts across the carrier group. It was a key event in the daily battle-rhythm. Orders and instructions would flow from this relatively small group of officers into the carrier and out round the Task Force. Staged in a tiny compartment behind the bridge, officers would crowd around a small, square mahogany table, most often with a nautical chart displayed before them. The Admiral sat on one side, the Captain of *Hermes* stood on another, to his right most often.

Euan and I would squeeze in at the back. He would do the talking for the two of us when needed, very rarely. I don't recall having received an invitation to join the meetings, but attendees all seemed to expect us to be there. After a review of that day's activities, Pebble was briefed in as an item of future business. The Captain of *Hermes* looked uncomfortable with the idea of his ship going forward probably with a much-reduced escort, for that was the plan, to get close enough inshore to launch and later recover a heliborne Special Forces raiding party. During a pause, he leant across the table, finger-tips of his right hand resting gently upon the chart, taking in the area off Pebble Island.

'Admiral, if I have this right, we are going to take this ship [and we all knew what he meant: vital, irreplaceable, one of only two aircraft-carriers, the flagship, if lost game over] into and through a known, enemy submarine-patrol area?'

---

[1] In the cloisters of Westminster Abbey there is a memorial dedicated to the Submarine Service, Commandos, Airborne Forces and the Special Air Service (the Long Range Desert Group added belatedly in 2013). It commemorates all those that served in those forces, the grouping reflecting something of the shared spirit that moved them, and continues to move them.

'Yes,' came the faintly quizzical, spare reply, delivered with another of those straight, penetrating gazes.

This was a display of strong will and courage all round. Where what should be said, could be said; where matters of gravity got aired objectively and free of emotion by all concerned; where a clear-sighted, thoughtful and daring commander exercised his leadership; and where equally strong, conscientious and confident subordinates could contribute knowing that was expected. The meeting moved on with us all eventually dispersing to 'make things so'.

I couldn't fully fathom the radar business though, confessing as much to Danny. The entire operation was turning emphatically upon the business of radar, to my mind reducing the better evidence that Pebble concerned aircraft dispersal. I saw inconsistency between the available intelligence, our analysis, the Navy's assumptions and what we were being expected to achieve. I could see no hard evidence for the presence of any radar, and yet Woodward and his staff were talking about it as a certainty, to the point of near-fixation. But then they knew of the CO's intervention specifying a radar by probable type and its threat to San Carlos, the favoured landing area. We didn't. I found the disparity unsettling. But I wasn't going to queer our pitch by asking too many questions. Raiding had been called off once before; I wasn't going to risk that again. I should rely on the recce to clear things up.

If we were to get recce ashore the following night, there was no time to lose. The task fell naturally to Ted and his people. He and his number two, Chippy, were called to join the SHQ planning team immediately after the Admiral's 'evening prayers'. We considered the situation, making deductions then agreeing things to be done that in effect constituted a set of operational orders. This bought us the time that Ted and his people needed for their own preparations.

Clearly the recce must confirm the presence of a target. I acknowledged the likelihood of finding only aircraft, and perhaps an amount of support equipment, stressing the importance the Navy attached to radar. I hoped that a good number of aircraft would do it, trigger the assault, but warned of the possibility that it might not: no radar, possibly no raid. If we did go in we must make a thorough job of everything: radar, aircraft, ground-support facilities, materiel. There followed a debate about pilots, all agreeing that they would be attacked. It would be one thing for the enemy to make good damaged or destroyed aircraft and equipment, altogether more difficult to replace aircrew. The recce must confirm a method of squadron assault and be prepared to guide the Squadron in. Civilian casualties must be avoided, along with undue damage to Falklands property. Precision and the proportionate use of force were stressed.

The Geminis were never mentioned. The Troop would canoe, the helicopters dropping them off in the area of Purvis Point, on the 'main land' opposite Pebble Island. During the day following drop off they would observe the narrows and far side, canoeing across at slack water that coming night. This gave us an attack-window from three nights hence. We went over all foreseeable eventualities——the 'what ifs' as we called them. What if the patrol was detected on insertion, on the West? What if they couldn't canoe across to Pebble? What if they were discovered on the Island? What if the raid got delayed? What if they found planes that then departed before we could get at them?

We covered the communication plan and its impact on my ability to give detailed orders for the raid. Ted would be using hand-speed Morse over a high frequency radio link, sending to *Hermes* via re-broadcast facilities at Ascension or in the UK. Consequently, he would be unable to pass large amounts of information. He need only confirm the presence of a target, or not. Otherwise he should signal by exception. If his observations fitted broadly with our pre-agreed outline plan, I needed nothing else. If they didn't, he better get the necessary back to me. Before departing to join him I would have issued the Squadron a concept of operations, together with a set of 'be prepared to' tasks. When we all came together on Pebble Island, at the entry point, he and I would rapidly confer to set the plan, before issuing the troops confirmatory orders and instructions.

Concluding the session, I stated with certainty that things would not go smoothly. On the night we would have a lot to do. We had a simple plan. It must be kept that way. We would be at near full squadron strength. We should be able to run a fair amount of risk. Provided we achieved surprise and superiority at the point of attack we should be able to impose our own certainties. Ted got the picture.

The following morning we ran into the usual, tiresome weather problems. The forecast apparently ruled out NVG, helicopter operations for the coming night: generally poor visibility in squally rain, not helped by high winds, all compounded by sub-optimal ambient light-levels. The senior pilot was adamant: No Go. We didn't know him and his team as well as 'G' did. I missed Ian Stanley and *Antrim*. I would trust Ian without question; if he said no, no it would be. But this man wasn't Ian. Nor did he know how to let one down sympathetically. Besides, if the moon/lux chart showed less than ideal flying conditions for the chosen night, why hadn't this bloody well come up before now? Tempers frayed.

War at sea was proving near unbearably frustrating. If it wasn't one thing it would be another, most commonly the elements. At every turn we appeared to be blocked. We desperately wanted to get off the ships, to gain greater control over our affairs. Postponement was almost too much to handle. The senior pilot remained unmoved by our increasingly evident determination. We tried one 'work-around' on him after another. Nothing got through. Given the Admiral's 'drop-dead' time, we feared that delay could lead to outright cancellation. He didn't care about that either. It was a matter of numbers. If the lux levels said no NVG flying, the answer was no. End of the matter. What to debate?

In near-despair, yet resolved not to give up until absolutely all avenues had been exhausted, I turned to *Brilliant*, asking if Ted could come across to talk over a matter on my behalf, best not discussed over the air. I had in mind insertion from sea, perhaps by ship's boat, possibly by canoe, if *Brilliant* could only get us close inshore, into reasonably sheltered water. If anyone was up for a bit of stealthy, nautical derring-do at dead of night, I guessed it had to be John Coward. He was.

Without hesitation he sent his Lynx over to collect Ted. Shortly the two of them came up with an insertion-plan, subject to the ship being released from its goal-keeping duties for the night. More than that, John went on to explain to Ted that he had managed to tweak the software of his Sea Wolf. It might be an anti-aircraft missile, but he was now convinced that he could get it to engage ground targets. Perhaps that would be useful for the raid itself. Incorrigible!

Meanwhile things had moved on with the helicopters. Apparently the forecast had improved for the coming night. Or perhaps someone had had a word with the senior pilot. One way or another, he had come round and was now prepared to give it a go. I informed John Coward, thanking him, noting the Sea Wolf tweaks. He wished us well.

As the time neared, I made my way to the hangar deck to have a final word with Ted and his people before their departure. The hangar deck never ceased, a hive of activity under harsh, bright lights whatever the time of day. The sounds of engineering echoed, accented by the heady smells of aviation, a mix of oil, kerosene, electrics, metal, machinery, even nylon from seats and harnesses. The combination might be found elsewhere, in other aircraft hangars, in other places, but in a carrier it has intensity, the product of limited space, constant usage and the incongruity of its all happening out at sea.

The eight men of the recce patrol had gathered in one corner, where Graham had stowed most of our stores. They were quiet, almost still compared to the industry all around them, talking fitfully in low voices. Previously, I had gone over things with Ted and Chippy, not least to ensure that we had taken into account all that we had learnt down in South Georgia. We couldn't afford any more hiccups on insertion.

The South Atlantic and its weather had our utmost respect. The plan reflected this. It appeared to take no liberties. Save for the short passage across the narrows to Pebble, the troops should not be unduly exposed to the sea's changeable, often violent moods. Indeed, I liked to think that the potential, tactical benefits of the water-gap between the 'mainland' and Pebble Island tempered by weather were being exploited with a degree of respectful sophistication. It offered security: an obstacle between our insertion-point and the enemy. And it afforded surprise, an approach that the Argentinians might not expect. What more? We could have done with some of that Gore-Tex stuff that people were talking about. We had little by way of issue water-proof clothing. Perhaps Hereford would get some down to us before too long.

As for the enemy, the ones we had met in South Georgia, how typical were they? The intelligence file referred to marines. Were they of a higher quality, better motivated, than their colleagues at Grytviken? Would they remain close to shelter like the garrison at Leith, or patrol beyond their immediate localities? Would they similarly site their defences mainly to cover the obvious approaches and the sea? Had we done all we could to mitigate the risks as we knew them? For instance, did our currently planned direction of attack bring us in on them from behind? Again, Ted had assured me that as far as he could tell he had taken all into account.

As for the ground, the Falkland Islands, none of us had set foot on the archipelago before. We knew to expect an extreme form of Dartmoor, hemmed by water, beaten by wind, cold and wet. That had to be right, surely. But how easy was it to find concealment? The land sounded notably open. The recce must conceal quite a bit of kit, the canoes, besides themselves. Would they manage? Once more, Ted and Chippy thought that they had things covered as best they could, having consulted members of G Squadron who were addressing similar issues.

And so it had churned. But now the die was cast. No point in going over it all yet again. I asked about the canoes, mostly for want of a subject. Definitely the right choice. They were stable, tough, a known quantity, a little short on stowage, limiting how much kit might be carried in, but good for sheltered waters. Nobody wanted to use the Geminis. Ted confirmed that they would keep close to the shore-line, before making their dash across the narrows. Even then, they would keep a close eye on the winds and sea state.

I did not go over the procedures we had agreed for use in the event that things went badly wrong, the emergency RVs, where, when and how often we might visit them, and in what sequence. That would have been unnecessary. Ted had earlier rehearsed those and left the details with the ops room. His patrols would have a firm handle on such Standard Operating Procedures. I didn't want to unsettle them in any way.

I did ask one final time that they keep things simple though, going on to stress that the Squadron's broad, conceptual plan for the raid would become their plan when confirmed in its detail by them for us all to execute. They would have to refine it in the field from observations they had yet to make, information they had yet to gather. It would be for them to present the final plan to us when we gathered at the squadron insertion-point. As a way of doing things, it was pretty well as we had intended for Leith two or three weeks previously.

Eventually the time came for them to step onto the hangar lift that would carry them the short distance up to the flight deck and their waiting helicopter. Unnecessarily, I told them to take care. They nodded, a few parting words, a couple of 'see you later Boss', and then they were gone.

Back in the calm of the ops room, Danny rolled and passed me a cigarette. We settled down to our long, anxious night, joined by Geordie and Lawrence.

We heard later that the insertion had gone well, and that the patrol had been dropped off at the agreed place, undetected as far as the helicopter crew could tell. They warned that the weather had been sporting: strong westerly winds with squally rain.

Ashore, the weather was indeed making life difficult. Rising winds whipped up a strong surf; combined with the rip tide surging in through the Purvis Narrows, it made canoeing along the coast an unwise, probably impossible venture. The elements were dictating things once more.

I have seen these waters myself since, in peaceful times. As you gaze out over to Pebble on a fine summer's day from the north coast at the extreme end of Critta Lee's 250,000 acre Port Howard farm, the remote beauty touches the soul. Everything appears untouched, natural, unchanged, almost impossibly, painfully pure. One of the few signs of man is 'Yorkshire Fog', the wispy, golden grass introduced along with the Corriedale sheep long ago now. Sunlight sparkles. The air is crystal clear save for the occasional flurry of dazzling salt spray. The sea boils in the narrows as the water drives in and out bringing food to the surface for the countless thousands of seabirds. The birds swarm. Shags predominate, coming from the breeding sites they share up and down the coast with that most courageous, endearing penguin, the tiny rock-hopper.

But this was winter and anything but peaceful. Ted and his troop had a job to do. If they couldn't canoe, they would have to walk. In a straight line it would be five or six kilometres from the helicopter drop-off point over to Whale Bay, from where they hoped to cross to Pebble on the second night. Easier said than done. They had a full fighting load to carry as well as the canoes. The wind's direction didn't help, more or less across their path, awkward both ways, tugging and shoving powerfully without let up.

It took them most of the night. Exhausted, wet through, mainly from rain, partly through exertion, shortly before dawn they had completed the portage. Tired maybe, but they had managed to find a sheltered and reasonably secure Lying Up Position (LUP) from which to observe the next leg of their journey. They were where they planned to be that first morning. They took the opportunity to grab a bite, rest and gather themselves for the challenges of the coming night, getting off a SITREP to *Hermes*.

It took a while to send the SITREP, for even by the standards of the day, our patrol-level communications were backward. They were based on a High Frequency architecture running out of the UK, the patrol radio being notably heavy, a wonder that such an item of equipment could have been accepted into service. However, it came with the then brand-spanking new lithium batteries, lighter and relatively longer lasting than previous types. The radio demanded much of the operator; skilful orientation of the lengthy wire antenna, and above all an ability to read and send hand-keyed Morse code.

Slow at the best of times, hand-keyed Morse proved hugely testing in the freezing, near-Antarctic conditions of a Falklands winter. With

Morse came off-line encryption, involving the use of a paper one-time-pad, another Second World War legacy. One-time-pad encryption provided complete security but demanded patience and painstaking attention to detail in use. Messages had to be kept taut, occasionally to the point of cryptic.

While TACSAT linked the CO back to Hereford and forward to his squadrons, there were not enough sets for issue down to patrols, nor band-width to support the necessary number of discrete channels. It had to be HF.[2]

The blustery winds of the previous night had heralded deep low pressure. By mid-morning the Falkland Islands were in the grip of a severe weather system driving up from the Antarctic. Stronger gusts were reaching the upper end of the Beaufort Scale, making it difficult to stand up, reminding Ted and his Troop of South Georgia. They watched as the waters they had planned to cross that night were thrashed into a furious, heaving, chaotic mess, the rip-tide powering in from the opposite direction adding to the ferment, the air dense with driving spume torn from mounting waves. What little rain there was lashed with blinding, stinging fury. Sea-water in the air cast a greenish, unearthly light over the scene. Visibility reduced to yards, offering only the occasional snatched glimpse of the opposite shore. Waves grew feet in height. And these were sheltered waters! The team knew enough not to risk it. Neither they nor the canoes would last long. They would have to wait for the storm to pass. They settled down as best they could, to sit things out.

The weather in the Falklands is nothing if not volatile. Changeability is one of its few predictable features, that and the near-constant wind mostly out of the west. By late afternoon the winds were falling fast, eventually settling at a moderate breeze. The sea became quieter.

The team crossed shortly after dark, landing at Philips Cove in a far corner of the Pebble Island farm, Purvis Rincon, some five miles east of

[2] A description of SAS equipment in general, can be found in the Appendix.

the settlement. Having cached the canoes and their bergens, they took stock of the surrounding terrain. First impressions were encouraging. The cove should do for the Squadron Landing Zone, easily enough room for four or five helicopters to land simultaneously into what was likely to be a westerly wind. With rising ground all round, the aircraft should be able to mask their approach and landing from any radar down at the Pebble airstrip; and they would be well out of earshot.

A wider examination of the surrounding area confirmed the initial, favourable impression. A vehicle track skirted the cove from north round to the east, nothing untoward, given that Pebble was a working farm. They would check for recent tyre marks in the morning.

Leaving a couple of men to secure the hidden canoes and to complete a thorough, more detailed survey of the chosen LZ, the remainder of the patrol set off for the airstrip and settlement to conduct a close recce of the target area. It didn't take them long to get there. The going was good, generally firm, gently undulating grassland. There were boggy patches and lots of diddle-dee, a heather-like, low spreading shrub common to parts of Chile and the islands of the Patagonian shelf. Falkland Islanders use its berries to make a sour jam, very much an acquired taste.

As the patrol neared the objective, communication on the VHF intra-patrol radios back to Philips Cove started to become intermittent. VHF requires near line of sight. To overcome this, Ted dropped off two men to serve as a radio-relay station bridging the five-mile gap between front and rear of his force. Should the recce have to withdraw in contact, the relay-site might also serve as a defended rallying point, offering some scope for fending off an enemy hunter-force. The disposition would keep Ted's team balanced, the product of his sure feel for minor tactics. He instructed the relay team to check the surrounding area to establish whether or not it might also serve as a squadron rallying-point on the night of the raid, that and a possible mortar position. They should look for a fold in the ground, with sub-soil firm enough to support the mortar base-plate. He correctly assumed that we would be bringing a mortar; we liked to have one in the mix if possible.

With that under way, and now down to a four-man patrol, he went forward to get a view of the target itself. He had hoped to site an OP (Observation Post) in a place affording visibility of the strip and settle-ment, preferably a safe distance from both, keeping the observers clear of any enemy perimeter patrols. But with dawn approaching, it proved impossible to find the right place in time, and they had to settle for a view of the airstrip alone. As the light improved they saw laid out before them eleven enemy aircraft: six of the deadly Pucaras, a single Shorts Skyvan and four Beechcraft Mentor recce aircraft.

The OP team were thrilled to see that many aircraft. Our founder David Stirling, and his No. 2, Paddy Mayne, must have experienced a similar thrill coming across the Luftwaffe formed-up on some remote Western Desert airfield back in 1941. But our excitement came tinged with a faint sense of unreality. We were still close to peace-time norms, up against an enemy difficult to dislike, a wholly unexpected foe. There was still something faintly delinquent about doing them harm, notwith-standing the recent shocks out at sea. Indeed, I don't think we ever learnt to wish hurt on the Argentinians in any spiteful, hate-filled way. There came a point when we all felt that the conflict had gone on long enough. If inflicting more violence hard and fast could shorten the thing, so be it, for the good of all involved. But there was never any deep animosity.

Ted and his team saw nothing to suggest that the enemy made a first light stand-to up on the airstrip itself. A generator could be heard chug-ging into life down in the settlement, evidence of sorts that people had embarked on a new day. A couple of men emerged from the shack at the side of the strip, where the FIGAS, trailer-mounted fire tender should be housed, probably a night-watch. Two others eventually sauntered up from the direction of the settlement to relieve them. Further change-overs occurred at regular interval throughout the day, all rather leisurely. Mid-morning brought some desultory activity around one or two of the aircraft, a couple of ground crew checking and securing engine covers, that kind of routine chore. There appeared to be no tractors for towing aircraft or any other mechanical handling equipment. There was the odd fuel-drum, but otherwise no maintenance facilities or equipment of any description. Perhaps it really was just an emergency, dispersal field strictly for temporary use. Maybe the aircraft would fly off at any moment, back to where they had come, before we could get at them. We didn't know that the recent bad weather had worked in our favour for once. It had softened the ground making take-off and landing at Pebble inadvisable.

As for defences, the patrol detected little or nothing: no anti-aircraft weapons, no patrols, a few strands of some sort of wire along the western side of the perimeter and no radar. They saw only a handful of men all day, the whole place looked wide open. Ted got off a message that morning:

Eleven, repeat eleven aircraft. Believed real. Squadron attack tonight. LS Philips cove. Send ETA.

8. The Raid

The signal came in to *Hermes* about mid-morning, causing a bit of a stir. It was immediately apparent, despite the Admiral's wish to get the job done as soon as we could, that Ted's 'tonight' was too sharp. The plan might be simple on the ground, but it called for a lot of coordination out at sea. If *Hermes* was to serve as the helicopter launch-platform, to get the aircraft within range she would have to move closer in towards the Islands, this impacting every unit of the Task Force one way or another. She would need at least one escort ship to provide defence against aircraft and any submarine. And we planned to have a gun-ship offshore Pebble, to give us the needed fire support on the ground. As for the other ships, what might they do, be able to do, concurrently? Where should they be during the operation?

Each aspect of the raid generated its own considerable preoccupations for its respective proponent and command. In all the excitement it would be all too easy to lose sight of the detailed needs of the raiding party itself, the troops. I did not expect us to become the main tactical effort; protection of the aircraft-carriers as our operational centre of gravity probably carried that distinction, most certainly in the early stages of the war if not throughout. However, the Task Force intended' to run a lot of risk, the justification of which rested upon our shoulders. Our priorities might have been formally protected. Perhaps above all else, we needed time on the ground, as much of it as possible. There didn't appear to be an operational procedure in place to safeguard that essential fact from the many distractions. Anyway, all was set for the night 14/15 May, the following day.

Strangely, perhaps a casualty of noise, nobody asked about radar. There had been no mention of the elusive thing in Ted's signal. Everyone seemed content to be going after aircraft alone. I didn't press the point. Perhaps the recce would come up with a radar in the meantime. We should certainly devote time to finding one on the night if possible. Drive on.

The troop commanders received their orders with plenty of time for them in turn to issue instructions to their own people and make all necessary preparations. I started by passing on what we knew of the enemy on Pebble Island. It wasn't much, but I reminded them not to underestimate the opposition. We were probably going in on a dispersal airfield, involving destruction of aircraft and associated equipment. I stressed the importance attached to radar. If we found one, it had priority over all other targets.

I confirmed that it would be a noisy attack, more or less a frontal assault in squadron strength. We would have to be quick about it for time was bound to be short. The emphasis lay on destroying the enemy's equipment and materiel, but the plan allowed for an attempt on the aircrew, time permitting. Similarly, we might try to contact the locals in the settlement, to see what information they might have on the enemy and their activity elsewhere across the Islands. In outline, 17 Troop, already ashore, to act as guides; 16 Troop to go for the settlement; 18 Troop to go for the airstrip; 19 Troop in reserve, to be prepared to assist at either the settlement or airstrip. Everyone was to be prepared to go for radar if they happened across one.

It was a matter of no concern to me how they destroyed the enemy's equipment, offering that the quickest and easiest way had to be with small arms and disposable LAW (Light Anti-tank Weapons): step up, shoot up, move on. That had to be much easier than emplacing demolition charges, with their temperamental time pencils. We would take a mortar with a mix of illumination bombs and HE (High Explosive). HMS *Glamorgan*, sister ship of *Antrim*, would be in direct support with her guns. Chris Brown would direct her fire. He should start by putting fire onto First Mountain, well to the west of the airstrip, stepping it in on my order until we had it where we needed it. We would use a mix of HE and star shells. I didn't see NGS as part of the destructive effort, more there to confuse and intimidate the enemy, on standby to dig us out of trouble should we run into any. Precision destruction of enemy stuff would be for the troops.

To keep things simple and to save time on the ground, the helicopters would load by Troops or functional group. If for any reason the frame carrying me and Tactical HQ (TAC) didn't make it, Ted would assume command. Drop-off would be into Purvis Cove, pick-up on return would be about half a kilometre to the east of the squadron RV and mortar location, south of Big Pond.

I covered a range of other coordination points and communications instructions, not least those concerning the settlement. I could allow only so much time for 16 Troop to creep into the place, the entire attack triggering the instant they went noisy. But if 16 Troop was taking too long, I would have to release the airstrip assault. I would give 16 Troop due notice. I was worried about the settlement. I could see how it might unhinge everything. I would follow it in. In the event that I lost radio contact for any reason, Danny had authority to launch the airfield assault, based upon a pre-set timing that we would have agreed on the ground.

In concluding, I stressed that the Squadron must be re-assembled at the RV for helicopter pick-up absolutely no later than 0700 local, nautical twilight, first light being 0730 local. To underscore the point, I reminded everyone that the ships would have stuck their necks out for us. They would have come close inshore, putting themselves at severe risk from air attack. The ships must get well back out to sea in good time. Every mile, every minute counted. Besides, nor did we, ourselves, want to be caught out in broad daylight, on a small island with scant cover and no escape routes. Everyone assured me that they understood the importance of getting in and out fast, under cover of darkness.

Late the following day, as we started to make our moves, with downright tedious predictability the plan ran into trouble: weather again! It wasn't too bad on land, a clear evening offering a period of good visibility with a stiff breeze. However, out at sea the winds rose relentlessly. As

Hermes and her escorts turned from the rest of the Task Force, to make the dash to the helicopter launch point, we found ourselves driving into the teeth of a pounding storm-force 7 to 8. This made a severe impact. It slowed the ships, having to push hard into the mounting waves. And it made things impossible for the crews to get up onto the flight deck to prepare the helicopters, the lashing winds keeping them below during the passage forward. Nothing would happen topside until the ship slowed on reaching the launch area or the weather eased. Therein lay another problem. To battle the head-winds after launching, the helicopters must carry additional fuel, but they couldn't carry more fuel over the originally planned distance because of the troop loads. *Hermes* would have to get further forward than originally planned. And she could only do that slowly because of the driving wind and seas. If that were not bad enough, the heavy seas damaged *Broadsword*'s Sea Wolf anti-aircraft system. Without the protection of this close-in, air-defence system, *Hermes* shouldn't go any further. So not only did we have to go further, but we also had to slow further, to effect repairs to Sea Wolf. The various snags and changes ate into the plan's built-in margins for error.

As we eventually neared the launch point, with the clock running down, I started to think, somewhat unfairly, that the Navy had consumed an undue proportion of the available time on their supporting part of the plan, missing the centrality of ours. I came close to calling it off, more accurately, asking the Admiral to cancel or postpone. But I wavered. We were definitely getting down to the wire, but perhaps not quite there. Get ashore, and we might yet be able to sort something out. The ships may have started late for comfort. They had been fighting hard since. *Broadsword* had made her repairs. *Hermes'* navigator and air staff had worked and re-worked what they could. And *Glamorgan* wouldn't be holding back if anything like her sister ship *Antrim*, shouldering her way through the storm. We owed it to everyone to give it our best shot too.

We at last reached the re-calculated launch-point, having lost well over an hour. We were invited up to the flight deck to board the helicopters.

No sooner had we got there, staggering under our loads, thrashed by the howling gale, than we were ordered back below. Now the helicopters had too much fuel in their tanks. They would have to lift over the sea, dump some, return, only then embark us. In the midst of this, fighting to keep my footing on the heaving, storm thrashed deck, I became aware of Chris Brown tugging at my sleeve, straining to get my attention.

I was preoccupied, nonplussed, striving to make sense of my battered faculties, to say nothing of the latest instance of operational dissonance. The driving spray and rain made it almost impossible to see and hear properly, the numbing combination of wind and cold near overwhelming. There were the dark, unexpectedly familiar shapes of helicopters, oddly reassuring, solidly dependable in the tumult, part of us in a way, offering a kind of handrail to cling on to. There were the dark figures of the flight-deck crews, several out at the Sea Kings struggling against the storm, pulled and pushed as they attended to the business of getting the frames away, a small bunch sheltering by the carrier's island, hunched yet attentive, waiting to dash forward when needed. The flight-deck itself was awash with water, sheeting spindrift flying from its surface. Always in the background raged the unseen, savage sea, beyond the rhythmically rising and falling edge of the deck, the ship booming as waves crashed into her. The howling, roaring wind was confusing, near deafening. Disorientation heightened the unnervingly magnetic, mesmerising menace of the deck's open edge. Certain death lay in wait for anyone falling overboard.

I could hardly hear what Chris was shouting at me. I could barely take in a thing, fragments, the odd word. It had to concern the fire plan. I felt sure he mentioned *Glamorgan*'s fire support and a mountain, starting somewhere or other. I simply didn't get it.

'Whatever you say, Chris, whatever you think best,' I responded carelessly. I had absolute confidence in him. If this was about some gunnery technical matter, he would know best. He knew what was needed, what we were after by way of naval fire support.

'Whatever's best.'

My shouted words appeared to work. They seemed to satisfy what he was after. My attention returned to the even less familiar business of being up on an aircraft carrier's open deck at night, in the South Atlantic, gale force winds threatening to hurl one over the side.

Some psychologists say that men are particularly prone to this tendency of being attracted to the new, unusual, noisy and shiny over the less showy, perhaps more routine matters. It can catch us out for novelty and glitter are no true measures of importance, actual or relative. I should have focused more on what my 'gunner' had to tell me, than on the rarely-experienced, hugely-impressive yet transient commotion all about.

At last, emerging from our brief adjournment back below, we got underway. The Sea King was near-perfect for this kind of work. It had a cavernous interior, plenty of power, and was quiet for a helicopter, not inside, but outside. Its rotors made a swishing noise, its engines a low, muted sound, with an occasional, higher pitch somewhere in the blend. It had a single, straight-through deck, pilots and passengers being on the same level, this bringing the two together, helping with any necessary interaction.

I tucked myself into the forward left seat for take off, so as to stand behind the pilots during flight, taking care not to lean on the port side door, prone to fly open under pressure. I fancied I should be able to see what the two pilots might see. Fat chance as it turned out. They had NVG. I did not. It helped to think I might. Besides, from there it should be possible to watch them. You could tell a lot from body-language, even when the two bodies were firmly strapped to a Sea King Mk IV of 846 Naval Air Squadron, softly silhouetted by the dim, green glow of their instrument panel. Mostly though, I would be able to listen to them, using the intercom positioned there on the bulk-head, and discuss things if necessary.

The aircrewman down the back confirmed all were on board, equipment secured. The senior pilot checked all helicopters ready. They were. The collective rose, eased with a gentle twist on the friction wheel, power coming in, steadily pulled up to and gently through the point it took hold of the airframe, reaching for flight, pedal countering torque and wind, cyclic too, responding to the raging gale outside. There was little smooth about a Sea King's take-off, even under calm conditions; for an instant, that sensation of insufficient power. The aircraft would struggle, shuddering and shaking as if pulling apart. Then, still protesting, it would come up, reluctantly unsticking itself from ground or deck, a slight lurch to one side or another, settle and then transition with a gentle tilt forward before eventually flying, as intended, the rotors generating a faint rocking motion. This time, the driving wind helped, adding lift. We went in a near instant from lift to flight.

Clear of *Hermes*, we dropped down onto a heading more or less into the teeth of the gale, skimming above the water. I could just make out a heavy running sea, the occasional breaking wave throwing up spray, reaching out for us. Windscreen wipers thrashed, on and off. It seemed to take an age, and yet not: one moment we were departing *Hermes*, the next flaring to land. In came that all-enveloping juddering, the airframe protesting the act of landing: then bump, up, gentle bump, settle. We were down. Everyone scrambled out, loadmaster to one side of the door soundlessly ushering us forth.

Then they were gone, the helicopters. Our warm world of metal and machinery, its smells of anti-corrosion fluid, oil, nylon and burnt aviation fuel replaced abruptly, absolutely and emphatically by that more familiar place of earth and vegetation. At that moment it was a dark and cold place, stirred by a damp, breeze otherwise feeling unexpectedly still and quiet after the commotion of the flight. The fleeting, cut-adrift, abandoned sensation slowly subsided, disorientation lingering until displaced by activity; not the cold though, bitter and penetrating after the warmth of the ship. We radiated heat from every extremity. It would take a while for the body to draw back all warmth to its core. No such distractions for Ted and his people though: they were thoroughly of the place.

Quickly they had the Squadron shepherded into formation for the move down to the settlement and airstrip. Shivering almost uncontrollably, I rapidly went over the plan with Ted. It was pretty well unchanged, other than the odd detail. I issued the troop commanders and other team leaders their confirmatory orders. I hoped they understood that it was the cold and nothing else that made me shake so violently. I gave the troop commanders a few minutes for them in turn to brief their own people. On Ted's advice we had adopted a twin-file formation, the Squadron travelling in two columns, side-by-side. I didn't much care for it. It felt clumsy. If we went into contact from a flank, the troops on that side alone would be free to engage, effectively halving our potential fire-power.

Go with it. No time for faffing over that sort of detail. Accept the risk. Must get to the target. I checked the time: 0400 local. We were very late. I went over things in my head as we stumbled along. Say four to five miles to the Squadron RV: an hour, depending on the going and a clear run, no enemy. Then forward to the edge of the airstrip and settlement by stealth, not forgetting the mortar: thirty to forty minutes. That gave us about an hour for breaking stuff; more than enough for the airstrip, probably insufficient for the settlement? Still nothing on radar. Too bad. Crack on.

After half a mile or more, the impracticality of the twin file became evident. It proved impossible to maintain formation, the two columns never simultaneously sharing the same going underfoot, and they experienced acute difficulty matching each other's speed. I ordered single file, taking the point with Ted. Trading security, tactical balance, everything for speed, we tabbed off PARA fashion as fast as we dared.[1] I was desperate to have that full hour.

It took longer than expected. Despite the change of formation and throwing caution to the wind, we reached the area south of Big Pond, the Squadron RV and mortar position, an hour or more adrift of the re-calculated ETA. This left less than an hour in which to do it all: creep forward, get into position, attack and withdraw. *Glamorgan* had already reminded Chris that they should leave soon, no later than 0730 local. I

---

[1] PARAs' 'tab'; the word refers to their quick, shuffling gait on a route march; for me it says something about their restless, energetic spirit. Marines 'yomp'.

shared the ship's anxiety. I could sense the troops coming in from the march. Danny came across with Lawrence to join me and Ted. We should be ready to move forward in a couple of minutes. We conferred. Give it a go? We all agreed. Give it a go. Okay then.

The ground underfoot gave a little, soft if not spongy, hardly ideal for the mortar. Too bad; it would have to do. They would have to find somewhere firm in the immediate area. Worse, we had lost one of the troops, detached during our headlong dash, which was not altogether surprising. One of the dynamics of single file is that speed at the back of the column will be twice that at the front, or so it seems. We had made no allowance for this during our tab, setting a pace at the front that must have been nightmarish at the back.

I gave the missing Troop a few minutes before making adjustments. 16 Troop should do no more than screen off the settlement from a position just off the airstrip; no time for anything more complicated. On being told, Stuart Harper looked crestfallen.

'All right, to the edge of the settlement, no further.'

I simply couldn't allow them to get drawn into anything that might lose us the initiative, require us to divert resources to their assistance, effectively have us reinforcing a failure. An untidy, protracted engagement could severely complicate the entire affair, perhaps cause us to miss the helicopter pick up. That could result in a right royal mess. We would end up on the island through the coming day, holding off a stirred up enemy. And what if the Task Force couldn't make it back in the following night: loss of the Squadron? I drove the thought to the back of my mind.

19 Troop, previously reserve, would now do the airstrip. John Hamilton's face was a picture when I told him. He assured me they had everything necessary, including 1lb standard demolition charges. I told him okay, but forget about orthodoxy, shoot the bloody things and keep searching for radar.

18 Troop would go into reserve on arrival. Ted, 17 Troop, no change: up to the airfield, act as guides and do what damage they could with the weapons they had.

We would go noisy with an illuminating round from the mortar. I finished by confirming that we were standing on what would serve as the Squadron RV. The Troops were to drop whatever they might be doing to be back at the RV no later than 0700 local, giving them about twenty minutes on target, likely less. I kept back a little spare time, knowing that they were sure to overrun. It was desperately tight. I wondered again at the wisdom of pressing on.

'And don't forget radar', I reminded everyone as they scampered off to brief their Troops, probably unheeding, all of them acting as though they had just won big on the football pools. A pointless urging, for they were going to biff all and everything they came across anyway.

The constant worry over time put the dampers on things for me; I could take little pleasure in the excitements of the moment. Instead, my mind kept turning on the consequences of getting stuck out on the island, the possible eventualities beyond those coming up immediately next. What were the options? Nothing appealed. Hell, it could wait. Should wait. If we didn't sort out the current situation, we might not achieve a thing. That said, be prepared. So my thoughts kept tumbling, moving back and forth from one timeframe to another.

I ran over things within SHQ. Lawrence would man the RV, not least to check the Troops back in. Accounting for our numbers was most important. We didn't want to leave anyone behind. When they arrived 18 Troop was to be held in reserve at the RV. I told Danny that I remained concerned about the settlement part of the operation, and would follow behind 16 Troop as originally planned. He should keep an eye on the airstrip for me, from the RV preferably, or move forward behind the assault if absolutely necessary. If he did go forward Lawrence must take over defence of the RV during his absence. I should be consulted before committing the reserve for any reason; however, I gave Danny authority to use the reserve should he be unable to contact me.

Danny and Lawrence both saw it the same way as me. The settlement end of the action may not have been mission-critical, but it could get us into a lot of trouble. By comparison the airstrip should be straightforward requiring little more than the execution of 17 Troop's pre-deter-mined tactical plan. They had had the thing under observation all day. There should be no nasty surprises. Yes, if this operation was going to go even more awry than it already had, it would most likely trigger down at the settlement end of things.

Turning to Chris, I told him to get the ship going with a star-shell immediately, the mortar fired, and then start stepping in her fire. I unnecessarily reminded him that we expected a mix of illumination and HE employing both mortar and ship, enough to keep the airstrip visible to the attackers, and the enemy's heads down. At about that moment 18 Troop turned up to hear their bad news: into reserve. They were not happy, their disappointment and anger palpable. I couldn't help that. But felt much better for having them back as a reserve briefed and in place. I gave Pete Sutherby the Troop Commander a quick and dirty assessment, emphasising that the airstrip should be straightforward, the settlement subject to more unknowns. If anything then, he must be prepared to help extract 16 Troop from the settlement—extract, *not* get drawn in!

Ted confirmed that he and John had got to the edge of the airstrip. I knew that Stuart must be close to the Settlement. Chris was ready with the ship. Reserve poised. All was set.

I told the Mortar Fire Controller (MFC) that he might start. The mortar fired its ILLUM, only for the tube to drive deep down into the peat, nothing but some six inches of it remaining visible. And that was it for the mortar. Lawrence laughed in that equable, good natured, way of his, and went over to help. He and the mortar team spent most of the rest of their raid digging the tube out from the clinging bog.

As the ILLUM burst, not exactly where intended, casting its orange, scudding light, pandemonium broke out up on the airstrip. The good sort of our making with everything going out, nothing coming in: star shells, tracer, rocket-flares, bangs, crumps, cracks. An aircraft cooked-off with a ripping shriek from its guns; another burst into flames, add-ing a vivid, dancing light to the illumination of the flares. Nothing untoward came in over the radio. All in hand, troops having a whale of a time. I noted that the radio net was relatively quiet, no unnecessary chatter, a few short, sharp co-ordinations as the troops made their way round their targets: slick. Still no mention of radar. Shame. I moved off with Chris and a signaller to catch up with 16 Troop. We found them at the edge of a mass of gorse a few hundred yards back from the settlement, Stuart in a huddle with a couple of his people, obviously working out their next move. From the gorse, the ground to their front sloped gently down towards what appeared to be a shed or wood building at the very edge of our field of vision; open grassland with wire fencing. Mines? I hung back, Chris talking to *Glamorgan*.

'Step it in, Chris,' I said unnecessarily, having little better to do, instructing him to start what he had already started, bringing the naval fire closer. Then almost immediately, 'step it in,' and again, 'step it in.'

I didn't know where the ship was exactly, apart from offshore to the north, but I reckoned that her incoming shells travelling at about a mile in two seconds could be in the air for ten or twelve seconds, possibly less. Anyway, keep it coming.

I moved forward to join Stuart and his huddle. By now we had quite a bit of light from the ship's star shells and our own Schermuly rockets. The scudding flares cast a dull, almost opaque, orange light, fast-gliding shadows adding to an impression of theatre, a stage-like artificiality. We scanned the open, empty ground to our front. No sign of enemy. It wasn't going to work though, any move closer to the edge of the settlement. Surprise had been lost. We would be badly exposed crossing the wide, grassy expanse, forward sloped and dangerously backlit by the goings-on up on the airstrip. And I didn't trust that fencing. It might be normal around a farm settlement, but equally it could be marking minefields? This would have to do. Close enough. No need to run more risk than we had to. We had sufficient to be getting on with.

I called it off there and then. Stuart showed understandable disappointment, but he knew it made sense. Let the enemy come up to us if they cared. I left him to mask off the settlement, to set an ambush from in and around his current position, to catch any enemy coming up to the strip. He shouldn't let any pass.

Screening off the settlement had to be the right thing to do. One less worry, and it afforded us all added protection. A weight had been lifted. And with still no enemy reported up on the airstrip it had to be time to start enjoying oneself. Feeling not only a lot easier, but even a touch full of myself, I turned more of my attention to the pleasurable business of passing fire orders to one of Her Majesty's Ships. 'Step it in Chris, step it in.'

I looked over to the airstrip where the light and noise continued unabated. It looked and sounded like a lot of fun. I thought about joining in. On quick reflection, it wasn't a good idea, entering anything as fluid as that in mid flow. All too easy to be mistaken for enemy, wander into someone's arc of fire, get in the way. Forget it. Get on with one's own job. The troops had it all in hand. We made our way back to the Squadron RV instead.

In a short while it would be time to go home, the RV had to be the place for Chris and I. It had good observation forward, and the reserve poised to respond in any direction. It offered tactical control. And until I gave the order to retire, the troops needed nothing more from me at that moment, other than to keep out of their way.

So, 'step it in, Chris' I said expansively, feeling for once pretty well on top of things, certainly enjoying the thrill of a one sided engagement. 'Step it in.'

And then Ted came up on the net, asking for me personally.

'Fetch sunray.'

'Send.'

Promptly, calmly, controlled but clearly not in good humour he went on to say, 'I don't want to sound as if I'm complaining, but do we need all this naval gunfire? I am going to start taking casualties at any moment.'

'Bloody hell!' I snapped at Chris. 'Stop, stop, stop!'

In all the goings-on I had clean forgotten about the snatched, half discerned communication with Chris on *Hermes'* turbulent flight-deck a few hours previously. Now it came rushing in on me, crashing in with shocking realisation: First Mountain a long way out, would it be okay to start stepping-in the gunfire from a point closer to the airstrip? It all now made terrible sense.

We must have started bringing gunfire in not from miles distant thereabouts, not from the clearly visible, outlined slopes of First Mountain, but from somewhere between the mountain and the western edge of the airstrip. Given the number of adjustments I had blithely instructed with such thoughtless abandon, it was a wonder I hadn't killed us all well before now.

And it might not be too late for that. We could have rounds still in the air, on their way onto the airstrip, onto Ted and John's troops at that very instant. It crossed my mind to advise them to dive for cover.

'Shouldn't have,' Chris responded to my obvious question, in that steady, easy and modest way of his. 'I told them to stop HE and switch to star shells.'

'Good. Good. No more HE then,' I affirmed rather feebly, suddenly feeling a lot less cocky. Chris acknowledged, and sent an appropriate message over his radio in measured, even tones.

'I'll ask for HE if we need any more,' I said unnecessarily, for my own peace of mind, to ensure he had it. He nodded, continuing with his instructions to the ship. I got back to Ted, composing myself.

'Roger,' I said, as breezily as I could, certainly more calmly than I had any right to feel, smoothly, as though with everything under perfect control, at my finger-tips, all going as if by design.

'Star shells from now on, okay?'

'Roger,' came Ted's clipped reply

So much for keeping out of the troops' way. On reflection, I would say that Chris had been onto things well before Ted came up on the net. But the HE must have been getting uncomfortably close for him to have made the call.

And so there it is, my part in the Pebble Island raid, a Special Forces operation regarded by many as a model of its type, a fine example of the precise, judicious, restrained use of force, faultless in planning, flawless in execution? For much, if not most, of my time on target I shelled my own troops.

Glancing across the RV I caught sight of the reassuring presence of Lawrence. I hoped he wouldn't get wind of the NGS business. I saw that he and the mortar crew had managed to extract the tube and its base plate from its hole. He came over splattered in mud, a wry grin lighting his face; with a shrug of his wide shoulders he nodded towards the mortar team before offering me one of his Rolos.[2] We could both sense the approaching dawn, agreeing in whispers that we now needed to get away. As if to underscore this, Chris reported that the ship sounded slightly anxious. They were not pushing, but they clearly wanted to turn back out to sea before long. I got onto Ted to tell him to break it off, to withdraw. He 'Wilcoed',[3] saying they were about done. I repeated that I meant him to break it off there and then, even if he was not yet 'done'. I was pretty sure that they must have destroyed all the aircraft by then. Time to go.

I gave it a few minutes, sufficient for 17 and 19 Troops to make their initial moves back before instructing Stuart to start bringing his troop in from the settlement. I would have preferred to have kept 16 Troop in place to cover us a while longer, to give us a more distinctly sequential withdrawal of forces. But time was getting drastically tight. We had to accept risks. Lawrence turned to check people in and through the RV. I knew that he felt it too, the vulnerability of drawing everything in at once, most of the force on the move. Any half-decent enemy could easily throw a spanner in the works.

Danny arrived, confirming that Ted was not far behind, a clean break, no enemy follow up. I told Chris to release the ship. No heavy fire sup-

[2] Rolo caramel chocolates, advertised for many years under the slogan: 'Do you love anyone enough to give them your last Rolo.'

[3] WILCO (Will Comply) a useful bit of jargon often used as an adjective as in: he's a WILCO person, meaning helpful, positive, optimistic, compliant even but not normally in any pejorative way.

port from then on, just when we might have needed it most. Couldn't be helped. The ship must go. And the mortar was out of it too, packed up. I glanced in the direction of the settlement, then towards the airstrip, silently urging the troops back, noting the faintly discernible light bleeding into the night sky. Where were they? I reached for some chocolate, preferring a cigarette. All gone. Damn.

'Ship on its way,' reported Chris.

Good. One less thing to worry about. The risk-taking was oddly thrilling. Danny had moved across to Lawrence. The two of them stood, quietly conferring, Lawrence turning to point back towards where the mortar had been. Their companionable stillness imparted calm and reassurance. At last, the troops started to arrive. Ted made his way over to report a couple of walking wounded, nothing serious, otherwise everyone okay, all aircraft destroyed. No radar! With little time for more he left to re-join his troops. Still no follow up by the enemy.

My mind turned on the next concern: helicopters. Would they find us, be on time? What if they didn't return? Should we go back in towards the settlement to take the enemy on? Or should we high tail it down to the end of the Island? And then what?

'That's it', Lawrence reported as 16 Troop passed, 'everyone through the RV.'

With that he cast around one last time to ensure that we had everyone we should have in SHQ itself. Everyone accounted for. We both caught sight of the pile of unexpended mortar bombs. They would have to stay. We must go. Still no enemy. Where were they?

By now, the eastern horizon was starting to take on colour, a deep dark blue, with a touch of mauve. A gentle pre-dawn breeze picked up. It was bitterly cold; although we barely felt it. We closed the RV, setting off for the Landing Zone more or less back the way we had come, tabbing fast to put distance between us and the settlement and its airstrip. Hell, I wouldn't want to be the enemy commander, having to answer for the night's goings-on. We had left him a right mess.

Presently, we reached the helicopter pick-up-point. Danny, Lawrence and Geordie got the Squadron into stick order, ready for a rapid load.

It was another gamble, doing it without a covering force to shield the LZ from enemy interference, gearing everything to speed. I anxiously glanced down at my watch, and then back the way we had just come. I was pretty certain that we hadn't been followed. But perhaps we should put out a guard. How much longer? My watch said any moment. The dark shapes of the troops were still, ready, patiently waiting. All stood or crouched, composed, but there was an alert quality, a tension.

If the helicopters didn't come very, very soon, it would have to be 'Plan B'; and definitely start by putting out a screen. My mind began to churn again. We had left the canoes at the squadron entry point, intending to pick them up on our extraction. Surely no solution there: ferrying the Squadron by canoe over to West Falkland to evade. Stupid thought. What about the settlement option, going back in? We might then be the ones dictating events. Pin them down. Keeping close-in on the Pebble garrison might make it difficult for them to employ ground-attack aircraft against us, for fear of hitting their own troops. But, what of the civilians? Should we start at the settlement and then fight our way back to an area for pick up the coming night, conduct a fighting withdrawal through the day? How much ammo did we have? Could we recover the mortar bombs? Round and round it went. The helicopters had to come.

Lawrence, sitting alongside Geordie, reached into his right breast pocket. 'Geordie, old chap, have my last Rolo.' He too must have been feeling it, making light of matters.

Then, there they were, the Sea Kings hover taxiing towards us merely feet above the ground, shadowy shapes against the darkness, night giving way to stealthily approaching dawn. A surge of relief: absolutely spot-on time, 0730 local to the second. How could I have ever doubted the Fleet Air Arm? They settled on the ground in front of each stick of awaiting troops, not needing our marshals. We emplaned in as many seconds as it can take; we had been right to emphasise speed. I jammed myself in behind the left seat pilot, took the headset from the bulkhead pocket, exchanged good mornings, the captain of the helicopter turning my way with a gentle nod of his head, in what I took to be an easy, comradely salute. The horizon to our front appeared ablaze with burning enemy aircraft. Our aircrewman reported ready. Near simultaneously all the other frames called in, loaded. And with that we lifted to go back out to sea, to *Hermes*, in time for a hearty breakfast, tired and contented.

Before my 'Full English', that would include black pudding and fried bread, I reported to the battle staff: eleven aircraft destroyed along with a quantity of fuel and other items. We weren't sure if we had killed or injured any enemy. There had been little resistance. I explained that we had found no radar of any sort and that we hadn't had much time in which to seek one out. We had arrived late and had time for the airstrip alone. They seemed unsurprised and content. Perhaps they were merely relieved to have it done, us back and the ship able to return to the cover of the Task Force to resume a role more familiar and suited to her stature. And maybe this never had been purely a matter of radar.

I went on to explain that we had two injured, one with minor shrapnel wounds to his leg, probably a splinter from his own 40mm grenade. Another had been concussed when the Argentinians detonated a demolition charge on one of the runway intersections. The whole area up on the airstrip was boggy, save for the main runway itself. But the bogginess of the adjacent parking and marshalling areas, together with the crater from the demolition charge, probably rendered the place unusable for the time being. We had made no contact with the settlement.

As Danny noted in his diary:

'An exercise, only easier. Boat was late, weather was bad, heli was late [he meant for drop-off, not pick-up], assault troop lost itself and still a repeat of a Paddy Mayne type action.'

The raid confirmed for me that no operation would ever go as planned or intended. This had been my experience in Dhofar, Northern Ireland, South Georgia and over the last hours. It seemed that war would remain nine parts the management of cock-up.

And Captain Coward of *Brilliant* would say that 'the essence of war is violence, moderation in war is imbecility'. On the face of it, the matter of the enemy's aircrew at Pebble would bear this out. Our late arrival had ruled out any attempt on their lives. Instead, we had no option other than to go after the aircraft alone. However, the enemy made good the destruction of the Pucaras ferrying four replacement airframes from Rio Gallegos that very day, giving them a net loss of two, bringing the total number of Pucaras in the Falklands to fifteen. The rapidity of the Argentinians' response suggested that they may have thought the raid an immediate preliminary to our main landings. It certainly underscored the importance they attached to Pucara as a weapon system, part of their counter-landing plans. The relative ease with which they brought the number of aircraft on the Falklands back up to strength served to emphasise the significance of the aircrew and key technicians, making them legitimate targets altogether more diffi-cult to replace.

But there had to be more to it than that. From something teetering on failure we salvaged matters of note. To the enemy and indeed the world, the Task Force must have come across as tough and deadly effec-tive. In addition, there was a discernible decency emerging. Aspects of South Georgia had been positively gentlemanly. Now there was this example of restraint matched to precision. I believe the Squadron's instincts were inclined that way all along; I don't think many, if any, of us would have taken the slightest satisfaction in killing pilots in their beds had we the time to get at them. It was a genuine relief to have failed to land that punch. The absence of any hint of brutality enabled us all to take unalloyed pleasure in our success. Concentrating upon the destruction of materiel alone kept us on a certain moral plain. Indeed, I liked to think the tone of the Pebble operation, following the example of South Georgia, went some way in keeping the conflict within bounds, suggesting that some moderation in war had its place.

Certainly, for the entire Task Force it came as a timely, reassuring shot in the arm. We might have taken a knock or two, *Sheffield* notably, but mostly the hits continued to go out the other way. We were more than getting the measure of our opponent. Our professionalism would seem to have us coming out on top. It came at a good time for the Squadron too, moving us on from the disappointments and frustrations of South Georgia. And not to be underrated, Roger Edwards felt certain that word of our success would get out round the Islands, buoying our people ashore, correspondingly dampening the morale of their occupiers.

The raid must have given Argentine spirits a further, powerful knock at home as well as abroad on the 'Malvinas'. The first contact with us on land, on the Falklands themselves, and it results in their outright humiliation, an embarrassment surely heightened by our apparent disregard of their fighting men: cutting out the airframes to the exclusion of airmen and troops. The latest in a growing catalogue of reverses, it could be expected to intensify any growing sense of gloom across their nation, and isolation among the garrison on the Falklands.

The Squadron had done a 'proper job', as they might say in and around Devonport. And so it was with a sense of satisfaction that I eventually got stuck into my handsome navy breakfast, save that by the time I did it was to find that Jolly Jack had been at the black pudding!

9. Campaign Plans

For the past month strategists and operational-level planners had been wrestling with the problem of how to confound the Argentinians given that on the face of it things were stacked in their favour. They were close to home, with a capable navy and a sizeable, modern air-force that included fast jets operating off mainland bases. On the Falklands their ground forces were numerous, well-equipped and in prepared positions, backed by ground-attack aircraft and helicopters, enabling them to conduct a mobile defence should they choose.

We, on the other hand, were operating over extended lines of communication 8,000 miles long, putting us at an immediate and severe disadvantage. Wear and tear on ships and other essential equipment would limit our duration. Ground forces would be lightly equipped, available shipping unable to transport or off-load our heavier equipment such as tanks. Similarly, we could carry only so many troops and so much materiel forward. We were unlikely to get anywhere near the three-to-one ratio, attacker to defender, that orthodoxy dictates; at best, we might achieve near-parity with our enemy on land.

The challenges for both sides would be compounded by weather: cold, frequent storms, gales on average every few days, and rain on fifteen days every month, throughout the winter. And the Argentinians had a head start on us. They were in position, and prepared for the Falklands' winter, we out in the open, having to bear the brunt of it. Little wonder that back in the UK other options than straight eviction of the enemy were under consideration.

In mid-April a paper for the Chiefs of Staff addressed the problem.[1] It offered that the two pre-conditions to be met before undertaking a

[1] This section draws on p. 194ff. in Sir Lawrence Freedman, *The Official History of the Falklands Campaign*, vol. II, Abingdon: Routledge, 2005.

landing, namely sea control and a reasonable degree of air superiority over the Falklands, should be achievable. The assessment noted that the mountainous ground in front of Stanley favoured defence, expressing concern over the prospect of civilian casualties were the fight to carry into the town. If at all possible Fighting in Built Up Areas (FIBUA) should be avoided. It involved large numbers of troops; heavy casualties, military and civilian; and widespread damage and destruction to property. The planners identified three broad landing options, although the paper before the Chiefs conceded that a landing in the Stanley area was the one most suitable in terms of delivering 'early and decisive military results':

> West Falkland. A landing in the west should be relatively easy to achieve and secure. But it would put only modest pressure on the enemy then based mainly in and around Stanley on East Falkland; it would require us to make a second landing should it become necessary to close with them.

> Lafonia (the Southern part of East Falkland). Again, this should involve relatively light enemy opposition and very low risk to civilians. Any move on Stanley must channel through the isthmus at Goose Green.

> East Falkland (North Coast). Landing in proximity to Stanley and his main defences could be expected to put considerable pressure on the enemy; but it would put the landings at greatest risk from enemy counter-action.

To an extent, these options hint at some early uncertainty within the higher military-strategic levels over how best to proceed if and when we did get ashore. There was as yet no consensus. It stemmed from the grave concerns over our strength relative to that of the enemy. And so planners were obliged to search for courses of action short of wholesale re-possession of the Islands. Thoughts ranged widely. One idea involved the establishment of an enclave from which to exert pressure on the Argentine garrison by conducting raids. Another imagined an airstrip capable of supporting RAF air-defence aircraft, this relieving the aircraft-carriers. Yet another envisaged a naval and air blockade, to starve out the enemy garrison, acknowledging that this would bring down equal misery upon our own people under occupation.

At our level, we never picked up on the strategic planning churn. For us it was always a simple matter: get the Argentines out, our people and Islands back. There was going to be a fight, details to follow. We would have been bewildered, perhaps even dismayed, to discover our higher leadership considering anything other than the straightforward expulsion of the invader. At our 'fighter' level, we simply had confidence in one another to get the job done.

Over time we did become aware of untidiness within the operational command-chain. We knew that Admiral Fieldhouse, C-in-C Fleet, at Northwood was the overall commander. We were less familiar with detailed command arrangements below that. FLEET had scant feel for land operations; accordingly, they co-opted Major General Jeremy Moore, Royal Marines, to advise them. In time, he became Commander Land Forces Falkland Islands (CLFFI, pronounced 'Cliffy'). We 'foot soldiers' never really got to know Moore as our leader, even after he joined us in theatre. For a period, Rear Admiral Woodward thought he was the commander of everything forward, in, on and around the Falklands; as did we. To an extent FLEET encouraged him to think in those terms. Consequently, until eventually put straight, he imagined himself exercising command of the Amphibious Force, including the embarked troops of 3 Commando Brigade. He didn't. Northwood held command of the amphibians to itself. During a brief critical period of the operation strong tensions developed between Woodward and the principals of the Amphibious Force: Commander Amphibious Warfare (COMAW) and Commander 3 Commando Brigade, Commodore Clapp and Brigadier Thompson respectively.

Positioning ourselves always alongside the higher-level commanders, we were quick to pick up on the inherent C2 complexities. It was a frequent topic of conversation on the TACSAT between the CO and Ops in Hereford. Careless of the rights and wrongs, Euan and I regarded Woodward as the 'Boss', the *de facto* in-theatre, joint force commander. And we continued to do so pretty well right through to the end, even with Moore on the ground. This could have been wishful thinking, but it also spoke to Woodward's stature, if not his status, as a war fighter. We had been with him up close, during some tough moments. We saw he had what it took. He held our trust and confidence. We liked him.

On 17 April Admiral Fieldhouse gathered his commanders off Ascension Island, where a general plan was agreed, differences resolved, and a degree of clarity achieved. They first considered our own physical and moral resilience, hence the amount of time we might have available to fight. They were particularly concerned about the serviceability of the aircraft carriers and SSNs. They ran over the enemy's relative strengths and the matter of the defences in front of Stanley. They took into account all other relevant military, geo-strategic factors. Then operational Courses of Action were discussed. They could see how any option short of full re-possession was likely to lead to stalemate. 'Repossession' emerged as the clearly favoured option: the eviction of the Argentinians at the point of the bayonet if necessary, taking back the entire Falklands archipelago. However, details could not be pinned down at that juncture.

Fieldhouse and his command-team went on to draw up an outline timetable that had the carrier group establishing the TEZ by 19 April; the aircraft carriers themselves could probably operate at intensive rates for up to six weeks, not much beyond that. They allowed fifteen days for advance-force operations, including information gathering by Special Forces (G Squadron and SBS), and a further twenty-one days for post-landing operations. So, a landing would have to be made no later than 23 May.

Back home notwithstanding Northwood's adoption of 're-possession', within the MOD the assessment and re-assessment of options continued. The work included a review of the physical imbalance of forces in favour of the Argentinians. About every fighting ship that could be deployed had been deployed, as had war-planes. Turning to forces on land, after much agonising, the decision was taken to deploy 5 Infantry Brigade, the Army's agile 'strategic reserve', probably a misleading title for a formation lightly equipped more by omission than design.

For years the Army's equipment priorities had been on its heavy mechanised and armoured forces stationed in Germany, almost wholly unusable in this particular national crisis. By comparison, the needs of our Light forces, including 5 Brigade, had been getting relatively little attention. To compound matters, at the outset of the current emergency 5 Brigade had been hollowed-out, its two Parachute battalions, 2 PARA and 3 PARA, re-subordinated to 3 Commando Brigade. Reinforcement by two Guards battalions, Scots and Welsh, brought the Brigade back up to strength, all acknowledging that it hadn't been the best way to mobilise a formation for war: first taking it apart, then re-assembling it with units unfamiliar with one another.

The Army showed a tendency to commoditise brigades, the dual meaning of the word 'brigade' itself serving to internalise the trait, being as much verb as noun. The Army's essential building blocks were its 'units'. And units got brigaded in mixes considered best suited to any given set of circumstances, a method referred to as 'task organization'. Aside from the distinct advantages of bespoke tailoring of forces to mission, it made for ease of management of increasingly scarce resources. Operational commitments staff were able to field formations by taking a unit from here, another from there, according to a wide range of managerial factors. It took a keenly conscientious operational commitments staff to ensure pure war-fighting considerations would always, and emphatically outweigh administrative convenience when task organising.

And understandably, physical capabilities tended to carry greater weight than the other aspects of combat readiness, such as the units' familiarity with one another's techniques and ways, and the intangibles of team spirit, and shared identity.[2] Of course tactics, practices and

[2] British Army doctrine sees fighting-power as consisting of three inter-acting components. There is the physical: troop numbers, their weapons, equipment and such-like. There is the moral: essentially fighting-spirit, the will-

procedures were things to be held in common, facilitating ad hoc task organisation; but there could be rough edges as we found at South Georgia. The risks of unfamiliarity could be mitigated through a suitable programme of pre-deployment training, covering both individual and collective skills. A well run programme should fuse units into a polished, all arms formation (brigade). Besides, there was also the renowned regimental system to draw upon, that built in moral strengths at unit level. A unit could be expected to behave well on operations, because that was what it had always done, and would forever continue to do, or strive to do, whatever the circumstances, whatever the company. This could be expected to compensate for any lack of esprit at formation level.

However, the full preparation of a specifically task-organised brigade takes time, a good six months to ready a formation for operations in Afghanistan recently. But the Falklands War was a come-as-you-are-party, with no time for exhaustive, pre-deployment training. It would take a very special brigade commander and staff to sort 5 Brigade without benefit of a thorough period of pre-deployment training; while in contact; under the wholly-unfamiliar circumstances of amphibious warfare; and out in the open of a South Atlantic winter. On paper then, the correlation of ground forces improved markedly with the addition of 5 Brigade, bringing the Task Force on land up to near numerical parity with our enemy on the Islands. But there was fragility. It would show.

Fortunately, 3 Commando Brigade was in superb shape, a shining example of organisational stability. Comprising the one commando 'clan', whether Army or Navy, it was blessed with an intense, near spiritual, fighting ethos that made it surprisingly well able to absorb additional units. The PARAs fitted in notably well, Marine and 'Airborne'

---

ingness to take the fight to an enemy. Finally there is the conceptual: how it is all put together and employed in terms of doctrine (what is practised and taught). The Falklands can be viewed as a case where a physical deficit was overcome by fighting spirit and the skilful use of what little we did have.

instinctively trusting and respecting one another, recognising kindred things deeply shared, including a wholly healthy, professional rivalry. And of course the Brigade was expert in the theories and practices of fighting from the sea, including under harsh climatic conditions.

Notwithstanding the Ascension meeting, and even though the Task Force would be brought up to greater strength, the essential uncertainty persisted: how exactly should the campaign proceed after the landings? This was never fully resolved. Instead, things unfolded less by design than in response to circumstances as they developed. Sir Lawrence Freedman puts it clearly in his history:

> At each stage of the campaign going back was politically unthinkable, staying still logistically impractical, so the only option was to move on to the next stage, without any firm plan for the stage after that.[3]

Admiral Fieldhouse was aware of the uncertainty. He did what he could to crystallise things in the orders he issued for the invasion on 12 May. No more reference to enclaves, no more graduated pressure by air, sea, SF or whatnot. He ordered a six-phase operation with the mission:

> To re-possess the Falkland Islands as quickly as possible.[4]

One man might have brought the land campaign into sharp relief: Major General Moore, as CLFFI. It was for him to come up with the design for battle ashore, and to obtain the authorities and wherewithal to enable it. His direction to Commander 3 Commando Brigade, issued on the same day that CINCFLEET sent out his formal orders to repossess the Islands as quickly as possible is revealing and worth quoting in full:

1. You are to secure a bridgehead on East Falkland, into which reinforcements can be landed, in which an airstrip can be established, and from which operations to re-possess the Falkland Islands can be developed.

---

[3] Sir Lawrence Freedman, *The Official History of the Falklands Campaign*, vol. II, Abingdon: Routledge, 2005, p. 445.

[4] CINCFLEET Operation Order 3/82 dated 12 May 1982: Operation Sutton.

2. You are to push forward from the bridgehead area, so far as the maintenance of its security allows, to gain information, to establish moral and physical domination over the enemy, and to forward the ultimate objective of re-possession.

3. You will retain operational control of all forces landed in the Falklands until I establish my headquarters in the area. It is my intention to do this, aboard Fearless, as early as practicable after landing. I expect this to be approximately on D+7.

4. It is then my intention to land 5 Infantry Bde into the beachhead area and to develop operations for the complete re-possession of the Falklands.[5]

It could be inferred from the fourth instruction above that Moore may have had a plan, one intended for implementation by two brigades, requiring him to be present to command it. But there is little or nothing explicit to support this in the preceding three. There may have been nascent thoughts. He did hold discussions and test ideas with Commander 5 Brigade during their passage south together.

Rather, the instructions are narrow in purpose: directions for the lead brigade alone. They hint at in-theatre C2 defects, for which Moore was blameless. Focusing on land aspects to the near exclusion of all else, his orders appear to overlook the impact they would have upon others, the Navy most notably, whose capabilities probably constituted our operational centre of gravity throughout.

They did give licence for an amount of tactical forward movement, probably no more than a vigorous patrol programme, for they effectively circumscribe this by emphasising the primacy of the bridgehead's security. Furthermore, the choice of words, 'gain information', and 'establish moral and physical domination', are customarily associated with aggressive patrolling pending anything else, something that a professional such as Thompson could certainly have been expected to rec-

---

[5] Sir Lawrence Freedman, *The Official History of the Falklands Campaign*, vol. II, Abingdon: Routledge, 2005, p. 446.

ognise. The implication running through the instruction would seem to be that Moore wants 3 Brigade to do nothing substantial that might then have the force committed to a particular operational course of action before he himself arrives, together with his full combat power, to determine, direct and conduct one.

There is now no escaping the static nature of these instructions that appear to have gone unnoticed by all concerned at the time, probably including their author. They have the Task Force put forces ashore only for them to wait a week or thereabouts for CLFFI to arrive with 5 Brigade. In effect, the ground campaign was to start with an 'operational pause'.[6]

This was dangerous. The enemy could be expected to react vigorously to our arrival, throwing everything in to defeat us while we were at our most vulnerable. Going ashore with half our available ground force, waiting a week or so for the remainder, was to allow the enemy to mount their counter-landing operations without distraction. It gifted them the initiative, inviting our piecemeal defeat. The Navy would be somewhat fixed, obliged to conduct a prolonged air battle for the amphibious operating area, with many of its ships close in shore unable to use their weapons to best effect.

We could all have done with something more forward leaning, ideally involving a tighter flow of 3 Brigade and 5 Brigade into the joint operating area; a course of action designed to minimise the exposure of ships to air attack, one making best use of our air defence capabilities, one that had the landed forces off the beaches and on the offensive if not immediately, very shortly thereafter. But we had no single, in-theatre

---

[6] 'Operational pause' is defined as 'a temporary halt in operations', enabling a force to be reorganised and re-generated so as to avoid its running out of steam. It acknowledges the cyclical nature of warfare, opponents drawing down on their respective resources, needing time to recover before resuming their efforts. Operational pauses are sequenced to accommodate this need in a way that keeps the initiative from passing to the other side. It would be unusual to start with a pause.

commander charged with overall responsibility for the actual fight, thereby enabled to see the operational level picture and view the inter-acting whole, positioned to read and respond to his '*fingerspitzengefuhl* (fingertips feeling)'.

If CLFFI's instructions pointed to uncertainty over how we were to proceed after the landings, he was not alone. It was a hesitancy shared at the highest strategic levels, a number of people still holding out hope that we might achieve our war aims without recourse to major land-operations in and around Stanley. But once troops are committed, it is time to get on. We needed clarity. Knowing what we did about our enemy and their likely reaction, simply going ashore to wait should never have passed muster. Eventually the Squadron would be drawn into the hiatus, finding ourselves operating as much to put life into our own campaign as to confound the enemy in the conduct of theirs.

10. Towards the Landings

The Task Force came together four days after the Pebble Island operation, the embarked forces fresh from their spell of sunshine off Ascension joining the visibly sea-stained, battered-looking units of the carrier group on 18 May. For the first time since the start of operations the Squadron found itself in close proximity to RHQ, then on board HMS *Fearless*, the principal amphibious landing ship, collocated with COMAW and Commander 3 Commando Brigade.

I am not sure how much can derive from a ship's name: *Fearless* and *Intrepid*, being examples that might be expected to bolster fighting spirit. I suspect reputation might count for more. Nonetheless, every little helps. There came a moment of irrational searching when embarked HMS *Intrepid* for a few hours, a time hard to forget, when inner fortification was at a premium. They were impressive ships, *Fearless* and *Intrepid*, Landing Platform Docks (LPDs), perfect for the job coming up, designed for the transport and landing of assault troops. Each had a cavernous dock below an equally spacious flight-deck capable of handling five Sea Kings. The ships could flood their stern to enable assault landing-craft to float in and out, making for rapid on-and-off loading of troops and materiel.

It didn't take the CO long to get himself across from *Fearless* to *Hermes*, to catch up and instruct us on upcoming events and our part in them. I say 'instruct', for I don't ever recall being in receipt of a formal set of orders from him, delivered in any customarily structured form, with a beginning, a middle and an end, tabulated by subject heading, complete with signal and coordinating instructions. He preferred to indicate what he had in mind, leaving the rest to us. One had to be alert, for his train of thought could rocket about. One needed to be able to recognise the intended items from the more discursive or illustrative pieces. There were those that found it difficult to cope with, those with a more schooled approach, a preference for orthodoxy, certainly people without an SAS background. We could handle it, his style was more than good enough for us. Indeed it was much appreciated.

· Mike Rose eventually rose to membership of the Army Board in the rank of full general. Regimentally, to a man we were always pleased at his promotions, some of us perhaps surprised, though only faintly, with each rise standing full testament not only to his leadership qualities, but also to the Army's most encouraging preparedness to recognise and embrace originality and healthy, genuine eccentricity. He had highly-developed, soldierly instincts and a lightning-fast brain. He was good to be around, energising, positive, entertaining too, with a quick eye for claptrap and an incisive turn of phrase.

On *Hermes* we kept things tight for the CO's Orders: Euan and his planning team, myself and mine that included Danny and Geordie who would handle aspects of radio communications. Some of us were due to go ashore behind enemy lines. In the event of capture and possible inter-rogation under duress, one wouldn't be able to reveal what one didn't know. Hence, I tried hard to limit my knowledge. In turn, I would pass on to the Squadron's leadership solely that needed for the accomplish-ment of their specific part in any operation.

This was a touch at odds with the Army's customary practice where junior commanders should understand the bigger picture and their higher commander's overall intentions sufficiently to enable them to extemporise or otherwise make adjustments as an operation unfolds, almost certainly not as wholly expected. But only a touch, for the SAS was a strong proponent of the method. It was just that operational secu-rity could circumscribe its application on occasions, particularly when an opponent might have time to react to any significant breach of secu-rity. This was one of those occasions, nobody from the Troops being invited in order to restrict awareness of what the CO must pass on to us.

Mike confirmed that the landing would be made two nights hence at San Carlos. He explained the choice of landing-area: a natural, sheltered deep water harbour lying about sixty miles west of Stanley at the northern end of Falkland Sound. It was defensible and difficult for the enemy to get at whether by air, sea or land. At that moment it was protected by a mere handful of enemy at its entrance, on Fanning Head. There was more to it than that, but we skated over the other reasons for its choice. We were all, Mike included, of the impression that the next phase of the campaign would be characterised by momentum, making it ashore and then getting going. He informed us that the area and its beaches had been reported clear of enemy by the SBS, save for Fanning Head to the immediate north; with views out across the main sea approaches of Falkland Sound, it had been occupied by a group of about sixty Argentine infantry equipped with two recoilless anti-tank guns and a mortar.

On the night of the landing, Fanning Head was to be cleared of enemy by an SBS team of about twenty or so, supported by our dear friend *Antrim:* it could have been the other way round. The SBS would take along a fluent Spanish-speaking marine armed with a megaphone, to enable them to call upon the enemy's surrender. That sounded a touch condescending. It crossed my mind that this would have been better as a task for D Squadron, perhaps reinforced by 'G'. We were getting a fairly good feel for the disciplines involved in attacking from the sea. We knew *Antrim*. And we had met our enemy who we were still inclined to give the benefit of any doubt, noting that these ones would be in prepared positions, defending land to which they appeared to be strongly, emotionally attached. The Squadron alone could muster three times the available numbers of SBS, and we came with all manner of relatively heavy weapons. The SBS was being asked to take on a great deal with small numbers, sparse resources and perhaps minds fed by someone's too-ready dismissal of the qualities of our enemy.

The SBS would be as keen as mustard. I just didn't think it particularly fair on them, an unexpected choice, chosen we guessed because they had found the enemy in the first instance, having thereby a form of proprietary right. We saw it as another example of the relatively loosely connected approach to SF operations as a whole. A single Special Forces commander with authority over all available in-theatre SF, in a position to weigh the pros and cons of his various assets would likely have made a different selection, we liked to think. We didn't dwell on it, and besides the SBS had *Antrim* in support, to tilt things in their favour. They should be fine.

The main landings would be conducted by stealth in three phases, over all of one night into the following morning. First, 2 PARA and 40 Commando would go in to take up positions guarding against an incursion from the direction of Darwin/Goose Green, requiring the Paras to sit astride Sussex Mountain in the south. Next came 3 PARA and 45 Commando, to take hold of the remainder of the beach-head, respectively Port San Carlos in the north and Ajax Bay in the west. Then artillery and air defences would go ashore to cover the entire beach-head, followed finally by 42 Commando to take up positions in the north looking out towards Douglas settlement and Teal Inlet.

The first landings were scheduled for 0630 ZULU, giving about five hours of darkness. Because of the EXOCET threat the carriers would stay well out to sea, protected by the Type 22 frigates. Given the distances involved, the SHAR CAP would be limited to about thirty minutes operating time astride the principal approaches to the amphibious operating area. This placed a heavy responsibility upon the capabilities of the escort-ships and Royal Artillery Rapier for Air Defence (AD) within the San Carlos area itself. Everyone expected an energetic counter-attack by Argentinian air: fast jets, Pucaras and possibly attack helicopters.

Mike explained that Thompson wanted to get his brigade into strong defensive positions within hours, well dug-in, able to withstand attack no matter what form that might take, quoting him as going on to say:

'Once firmly established and not before, the Brigade will patrol aggressively and mount operations to sap enemy morale and will to fight.'

This faithful reflection of CLFFI's instructions held no suggestion of caution for us. None of us then saw that 'firmly established and not before' referenced a sequence starting with what would feel like an over long pause. Indeed, Mike, who had been close to the landings' planning team for the past weeks, underscored that the landing must not to be regarded as an end in itself, nor treated as a 'given'. There could well be a tussle for the initial lodgement, but we all imagined that the offensive was about to begin in earnest, and that it would be flat out from thereon.

Mike emphasised that the Brigade would find itself digging-in during daylight. In places trenches might go down quickly, through peat. In others, where bedrock came close to the surface, sangars[1] might have to be built up. The troops needed as much time as possible on the first day free from enemy interference. Accordingly, an exhaustive deception-plan had been designed to gain needed breathing space. It involved us.

The stratagem came in two parts, its purpose to give the impression of a major landing between Choiseul Sound and Stanley, on the south coast of East Falkland. This logical landing-site offered deep-water approaches to numerous bays and beaches, all suitable for the disembarkation of troops and materiel. Apparently the deception had been building for days with spoof radio transmissions, air activity and the nightly shelling by ships of locations on land that could be expected to concern us. It even involved an SBS patrol going ashore to contact local people in order to spread disinformation. This activity would be brought to a high pitch on the night of the actual landings. To add to it all, the Squadron was to make a diversion in the area of Darwin.

Unknown to us, a third, strategic level element sought to deceive Argentina's high command, creating uncertainty over our most fundamental, operational intentions. Official comment back in London would build an impression that there might be a series of initiatives designed progressively to increase the military and political pressure on the enemy. Observers and commentators were encouraged not to

---

[1] Pashtun word, much used by the British Army, referring to defensive positions constructed of stone or sandbags where the digging of trenches is impractical.

expect a D-Day event such as that of Normandy in 1944. Before any-thing such as that might be undertaken, there would be a tightening of the screws here and there. The various raids to date could be seen to fit the pattern, including ours, this perhaps explaining in part Woodward's eventual interest in 'Pebble'.

Strategic deception was a delicate matter for HM Government remained determined to avoid the dissemination of lies. It would involve the most careful use of words and phrases, relying on journalists to make their own interpretations, feeding off their own predispositions. By all accounts it worked. On the eve of the landing one American journalist reported to Washington that he had it on authority of a Cabinet Minister that there would be no invasion that night, a message sure to be heard in Buenos Aires, passed on to Stanley.

Having explained our part in the landings, and otherwise brought us up to speed, Mike went off to spend an hour or so with the 'Merry Men', as Danny called the troops. I got down to the business of clearing my mind on what I had just been ordered to do.

I started by considering a raid on Darwin/Goose Green, the obvious thing to do (Map 6). But I quickly went off the idea. It was the location of the enemy's operational level reaction forces comprising a battle group of the 12th Infantry Regiment and Pucaras. They would be in strong, well prepared positions, the airfield protected by rapid firing anti-aircraft artillery/guns (AAA), utterly devastating in the ground role. Routes into the isthmus were predictable, easily covered and prob-ably protected by mines. After Pebble, and having an airstrip, the defenders were sure to be fully on the alert.

It was not that I thought Darwin/Goose Green too strong to take on. Only, the very idea of a raid itself didn't seem to stack up. To start with, I couldn't see how we could mount one in the time available: twenty-four hours, thereabouts. The recce should take two or three days. If that went well, we might get a force onto target to cause an amount of damage. Timings alone would appear to rule out an a raid. And did inflicting a bit of damage really deliver the requirement? My instincts signalled not.

In an attempt to make better sense of it all I returned to first principles, going back to what the CO had told me about the mission, its 'intent', and the other elements of the deception arrangements. Our diversion(s) needed to add plausibly to a scheme that had been running for a while, reaching maturity. Presumably, this already had the enemy thinking and looking the wrong way. Thus, we didn't need to draw their attention in any particular direction so much as reinforce an operational picture by then well developed. If the heightened 'maskirovka'[2] was working as intended on the night, they should believe that the invasion had started a short distance up the coast towards Choiseul Sound, and be preparing to respond.

Their contingency plans must involve the air/land forces poised at Goose Green. If those forces were to come out they could severely complicate, even set back the real landings, catch 3 Brigade at a vulnerable moment. The Squadron should work to prevent that. Our diversionary efforts needed to delay if not stop any enemy move out from their current positions. A raid was unlikely to achieve this, being easy to read for what it was: an offensive act followed by a planned withdrawal, nothing more, nothing less. Of course, it might cause an amount of damage and some momentary consternation, but was unlikely to sow any lasting operational confusion or keep an alerted enemy from moving.

Whereas, if we pushed at the approaches to their location from the north they might read this as the preliminary, albeit tentative, moves of a full-blown attack on Darwin/Goose Green itself. It little mattered whether they saw this as coming in from the direction of Choiseul or not. They would know that we had landed. But it might just persuade them to hold their ground for a period, as we appeared to be coming to them, onto ground that they had prepared for defence, pre-registered killing grounds and all. It would play to their preference. They might

---

[2] *Maskirovka*—Russian military doctrine of deception, developed in the early-twentieth century and brought to a fine art by the Red Army in the 1940s.

not delay long, but it could buy an amount of time, every minute of which should see our forces better established in San Carlos.

Danny and I chewed it over, deciding that it did indeed make sense. We should portray ourselves as the forward element of a much bigger effort, a recce screen perhaps, pushing at the enemy's outer perimeter from the general direction of Choiseul. It should get them guessing. And that might keep them fixed in place for a while. I didn't think to bother RHQ with an explanation. The scheme of manoeuvre appeared to fit the picture we had been given and the CO's intention: good enough.

I had always wondered what it must feel like to be part of a diversion, to step into harm's way in order to distract from the main thing. Now I knew. It was okay, provided one could believe that it stood to add substantially to success. If by our efforts the enemy's operational reserve remained in place for a few hours, preferably more, we should have made a significant contribution.

Besides instructing us on the landing plan and our part in the operation—the diversionary role—the CO had told us of the last-minute decision to redistribute troops from *Canberra* to the amphibious assault ships. She had departed Ascension with three major units embarked: 40 and 42 Commando and 3 PARA. Moore forbade her from entering San Carlos with that many troops on board, 2,400 approximately: the better part of the entire Brigade. This made absolute sense, but someone might have spotted the danger earlier than a few days before the landings. Fortunately fair weather held, enabling the necessary, major 'cross-decking' to be achieved in mid ocean using the LPDs' assault craft as well as helicopters.

Much as expected, as part of the redistribution of forces the two squadrons were ordered from *Hermes*. We needed to keep close to the new, main effort ashore. We were to embark the San Carlos-bound *Intrepid*. This caused little disappointment. It had been most useful to be close to the Admiral over a seminal period. Euan and I had certainly grown to like and respect Sandy Woodward. But *Hermes* was large and thus inevitably a shade impersonal; she was also the carrier group Flag

Ship, encouraging people to be somewhat correct as befitted her status. We all missed the easier intimacy of the smaller ships. It struck us that the smaller the unit or grouping, the more likely it was to feel wholly as one, and all fighting men respond well to close comradeship. Perhaps we could get back to similar levels of amity on *Intrepid* as we had enjoyed on our respective ships off South Georgia.

We started our cross-decking from *Hermes* to *Intrepid* the following day. By then Danny and I had scoured the available intelligence and maps for possible enemy targets north of Darwin. We had identified five or six noteworthy, isolated houses in the area. It would be reasonable to expect the enemy to use one or two of these as forward bases from which to operate security patrols. With luck some of the houses would be in such use on the night. We didn't want particularly to destroy any patrols, so much as get them to feed back the impression we hoped to create.

We realised that civilians, our own people, could be in residence. I would have to make clear to the troops that despite its importance, since the task could be achieved through the threat of violence as much as by inflicting actual physical harm, so it would be correspondingly difficult to justify any collateral damage whatsoever. It would be enough to put on a show. We identified five targets.[3]

With that done, Danny went off to see how Graham was doing with the transfer of people and materiel to *Intrepid*. I settled down to draft a set of orders for the two of us to check through later. After a while, Danny came back to say that Graham had already cross-decked with an advance-party to receive our stuff, leaving Lawrence to despatch people and kit from the *Hermes* end. Everything was well in hand, nothing for us to do. If I had finished writing up the orders why didn't we go across early? I showed reluctance, tending to put things off to the latest possible moment.

[3] Each troop was tasked with a house apiece, one troop having two: 16 Tp Camilla Creek House; 17 Tp Burnside House; 18 Tp Teal Creek House and High Hill House; and 19 Tp Canterra House.

'Off your bum, Cedric. If we go now, we'll be in time for a beer before supper.'

That did it, the thought of a beer. I gathered up my kit and cross-decked to *Intrepid*. And that's how Danny most likely saved my life.

We got across to find the ship stiff with troops. Below decks paras and marines had been crammed into every conceivable space: many were attempting to 'go firm' in corridors, with large numbers in the docking area. The strays were mostly members of 3 PARA, alert in appearance, taking note of their new surroundings in the fashion of those accustomed to having their way yet finding themselves momentarily in unfamiliar circumstances, going about the business of re-asserting control. I could see they had that 'up for it' thing about them; what one expected of the Parachute Regiment.

As ever, Graham had secured me a pretty smart basha,[4] this time complete with an en suite shower/bath! I never fathomed how he achieved it. On each and every ship we embarked I got a bunk to myself. I didn't ask, suspecting that he must have been bumping up my rank or military stature in some way, relying on people's general lack of awareness of the specific workings of the SAS.

Having a soft spot for Paras, and feeling a shade guilty about my good fortune, I invited a lance corporal and his machine-gun team out in the corridor to share my space, making sure they left me the bed. I harboured second thoughts when I saw the size of their bergens and quantity of assorted gear they were to carry ashore. I left them to cram in as best they could, while I went off to find Danny in the bar.

I found my way without too much difficulty, displaying a faintly disturbing capacity to track down a beer under almost any circumstances. On this occasion in time of war, at sea, on one of Her Majesty's Ships, about to assault an enemy-held coast. More reassuring perhaps, my suc-

---

[4] A Malayan word for shelter, picked up by the Malayan Scouts (forerunners of 22 SAS) during the Malayan Emergency, employed by the Regiment ever since in reference to a living place. Used perhaps less freely across the British Army, it was also in common parlance among the Aussies and Kiwis.

cess demonstrated a nicely developing ability to navigate the interior of a warship, for I had deliberately taken in a detour of the docking area. The hangar struck me as somewhat improbable, faintly reminiscent of a scene from a James Bond film: a real, working dock, but inside a ship, a cavernous space complete with cranes and all the paraphernalia of a dockside, landing-craft bobbing gently. Voices echoed, things clanged, machinery hummed, all under bright arc lights. The huge chamber looked perfectly suited for its intended functions, reinforcing the favourable impression of the ship. The gathering gloom beyond the open stern-door suggested that the cross-decking must be nearing completion if it was to be achieved in daylight; that is, I hoped it did, having in mind Lawrence and the rear party across on *Hermes*. I needed to go over some things with the Squadron 'head-shed' that evening, in readiness for our upcoming foray ashore.

On finding Danny in the wardroom, queuing to be served at the small, crowded, yet beckoning bar, I told him about the dock. He too had paid it a visit. We both found it a thing of wonder, chatting contentedly. And then it came, a shaft of pure malice, sliding in from behind: contrived indignation, delivered as a sibilant aside, faintly sneering, clearly intended for the two of us to hear.

'Look at them; what do they think they're on?'

'Bloody hair' came into it, and for good measure, 'scruffy'; of the two of us, that distinction must surely be mine, singled out for special mention then.

We were a mixed throng: soldiers, sailors, marines, even the odd airman. I couldn't believe it had been Navy. It was not wholly surprising though. It happens, as we had experienced in Kenya. But I hadn't expected it at that moment in that place. We had been at war for a while. Gone through a bit. Helped things along, I liked to think. Learnt a sense of proportion. Dress had never mattered as much as a well-maintained weapon to us. And longish, thick hair helped keep the head warm when ashore. It was bloody cold out there. We were in the same boat, set on the same grand enterprise, going up against a shared enemy.

These were circumstances that should bind: band of brothers stuff. Not for this moron it would seem. I suppose very small, tidy and profoundly ignorant minds have their place even in times of war. But this was a bit rich. Hell's teeth we were going back in the following day, behind enemy lines to help this dimwit.

Could I have imagined it? I hadn't turned to confront him. Pointless, the likely blank stare in response challenging an accusation all too easy to deny in feigned indignation. I had looked at Danny instead. His face set, expressionless, he had heard. He concentrated on getting the beers. I also tried to ignore it, put out of mind the offended sense of fair play in particular, wondering if it hinted at the possibility of a rift between the seasoned veterans of the TEZ and the shiny, new arrivals from Ascension. We 'old lags' did feel different, not in any superior way. But, in a short period we had gone through much together, downs as well as ups. Probably not, and even if it did operations tended to get most people firmly grounded, pulling together. Forget it, there were more pressing things to be worrying about: getting that beer for starters.

And then proportionality did assert itself, powerfully, with a dreadful, merciless finality. A moment later the tannoy piped that a helicopter had gone down. We paid it little heed. The reporting of a helicopter down was becoming by then almost a matter of routine in the TEZ. The ASW helicopters in particular appeared prone to a mechanical occurrence that would cause them to drop into the sea from the hover. Only a couple of days previously a 'pinger', ASW Sea King, had ditched, all crew members surviving.

Then a naval officer came over to us. 'We think it could be yours,' he said quietly, into my ear.

At first, I didn't grasp what he meant, the gravity of his words. He guided Danny and me up to the bridge. It was hushed, the watch closed-up, everyone calmly attentive, information and instructions passed audibly, yet in low tones. The officer of the watch confirmed that it was ours, the downed helicopter, the last lift of the day. Rescuers were on the scene searching for survivors. The word brought me up short: survivors! The magnitude of the situation crashed in on me. I could sense people stealing glances our way, in curiosity while going about their business. They knew what all this meant.

We were all mariners at that moment, together confronted by the perils of the sea. How many had they recovered so far? They didn't know. It had to be Lawrence and his rear party. The bridge assured us that everything that could be done was being done. *Brilliant* had been tasked, boats ordered away, a helicopter at the scene. It helped, knowing that John Coward had control of the rescue operation. He would be doing everything humanly possible, striving to the utmost.

I went out onto the bridge wing, Danny to our ops room below. It was dark, bitterly cold outside. Rescue lights were visible, difficult to say how far away, an occasional glimpse of *Brilliant*, a hovering helicopter more sensed than seen. The lights bore out our faith. The Navy had thrown caution to the wind, weighing the risk of detection against the urgent needs of the rescue. The sea was ice-cold with a gentle swell. Crew might survive a while in their immersion suits, but the troops would fade fast. I went back in for news.

The bridge officers looked studiously to their duties. They had nothing more. A heavy, awkward silence descended, relieved by the quiet passing of routine communications. There was little that any of them might say or do by way of comfort. I went back out onto the bridge wing to gaze across at the searchlights sweeping back and forth. I felt empty, confused, uncertain, helpless. There was *Brilliant* visible from moment to moment as she held station, silhouetted by the lights. I wished I could be with John Coward, on his bridge, close to the rescue and drawing strength from his powerful, positive calm. Pulling myself together, I went back in to ask the officer of the watch to keep us informed, to say that I would be in our ops room where we would try to draw up a casualty list. I sensed his relief. He could see that I had been reaching for something, I didn't know what, something that he and his team were unable to give. Better for each of us to get on with what we could, to attend to what we must in our own ways. I left feeling numb.

Danny was in the ops room, along with Geordie and Graham. They were calm, strangely still, poised, waiting. They looked across at me. I had nothing for them. We had a fairly clear idea of the flight-manifest. It had been the last lift of the day. We had nobody left across on *Hermes*. Therefore, anyone not embarked *Intrepid* must have been on the helicopter. The ops room was in the process of double-checking the returns that had come in from the Troops and sub-units. A signaller informed me that one of the survivors had been recovered to the ship, now down in the Sick Bay. I went to have a word with him.

There I found Corporal Wilson, a signaller. The medics had him in a hot bath working to raise his core body temperature. He hadn't been in the sea long. He was shivering uncontrollably. I didn't want to burden him, but felt the need to know more. Showing extraordinary resilience, wholly in control of himself and collected, he explained that they had come up to the stern of *Intrepid* only to be turned away. They were going round again when it happened. One moment they were flying, the next they were in the sea. It had been a severe and sudden impact. He had been near the door. Rescue had been quick to arrive, but no, sorry, he had seen nobody else. He had found himself alone in the water. I went back up to the ops room fearing the worst.

Danny had a completed list, but it would be sensible to wait until *Brilliant* declared the rescue operation over before passing a Notification of Casualties (NOTICAS) report to RHQ. They were already aware of the incident. We knew of nine survivors: one from G Squadron, one signaller, five from D Squadron, and the two pilots. Otherwise, we had twenty people 'missing', including an attached team from the RAF, experts in laser target-designation. We knew that 'missing' meant killed in action, lost. We clung to hope for a while, even though each passing minute brought greater, dread certainty. Still we waited. It was almost too much to take in, the sense of powerlessness bemusing. Many of the Squadron's unaccounted people came from the one troop, Mountain Troop. Running down the list my finger paused on Lawrence's name.

'Yes', Danny said, softly, in a whisper. 'I know.'

The ops room fell silent, supressed movement, nothing said. We waited, each of us withdrawn, the silence lying thick and heavy. Then, came word from *Brilliant*. She had done all she could. There were no more survivors. Nor could she find bodies. We stirred ourselves, drawing some faint relief in activity, attending to what needed to be done. Our 'missing' were dead, gone, 'lost at sea'. The Task Force moved on.

We made our report to RHQ, myself direct to the Commanding Officer repeating each name over the TACSAT. It seemed only right that the two of us should do this personally, not pass the responsibility to anyone else. Woodward observed in reference to the cross-decking operations of that day, our losses: 'The price has to be paid possibly due to equipment failure or pilot error, but almost always in human life'.[5]

Once the NOTICAS had been sent, we took stock. D Squadron and G Squadron between them had lost twenty men, the biggest operational loss to have befallen the post war SAS in a single incident. For some, survivors of Fortuna, this had been their third helicopter crash. Seven people had been pulled from the sea, of whom four returned to the fight, three evacuated back to the UK wounded. Seven of the Squadron's dead or injured came from Mountain Troop, casting doubt over its viability as a specialist, insertion troop.

Geordie pointed out that our most pressing problem concerned communications; we must do something about it there and then. G's signallers had been covering the period of the cross-decking operation from the previously established COMCEN (communications centre) on *Hermes*, while D Troop, the Squadron's signallers, moved to set up on board *Intrepid*. Once D had got up and running, G would have closed to make their move. It had taken us longer than expected to re-establish ourselves, G's people eventually passing 'comms' to D before transferring to *Intrepid* on the last lift of the day. Consequently, G Squadron's communications had been lost almost in entirety: four out of their six

[5] Sir Lawrence Freedman, *The Official History of the Falklands Campaign*, vol. II, Abingdon: Routledge, 2005, p. 462.

signallers, radios and codes. With G Squadron patrols deployed in the field there wasn't a moment to lose. This drove home the severity of the blow we had suffered. The fighting capacities of both squadrons had been reduced in sabre and support troop strengths alike. Geordie assured us that by taking in the two surviving G Squadron signallers, he could and would assume responsibility for the communications of both squadrons for the remainder of the war: and so it proved.

At some point there occurred a three-way discussion over the TACSAT, between the CO, the Ops Officer in Hereford, Euan and myself on *Intrepid*. During the conference Hereford suggested that D Squadron had done enough and must be ready for relief by B Squadron. I reacted badly. It may have been well intended, but I viewed it as a sorry suggestion, even insensitive, coming at precisely the wrong moment. Right or more likely wrong, I interpreted this as an attempt by B to get into the act. Fair enough. And I could applaud their spirit. But I was in no mood to step down. And nor was the Squadron, of that I was absolutely certain. We had a job to do, a war to finish that had barely started, one that had just become very personal indeed. We had taken a bad knock, lost many good and dear friends. I knew that Lawrence, all of them, would have expected us to soldier on. I knew how we could adjust for our losses and still remain a potent force. No, if the concern related to our mental state or such, the best therapy would be action and plenty of it. As for the war itself, we were well stuck in, coming up to speed. We had become soldiers of the sea. This had involved some hard lessons. We had learnt from them. How could B immediately match that? It made little sense. We were in no mood to stop. Not then, not at any time as it turned out. The four of us agreed. It was a short conversation.

Shortly after, Mike Rose managed to find a helicopter to lift him across to *Intrepid*. He came to talk to me and the troops in person. There wasn't a lot to say. Though we were able to reassure him of our resolve and unbroken spirits.

The following morning the Squadron assembled to be told how we would move on. I went over what the CO had instructed us to do, that we would be going back in that coming night, conducting diversions as previously intended, no change. The troops clearly expected nothing less. Indeed, had I passed on Hereford's idea to replace them with B Squadron as soon as practicable they would have been dumbfounded. I believe we would all have conspired to make this near impossible to effect. I confirmed that we would remain with an ORBAT of four troops, roughly equal in strength, Mountain Troop being reinforced by re-distributing manpower from the other four troops. I explained that we would find it that much easier to maintain a squadron level of manoeuvre with four albeit under-strength troops, than it would be by readjusting to three strong troops.

It was a moot point. But, Danny and I had both concluded after talking it over the previous night that we should carry on looking and feeling as near normal as possible; reducing to three, nevertheless strong troops would have highlighted our loss in a visible, structural way. Better to carry on unchanged with four.

I asked troop commanders and troop staff-sergeants to get together straight after the briefing to make the necessary transfers, ensuring that they informed SHQ of the changes before that night's deployment. The troop commanders were advised that confirmatory orders for the diversionary operation would follow, once they had sorted the move of manpower. With that the Squadron dispersed to 'get on John'.

It had been a solemn moment. There were no questions, no comments, nothing emotional or dramatic, simply people absorbing bad news and its implications. The Squadron, whose business it was to do war, merely needed to understand what had happened, and how we were to adapt to carry on as a unit: the practicalities. They needed no stirring eve-of-battle words. And they didn't get any from me, not then, nor at any time. Events may have taken a severely bad turn, but we had a job to do. There were people relying on us. It didn't need anyone to tell them that. We all had our own developed sense of professional responsibility.

There probably is a place for exhortation. At one time the Army clearly favoured an 'Order of the Day', employing them regularly throughout the Second World War, to appeal to a force mainly made up of citizens under arms, engaged in a struggle for national survival. But if the words are to be more than expected blandishment, used to mark an occasion, they might get at the chords deep within.

We received only the one address during the war, as I recall, piped on board *Hermes*, spoken by the Captain I believe. It did strike a chord. It was delivered on the eve of the shooting war, before the SHARs' raids on Stanley and Goose Green airfields, the night before the first Vulcan bombing. It made reference in abbreviated form to *Henry V*: happy, few, England a-bed. I am sure I didn't imagine that. They are wonderfully theatrical words although they sounded rather hackneyed just then; perhaps because we soldiers were feeling off to one side, onlookers with consequently barely any sense of occasion.

However, I did register the mention of one's own family: making them proud, and of not letting them down. It felt odd at the time, to draw family into things. Needless to say we had a duty to perform in the manner of 'England Expects', but on reflection one could see that we all carried an additional, very personal responsibility to our families and friends. They should be able to take pride in our actions, no matter how things turned out. This would have concerned courage, but also decency and humanity, the upholding of our shared values. The Captain reminded us that our behaviour would impact not only nationally and on ourselves personally, but on those closest to us, our families. He appreciated how easy it was to overlook them and their needs, their feelings. So, yes, a few well-chosen words probably have their place.

11. The Home Base

The demands of service life on a soldier's family are acute. A cliché perhaps, but undeniably true. They say moving home represents one of the more stressful things undertaken in life, for many people involving a move across town or county. By the time of the Falklands conflict, Suzy and I had been married six years, moving house and home four times. Pretty well par for the course. She would tell me that it totalled seventeen moves, four overseas, by the time we completed our thirty years of 'accompanied' service, before her untimely death from cancer. This is not to moan. I wouldn't have pursued any other life; and Suzy was all right with it, aside from the moves. I mention it to offer but one measure of the turbulence a soldier's life can have on the home, a challenge acknowledged by Field Marshall Slim in his classic book *Defeat into Victory*. Concerning the achievements of the 14th Army in Burma during the Second World War, he dedicates the book to his wife Aileen:

> a soldier's wife who followed the drum and from mud-walled hut or Government House made a home.

Nothing new then, but aside from the turmoil of packing and unpacking home at relentlessly regular and frequent intervals, moving can be hugely disruptive in many other ways: on schooling, for instance, or anything else benefiting from stability. Many wives give up careers to follow the drum, finding it difficult to get work because of the seemingly constant relocations, often over substantial distances. Then there is the separation.

Regimental duty, service in a fighting unit, involves weeks, if not months, each year away on training exercises, even operations. Of my twenty-four months commanding D Squadron, sixteen were spent away from home, twelve of those on operations. Families do learn to cope. It was common when in the field to get a spell of Rest and Recuperation (R & R), enabling one to get in a few days at home. Ironically, Suzy never much appreciated R & R, telling me that it disturbed her and the children's routine. I could feel hurt, but knew what she meant; a settled routine can help one through most things.

About four weeks into the war and the families were well settled into their routines, albeit experiencing an amount of heightened anxiety given that this was a national crisis receiving near constant media attention. Rarely out of mind, the conflict became almost the sole topic of conversation. From the very outset, the Regiment had established a system to ensure that people received information promptly if necessary, and otherwise on a regular basis. At its most commonplace, word cascaded from RHQ and the Families' Officer down a structure that mirrored those of the deployed squadrons. A squadron commander's wife might have the contact details of the troop commanders' wives. In turn troop commanders' wives would know how to contact the wives and girlfriends of the troops. Of course, it was more nuanced and less formal than it sounds. In our case Val and Linda, Danny's and Lawrence's wives, and Suzy were close friends, making it that much easier to 'network' the Squadron. The important thing was to have a method spanning the Regiment, to have everyone connected.

The Families' Officer, Peter Davey, helped with any domestic problems and the prompt transmission of official notifications. In the event of having to inform next-of-kin of death or injury, it would be his, or in his absence another officer's, onerous duty to conduct the necessary house-call, ensuring all possible care became immediately available. It was an established and practised method about to meet its most severe test to date.

Anne, Ted Inshaw's wife, received the call moments before departing for work, asking her gently, but firmly to come into the 'lines' for an important meeting in the gym at 10 o'clock. She got the morning off from work.

The gym was full, the atmosphere one of curiosity mainly, no alarm, despite the unusual nature of the call to a meeting with no prior notice. None of them could recall such a thing. They all knew how casualty-notification worked, the dreaded business of the 'knock on the door', always an officer whenever possible accompanied by a friend with the padre in attendance. They knew enough about operations to know that we were bound to suffer hurt, given the scale of things, that we were engaged in a major war. Already ships had been lost on both sides. No, it couldn't be a NOTICAS, not like this, not *en masse*, not wholesale, openly and impersonally. What could it be?

Anne had faith in Ted, doing the job he loved in company with the best of professionals. Her friends and many of the other women felt much the same; confident, if a shade fretful on occasions. Many of them assumed that the call must have something to do with the incoming Commanding Officer Neville Hayward who had been due to take command about now.[1] That had to be it, for there he stood presumably, the unfamiliar officer up there alongside the adjutant. Perhaps, given the circumstances of the war, he wanted to introduce himself, put a face to the name. The adjutant asked for attention. The gym fell silent. Neville stepped forward.

'Your husbands are safe,' he stated bluntly, coming straight to the point, wishing to dispel any anxiety or fear as quickly as possible. 'Because you are here in this room—it means your husbands are all right.'

Most people were taken aback, not knowing what to make of it. Others looked about for friends who might be absent. Neville went on to inform them of the helicopter the evening before, stressing that those who had suffered loss had been informed and that all were being cared for. The Regiment would prefer to maintain its customary silence, but given the gravity of the matter and its circumstances the incident would be made known to the public by the BBC on the early-afternoon news programme; hence the urgency of the meeting. He went on to offer

[1] Sensibly, the handover/takeover had been postponed until after the war, nobody wishing to disturb a settled chain of command in mid hostilities.

advice on a range of related issues. They should never hesitate to contact Peter Davey, the Families' Officer, for help, whatever it might be, no matter how trivial it might seem. They were warned to beware the heightened press interest. If approached, people should refer the media to the Regiment. In the event of any pestering or harassment, again they should contact Peter immediately.

Back on *Intrepid*, I suspect most of us gave little or no consideration to how things would be handled back home, scant thought at the time for Linda or any of the other widows. The war absorbed our energies night and day, allowing us meagre opportunity to think beyond its horizons. The very next night we would be back in; we were moving relentlessly from one event to another.

This may sound insensitive, to risk confirming a received view of the SAS as soulless killers, an impression promoted in fiction, the entertainment industry, including the media at the time. This tommyrot took severe hold not long after the Iranian Embassy siege two years previously, when the Regiment had been propelled into the limelight.[2] Ever since, we had been portrayed as some latter day sect of warrior monks, capable of all and any martial art no matter how inane. The silliness took hold in part because that must have been what people wanted to believe.

Things were not helped much by a defence policy of neither confirming nor denying Special Forces activity, current or historic, the blanket application of which created an information-void, readily filled by the unscrupulous to promote sales of their creative conjecture or any other agenda or interest.[3] Newspapers could be particularly inventive, fabricating all manner of nonsense to shift copies. Over time, we would feel

---

[2] The Iranian Embassy, London was seized along with twenty-six hostages by a group of six armed men. The resulting siege lasted from 30 April–5 May 1980, ending when the SAS stormed the building, killing five of the terrorists, and rescuing all but one of the hostages.

[3] A policy of neither confirming nor denying Special Forces activity was intended to help protect the security of current SF operations and personnel from hostile scrutiny.

the impact, humility being difficult to maintain in its purest form when so much else relentlessly drove its antithesis. It would have been surprising if the odd head hadn't been turned, given how easy it could be to profess and feign modesty while inwardly taking pleasure in flummery.

In truth, an SAS soldier is like any other man, conforming to imagined type: best at doing one thing at a time, forgetful of anniversaries, inclined to put off until tomorrow the DIY that should have been done the day before, attracted to gizmos and so on. The Falklands and previous regimental generations did it mostly on 'beer and fags'; a fair number didn't. We then came in all shapes and sizes. But then as now the most superficially obvious distinguishing feature between an SAS man and any other decent soldier would be his capacity to carry a bergen of improbable weight over prodigious distances for protracted periods; that, and a natural capacity for operating in the jungle, or at least being able to cope in the jungle.[4] There were one or two other things, but that was about it; the essential, underlying, matter being one of mental toughness.

There were colourful warriors among them; Alfie Tasker, for instance, who I first met in the jungle. Ragged, with toes protruding from his canvas boots, he made a poor visual impression: he looked done in to my then untutored eye, a Borneo veteran who had seen better days. Huge mistake. He would glide elegantly with effortless grace through even the thickest undergrowth while we youngsters under tuition struggled along in his wake, crashing, bashing and snagging, barely able to keep up. He would wear a jungle hat on operations in Oman, Dhofar, mostly when attending *geysh* (the Sultan of Oman's regular army) planning conferences; it would have a bolt attached, under which he had penned 'Screw the Nut'. He didn't much like the desert, or British officers on loan service with the *geysh* come to think of it; yet, his soldiering in the open glare of the Jebel mountains was

---

[4] Both are major features of SAS selection: carrying a bergen plus full operational load, and jungle training. The first tests mental and physical stamina, and the jungle is good for bringing out and then developing basic soldierly skills.

every bit as accomplished as it had been in the enveloping shade of a primary jungle canopy.

Then there was the legendary Rover Slater, my first troop staff sergeant, who one day shortly after my initial six months in the troop suddenly declared in a loud voice, addressing me, but for all to hear: 'That's it. Okay. You're it from now on,' meaning I could command the Troop from that point. And there was I thinking that I had been 'it' all along, with him as my number two. Stupid boy. Rover, rumour would have it, had bitten off part of someone's ear in a bar brawl while soldiering in the Far East as a young man: hence the name. Another brilliant jungle soldier, but every bit as good elsewhere, he displayed a genius for the arts of war, making him one of the finest tacticians. I had never come across the like of him before, and I never came across the like of him after, nor many as brave. He raised my understanding of soldiering in ways that I would apply throughout my career, whatever the level of command.

But we were all, old hands and young alike, supported by strong, dependable wives or girlfriends. You might say our women had to be strong and self-sufficient to be able to put up with it all. The unforgiving tempo of the operational and training cycle was one thing, involving weeks and months of separation every year. The matter of the Regiment's 'unrelenting pursuit of excellence' was entirely another. It demanded near total professional immersion. In this respect, perhaps we did resemble military monks, the absorption leaving little room for family life. And yet, a stable home 'front' appeared to correspond to sound professional performance. This should be no surprise. If fear draws down a man's courage, so must stress and pressure generally erode performance.[5] A man under pressure from home, while having to cope with the demands of war, might be expected to struggle in

---

[5] As a young man Lord Moran had served in the trenches during the First World War. In his book *The Anatomy of Courage* he seeks to answer the question 'What can be done to delay or prevent the using-up of courage?' For he believed that a man had only so much courage to draw upon and that once expended he must break.

giving and maintaining his best. And in the SAS only the best would ever do.

At the time, I don't believe many of us fully understood how important home was to our ability to fight. Domestic stability, selflessly bestowed by our wives and families, granted us the freedom to give our all to the operation. If we thought about home, it would have been fleeting. For most of us it was just there, safe and secure, all the more sustaining for that. We would be going ashore in a few hours' time. There were many things to think about, to be done before we did. Grieving would have to wait, and with it all gentler thoughts, heartless as that might sound. But as the Captain of *Hermes* had so perceptively reminded us, we could get on and do what we must in ways that might bring pride to us all, families included.

12. Masking the Landings

By late afternoon we were all ready for the deception operation, including the aircrew over on *Hermes*. Personal kit had been stowed mostly with ammunition, some food in case we had to stay out longer than expected and a few items of dry clothing sealed in polybags with the customary duct tape. The ship was ready. And 3 PARA looked more than ready for their night too. At one point during the preparations Geordie reminded me that he was now short of people, including badged signallers, due to the helicopter incident, making it difficult for him to find fully qualified radio operators to go into the field behind enemy lines. Would it be okay this once for me to take an un-badged signaller? He assured me that the man showed much promise. Indeed, he would welcome the opportunity to give the lad a 'run-out', for the two of us to get a better feel for what he was made of. Geordie would value my opinion before encouraging him to go for Selection, or otherwise.

One is said to be 'badged' having passed Selection for service as a fully qualified member of the SAS. It was an unwritten rule that a patrol should comprise only badged members. Of course un-badged specialists might be taken forward, us supporting them or vice versa; but as far as practicable patrol members should be badged.

I appreciated Geordie's difficulties. He would not normally ask me to offend our own rules of war. These were truly exceptional circumstances. I hesitated, but reflected that the diversions shouldn't be unduly demanding. The distances to be covered were not remarkable at twenty to twenty-five kilometres, conceivably thirty with detours. As for tactical manoeuvre, the operation had been designed as a series of troop-level tasks. I planned to follow behind one of the troops, before re-positioning to cover any eventuality requiring a squadron level of response. It was difficult to see what that might be. If the deceptions failed there was the possibility of the enemy coming out to make for San Carlos. We might come across a target of opportunity. Unlikely. It all seemed fairly straightforward. I agreed to taking the un-badged signaller forward. It turned out to be a hellish night.

We mustered behind the flight-deck. It was bright and sunny with plenty of daylight left to go. I hoped the pilots had calculated this correctly, observing as much to Danny. I didn't care for daylight. When it came to going ashore we had become creatures of the night. My signaller tucked in at my shoulder, slightly too close, too attentive. Trying hard, otherwise he made a favourable impression: a big lad, with a big bergen.

I could have done with a last cigarette, but aviation and smoking didn't mix well. There were notices around the place making that clear. Instead, I went over things with Danny one last time. I reminded him that I planned to tuck in behind Pete Sutherby's 18 Troop and catch up with him at the Squadron RV an hour or so before first light west of Mount Usborne.

Unavoidably, we would be out in daylight the next morning for some of our walk back, perhaps ten kilometres before getting into 2 PARA's area on Sussex Mountain. I hoped to catch up with their CO H. Jones, a friend, originally of my Regiment the Devon and Dorsets. Danny too wanted to drop by to catch up with his son Garry also serving with 2 PARA.

Intrepid's huge flight-deck made it relatively easy to mount up. I noted that Danny was doing what Lawrence would have been doing, keeping an eye on things, ensuring people got to the right place, at the right time, in the right order. I hadn't needed to tell him. The Squadron's powers of recovery would prove formidable, and were already starting to show. Without prompting, at all levels people covered for those no longer there. We would absorb our losses to continue our evolution into a thoroughly-honed, highly-responsive instrument of war. Before the end, the Squadron could move from one complex tactical evolution to another with only a few sparse words of instruction covering matters mainly by exception. This high tempo would derive principally from practised drills, that and people just thinking for themselves as part of the whole, anticipating and knowing how and when to act. Of course we got to know our war: the enemy, our friends, the terrain and the weather. That helped.

I took up my customary place behind the left-hand pilot, strapping in for take-off. Then came the familiar intense vibration, the airframe protesting as the power came on, everything juddering deeply, that reluctant release of one side or the other as the wheels came clear of the surface, and then we were up, transitioned, banking gracefully out over the sea, the helicopter settling into flight. Around me percolated that heady smell of aviation fuel and all that made up the interior of a Sea King going about its business. I signalled to the aircrewman further down the back, over by the still-open door. It took a second or two to get his attention. He thumbed up. I unstrapped to stand behind the pilots, reaching for a headset, stowed as usual on the bulkhead opposite. Everything as it should be, an economical exchange of information going on between the two pilots and occasionally the aircrewman, business-like and relaxed.

We kept low, running across a relatively calm sea, crabbing slightly into a wind coming from the west, our starboard side. Before long we coasted in close to Cape Dolphin, just then bathed in a deep golden evening light, the sun flaring as it dipped the horizon; a beautiful coastline that in summer teems with wildlife, notably sealions. Not now though. I noted a few seabirds and felt a curious sense of trespass as sea changed abruptly to rocks and grass. How odd to see grass, brown grass and what looked like heather. How disturbing to be racing across it in daylight! I had expected us to hit land after dark, not on dusk. Had the pilots got this right? I knew they had a lot to do that night, beyond dropping us off; we may have been their first task, but darkness was every bit as important to us as it would be to their later serials. They didn't sound in any way perturbed, only the occasional exchange as way points were met, slight adjustments made. This and their body language spoke of things under control, going as expected. I said nothing.

We had about fifty kilometres to run, say a quarter of an hour. That must be Mount Usborne on the horizon, fading fast in the gathering gloom. The pilots reached up on their helmets for their NVG, first one then the other. A couple of words passed between them, each confirming himself 'night capable'. How could I have harboured doubts? We arrived as they said we would: in total darkness.

At drop off there was again that feeling of abandonment, that momentary disorientation as the senses raced to comprehend it all. The helicopters departed taking their noise and leaving a farewell draft of their near-intoxicating perfume, burnt AVTUR. Then the soft swish of wind as our new surroundings took hold; a damp, bitterly cold place after the warmth of the ship and the draughty shelter of the Sea King. We stumbled about uncertainly on the unfamiliar grass and humped tussocks of diddle-dee, the rocks. Maps orientated, kit adjusted, formation adopted, final instructions given, the Troop got underway, the signaller and myself bringing up the rear.

I didn't pay much attention to navigation, the occasional check of the compass, relying on Pete and his troops. We were going in the right direction as far as I could tell. I did note that my companion appeared to be labouring a bit, making faint noises. I was surprised, for we had barely started, the pace comfortable and the going not too bad: undulating heathland, some boggy patches. My ankles were feeling sore, still recovering from that night in Kenya. My belt-kit rubbed here and there, normal at the start of a patrol as body and kit came together, before settling. Everything more or less as it should be. It was good to be ashore in one's own element, rifle in hand, not having much to do apart from keep up with the man in front. I liked my Armalite for its lightness and the way my thumb tucked into the rear sight carriage as if made to fit my thumb and no other's, its comfortable familiarity reassuring.

Eventually, we slowed as we neared our objective, High Hill House. I hadn't noticed at what point the Troop had split, the other half separating to make its way to Teal Creek House. Perhaps I should have been more attentive, but all was unfolding much as expected. Then we stopped, my signaller obviously ready for the break. He settled heavily into the heather. He confirmed he was okay. After a while I started to get cold. Leaving the signaller, I went forward.

The patrol commander and one or two others were in a huddle. They thought there could be enemy out front. An OP perhaps, on a slight rise barely visible to the naked eye. I borrowed the patrol commander's binos for a better view. It was difficult to tell. There did seem to be some movement, but it could have been imagined? The consensus hardened on there being something. Asked my opinion, I offered it didn't much matter. I had made clear in the orders that before firing on any of the houses we had to be certain that we were engaging enemy not firing on civilians. If in doubt, fire to miss. In this instance the target was out in the open, most unlikely to be civilians. It was close to our objective and in the right kind of place for an enemy outpost. Then again, it could be sheep. I suggested the patrol engage, firing a shade high. If they got return fire, simply bring all to bear. If they didn't, we would have made a din, in the right area, sure to be noticed and reported.

This they did, plenty of tracer arcing into the night sky, a good show. We got nothing back. Even with the parachute flares it remained difficult to see what we had in front. I do know that what with this and the other demonstrations across a wide area that night, the enemy were for a while taken in, believing that we had made a major landing, not immediately clear where, and that we were pushing down onto them at Darwin; all pretty well as intended. We were soon heading back north towards the Squadron RV. And that's when the trouble began.

It started with a muffled gurgling sound, my signaller clearly in distress. The two of us stopped. He didn't answer. Leaning towards him I could see that he was hot, wearing far too many layers. I told him to take one or two of them off and take a drink of water. Meanwhile, with the rest of the patrol no longer in sight I checked my bearings. I wasn't unduly worried. The rear man of the patrol should eventually twig that we were missing and stop the others to enable us to catch up. Wrong. Perhaps they did stop. We never caught up.

We were out there on our own. I felt foolish, rather than anxious, having got separated. We eventually stepped off to go only a short number of paces before the gurgling resumed, changing to a low moan. I pushed on. He slowed. I glanced at my watch. This could take a while. I grew concerned. What if the enemy moved fast out of Darwin to follow up the various diversions, or to move on the landings? I must get back to the RV as soon as possible, to take control of the re-gathering squadron as planned. We made another couple of hundred yards before having to pause yet again. The moans had grown louder. I told him to keep quiet. It could attract the enemy. The volume increased. And then I compounded our problems.

The horizon to our front didn't show as I expected from the map. My compass pointed to ground much lower than anticipated. I decided to put in a touch of 'right hand down'. Mistake. A big one as it turned out, for this led up to the east of Mount Usborne, the Squadron RV being to the west. If that wasn't bad enough, it went straight into a vast area of stone runs. It would be my first encounter with these extraordinary geological features. They are much like glacial moraine in appearance, but formed differently, a jumbled mass of fairly uniform, angular rocks, often damp at night from mist or dew, an absolute nightmare to negotiate, each and every greasy footfall critical. A slip could all-too-easily result in a fractured limb, a snapped leg very likely. They needed to be treated with utmost respect, preferably avoided.

After a short distance we were right in among them, rocks in every direction. There seemed no alternative other than to press on in the hope that the going would improve. No such luck. It was pure hell. We made painfully slow progress, both of us slipping and sliding. My signaller was making little or no headway. I kept going back for him. I considered leaving him to find help, evidence of my growing desperation. Instead, I took his belt-kit and rifle. This got us a few more yards deeper into the rocks. His noise continued. He slowed some more. I tried carrying his bergen too. Impossible. Any moment I was going to slip, likely to break a leg. Where would that leave us? I decided to cache his kit among the rocks, all of it including his rifle, retaining only the codes.

We set off again. Going hand-in-hand didn't work, not among the rocks. I let go, crawling forward on all fours, returning from time to time to coax him on. I couldn't understand it though. He was a big, fit looking lad. We hadn't gone far or fast that night; less than a few miles, mostly at a cautious patrol speed. And he was now carrying nothing but himself. Yet still he hung back. He had effectively thrown in the towel. This baffled me most. How did giving up help exactly? How was that expected to improve his situation? I tried this reasoning on him. It didn't work. Little did.

Somehow we clawed our way up the hill to the saddle on the east, the wrong side of Mount Usborne's peak. I felt terrible about compounding our difficulties with my shoddy navigation, but kept that to myself. After a short rest, some water and a biscuit, we set off once more. I had needed the break possibly more than him. I was feeling done in, my ankles tender and fragile after the stone runs. The night was taking on aspects of Selection, perhaps worse: after all, we were behind enemy lines. As we neared the summit, I thought I could see something to our front, a sangar maybe? I didn't think it very likely, but it was in the kind of place an enemy might site an OP. I told him that I would go ahead for a quick scout around, to make certain our route lay clear. It meant leaving him on his own for a short while. At this, his noise actually increased.

I went forward regardless, feeling both baffled and fed up, leaving him where he sat, knowing that if we did have enemy up ahead they would be fully alerted waiting for us. Fortunately nothing, a pile of rocks; for good measure I checked further on up and over the summit, making the most of my momentary freedom to move as I liked. Still nothing. With the summit and surrounding area evidently clear of the enemy, I went back to retrieve the signaller. He was easy to find. We continued our laboured progress towards the Squadron RV.

Dawn. My companion was by then more or less quiet, shuffling along, barely lifting his feet, a picture of misery. We were hours late. I was tiring, my ankles the problem, really painful, feeling weak in a strangely brittle kind of way. At long last, coming down the west slope of Usborne I caught sight of our goal. There was Danny's ruddy face, glowing in the bright morning sunlight as he gazed up towards us from behind some rocks. Catching sight of the RV, my outwardly exhausted, spent companion flung off my hand and with a squeal of delight sprang forward to hare down the slope to the safety of the troops below. He rocketed off with a noticeable bounce, leaping away like a champion fell runner. I couldn't help but admire the style, the agility, not least the strength in his ankles! There was not the slightest hint of fatigue. None! I shambled down the hill in his wake, keeping to the grass and heather to cushion my footfall. I sloped in, feeling decidedly foolish. Danny handed me a rollup, somebody else a sip of his brew. I told Geordie that I didn't think much of his signaller, not right for Selection, and handed over the codes. A quick up-date, a few cubes of chocolate later and we all headed off for San Carlos.

We hadn't gone far before we met a patrol from 2 PARA, heads down, tabbing at a good pace, looking purposeful and utterly unsurprised at coming across us. They didn't stop or break step. With a few 'good mornings' they kept going for the spot we had just left, I guessed. It would give them a fine view out towards Darwin and Goose Green. They had to be ten to twelve kilometres forward of their own lines, beyond the range of their battalion's mortars, relying then on artillery for support. H was right. Get eyes well forward. That's what I liked about Paras, they had 'get up and go'.

We heard it before we saw it, a Pucara. I shot a glance back down the ridge to see the Squadron strung out, well spaced, but in a vulnerable, linear configuration. Then it came into view, a small speck from behind the Mount Usborne. Simultaneously the troops vanished from sight into folds in the ground, into the cover of the odd rocky outcrop. Excellent. It had needed no word of command, everyone alert doing the right thing. The Pucara continued its climb, turning to parallel us a couple of miles distant. Unknown to us we had been spotted.[1] The pilot was

---

[1] Mike Rose met the pilot some years later in Zagreb. They were both then serving together with the UN, Mike commanding UNPROFOR in Sarajevo. The pilot claimed that he had seen us as he came from behind Mt Usborne, the movement of our dash for cover catching his eye.

bringing his aircraft round for an attack from the west to give him a straight shoot down our length; to come in from the east would require him to jink round Usborne, complicating his strafing run. Blissfully unaware I lay back in the welcoming heather, taking opportunity of the pause to roll a cigarette. I was reaching for the makings when to my horror I saw two figures jump out from cover, one with a pole-like thing over his shoulder; two members of 16 Troop with a Stinger missile, Carl Rhodes and Kiwi.

'Bloody hell, Danny!'

I don't know why I blamed him. He looked every bit as startled as I felt. We knew very little about the Stinger. A dozen or more had been parachuted into us along with Pat Masters only a few days previously. He had collected them from our US Special Forces mates in North Carolina who had given him a crash course in their use. A gentle giant of a man, complete with broken nose, Pat had one of those disarming Southern Irish accents. He had been lost in the helicopter. With luck he had managed to pass on some instruction to 16 Troop in the short time he had been with us.

We were about to find out, for it was too late to stop them. They would be oblivious to all but the quarry before them, utterly engrossed in what they were attempting to do: namely, shoot down a deadly ground attack aircraft, with a wholly unfamiliar weapon, with no formal training, possibly no training, on operations, at the very first attempt that must not fail. And all that under sub-optimal conditions, for I had noticed that the sun, a reasonable heat source by heat-seeking missile standards, lay low on the horizon roughly in line with both them and the aircraft. I couldn't fault the enthusiasm, but I knew this must end badly.

The Stinger was essentially a tail-chaser optimised to find and enter an aircraft's exhaust. It needed to come in from behind. Pucaras had a low heat signature, reduced even further by their propeller-wash. The aircraft was coming in pretty well head-on, perhaps a degree or two off to one side as it steered for its eventual parallel course. This missile would have to be seriously good if not miraculous. Things were stacked wholly against success. Sod 16 Troop. If we survived this I vowed to give them hell.

I imagined more than heard a mighty *whoosh*, not much of a bang; a huge plume of smoke remained hanging in the relatively still, damp morning air, gently curling. The Pucara pilot could not have failed to notice the massive signature a mile or so left of his nose. We were in for it now. The missile streaked away. We could see it, a long pole-like thing desperately trying to turn, to come in from behind the aircraft, skidding round, quivering. And then a flash followed not long after by a muffled bang. A first-round hit. Indeed, unknown to us until much later, it turned out to be the first ever operational firing of Stinger. There was no cheer, no leaping to feet, silence, the rocket's exhaust plume still wafting wispily in the air. We must all have been sharing the same sense of relief, if not disbelief. 16 Troop had got away with it. We had got away with it! They were off the hook, faith in them wonderingly restored.

The Pucara struggled to gain height before the pilot ejected. A parachute deployed. Good. And then I remembered that there were two crew members. As the one canopy opened and the pilot drifted down, 16 Troop made to collect their prize. Danny called them back. The airman was a long way off and we still had a way to go. Let him be.

After that, enemy aircraft came in thick and fast, heading towards San Carlos down either side of our ridge. We were witnessing the Argentine counter-attack, with a grandstand view. It was quite an onslaught, vigorous and determined if a touch late in the day. Pucaras continued to come out from Darwin, some from the direction of Stanley, joined by mainland-based McDonnell Douglas A-4 Skyhawks. With skill and courage that all of us would acknowledge, they came in feet above the ground. Aside from fences and the odd line of telephone cabling there were few obstacles to low flying in the Falklands beyond weather, rock and earth. The odd tree around the settlements but no pylons or church steeples. Nonetheless, this was low flying at its impressive best, both skilled and brave. But perhaps too daring, too low for the bombs they dropped from those heights often had insufficient time in which to arm, failing to explode on impact.

The jets came mostly unheard from behind, from the east. Suddenly, there below us, we would peer down into the cockpits from our ridge-line, a fleeting glimpse of a pilot's helmet, their attention always fixed ahead, fully absorbed, paying us no heed as they crouched over their controls. They came in fours, paired in loose formations, one slightly behind the other. There seemed to be many of them.

I considered what best to do. We had useful fire-power to bring to bear on what I supposed to be a principal and practised pre-planned flight path. After our first attempt, subsequent engagements with Stinger had failed. If we deployed in more settled positions perhaps results would improve. On the other hand my instructions had been to get inside the San Carlos air defence envelope as soon as possible and back to *Intrepid* for re-tasking. The Navy had air-defence covered as one of their jobs, with the Army's RAPIER air defence missiles coming ashore as a priority to help them. I was also keen to come in on 2 PARA in daylight as they expected. H. Jones had provided a password to cover any night passage of lines: the challenge *semper*, the response *fidelis*, a maxim of our dear regiment, the Devon and Dorsets. On reflection, not much of a password though, known to many including the 195,000 members of the United States Marine Corps who to be fair to H were not on the Islands. Despite H's thoughtful anticipation, I still preferred to play it safe, to move through in daylight. And that was how re-tasking came out on top of air-defending.

We trudged on. To hedge the bet though, we would stop to engage aircraft as and when we detected them, as they flew past. But snap shooting in that fashion was a tall order. An additional five Stinger launches were attempted, none successful as the main motors failed to ignite, probably as a result of snatching the shot. We almost certainly achieved better results with our small arms, the aircraft going through that close, our weight of fire that intense. I certainly recall getting off one whole magazine with the sights absolutely on the right place, ahead of an A-4; but 5.56 is a light round that brings a moderate punch to bear on an aircraft retiring at around 300 knots. We downed no more aircraft. To be more accurate, none came down visibly as a result of our efforts. There were jets that returned to their bases that day damaged by small-arms fire. Some of it from the Squadron one would suppose and like to think.

Nearing 2 PARA's location towards the end of the afternoon, I looked out to sea. A warship circled slowly round in the bay to our south, obviously hurt, on fire, wispy, grey-green smoke rising lazily from openings in her upper structure. She was clearly in distress, seriously wounded. If we had been on one flight-path into San Carlos, she must have been on another coming in up Falkland Sound.

A terrible thought crashed in on me. 'Tell me,' I said turning to Chris Brown our fire-support officer, 'that isn't our ship down there?'

He knew what I meant. *Ardent* had been in position the previous night to support us during the diversions with gunfire, should we have needed it.

'Could be,' he responded.

'But we did release her, didn't we?' I asked, trying to hide a rising sense of foreboding.

'Absolutely,' he said, 'hours ago, before first light, once all the Troops were in [the RV].'

There it was again, people thinking for themselves. I may have been preoccupied with my signaller at the time, but the Squadron continued to function without me and the vital matter of releasing the ship in good time for her to make her withdrawal had not been overlooked. What a relief. We trudged on.

But the thought continued to nag at me, my relief tempered; if it was *Ardent*, and it had to be her, had we in any way contributed to her fate? Had she been caught as she came off the gun-line? Or her re-tasking, had it been consequent in any way of her previous positioning in support of us, a case of she's down that way, she might as well stay down there, to do this, that or another? Or had she been caught in a place and manner wholly without connection to all earlier tasking?

We learnt later that it was *Ardent*. She had been jumped by A4s while patrolling off North West Island in the early afternoon, several hours after her release by Chris. A key component of the amphibious area's air defences, she had been positioned to watch and fire down Falkland Sound, astride the enemy's principal air entry point into San Carlos it transpired. She had suffered repeated onslaught, gallantly taking fire that otherwise would have fallen upon the amphibious shipping and troops. She sank the following day after a heroic fight for survival.

There was no time to visit 2 PARA. We passed through their defences as the light was fading, in a hurry to get back to our base. Once embarked, I dropped in on the Amphibious Ops Room. There was nothing for us, but things looked to be going well, everyone ashore more or less as intended. The map showed Para patrols well forward. Fanning Head had been dealt with. The Navy was sanguine, having absorbed a furious enemy onslaught by air. Perhaps most reassuring from our perspective, the enemy had yet to counter-attack by land. If he left it much longer it should be too late. Perhaps the Squadron really had helped encourage him to stay put, hold back his operational reserve down at Darwin/Goose Green. If so, the *maskirovka* had worked. Along with others, including *Ardent* who had shelled the airstrip that night, we may have helped with a signal contribution. And we had done it discreetly, without ceremony, known to a well informed few, exactly as the Regiment liked it.

The next days would be interesting, but there was nothing for us at that time, no new tasks. I passed this on to the Squadron with advice to eat, rest and otherwise get ready for the next 'serial'. I did the same, finding time to reflect on the matter of the signaller.

It had been odd, all too easy to dismiss. He had not been badged. Therefore, I had been wrong to take him along. I broke one of our own cardinal rules: end of the matter. But surely there must be more to it than that. He was a physically fit and trained soldier with ambitions to join the Regiment. Shouldn't he bear some responsibility for his unsoldierly performance?

He had failed, quickly and emphatically, for no apparent reason. He had faced no real danger, fleeting or prolonged. Nor had he been unduly physically stressed. Up until the withdrawal the event had been little more than a walk in the park. But he had been out front, in a sense behind enemy lines. Did that have a bearing? Whatever the cause, he did appear to lose his grip for a number of hours. And therein lay another puzzle.

Shouldn't there be efficacy to disengagement? In this instance, his behaviour had in fact increased the danger for both of us. On the other hand perhaps it did make things better for him. He was relieved of his equipment, a significant physical benefit, and then effectively disarmed. Could he consciously or otherwise at the time have been expecting this to improve his lot? Possibly, but probably not; he had seemed to be beyond all reason. More assuredly, from thereon he was kept to base station duties. He never went back into the field. Nor was he sent home; we were too short of signallers for that.

We had strong social devices in place to encourage good performance, to help discourage any break down. At the time, a man's most-prized personal distinction would have been courage, its antithesis to be thought a coward. These were potent social sentiments rarely if ever voiced. People were simply expected to behave and perform properly without need of their express application. Across the Task Force the vast majority of people did perform correctly, keeping fears in check and to themselves. When the opportunity presented many rose above, to display heroism, the term then reserved scrupulously for those exhibiting selfless courage of the very highest order. There must be few people who would not warm to the thought of being considered heroic in the strict sense. By the same token, to be considered cowardly would then have been a matter of utter dread, given immediacy by the fears most of us harboured, gnawing away for much of the time, heightened in moments of crisis, threatening to tip toward failure more readily than rise to heroism.

Whether or not these attitudes unduly supressed any genuine, clinical cases of strain, I could not say. But concerning the Squadron, with this one exception we had no evident cases of excessive anxiety, not at 'the time nor in the years immediately following. If asked, we would probably have said that we merely performed as expected. If pressed, I would offer that performance is the sum of many things with fear of failure a notably strong motivator and activity a most powerful distraction. In this case, a man assessed to have good potential was found to be wanting, none of the customary mechanisms and safeguards proving effective.

I knew enough to guard against the over-zealous application of calls on bravery and the censure of cowardice, for they could also impair professional judgement. It is difficult enough to make sound decisions when confronted by all the other noises of war without adding to the clamour. I had first hand experience of this, from operations in Dhofar, Oman, five or more years previously. There a British officer on loan to the Sultan's Armed Forces was so mindful of the impression he felt he should be making that he would put those about him in danger with cavalier, trite and utterly unnecessary acts of staged bravado. In all like-lihood these were employed to mask his own short-comings, distrust of his own fears perhaps one of them. His irrational acts could have been some form of displacement. It certainly came across that way, for we needed no buoying.

Ever since, I had tried to be careful about courage and cowardice, most certainly as they might be employed to influence planning for they can contaminate objective thought. It will always be a matter of balance.

13. San Carlos

It took three days and increasing frustration with the course of events for us to achieve re-tasking, days during which the Navy fought a battle of attrition with courage and steady determination against an enemy air force every bit as committed. It was the higher direction of the war playing out.

In line with Major General Jeremy Moore's strictures the infantry battle groups had gone firm in the beachhead to await their general and his additional forces. Concurrently, 3 Commando's logistic regiment and the amphibious and logistic ships had started to build a maintenance area ashore to support the eventual offensive. This served to keep a significant number of warships in and around San Carlos to protect the offload and what we took to be a stalled operation.

The Navy was not wholly trained nor optimally equipped for an inshore air battle. It had been prepared primarily for operations in mid-ocean keeping the North Atlantic free of Soviet submarines and maritime aircraft so that the US might reinforce NATO in the event of war in Europe. Operations close inshore against an enemy, ground-based air force were an unanticipated eventuality that put severe strain on its men, machines and doctrine. Nor should the gallantry and commitment of the merchant marine be overlooked; many of the ships going into the bomb-alley of San Carlos were RFAs or Ships Taken Up From Trade (STUFT).

Few of the ships, warships included, mounted modern, high-volume-fire anti-aircraft guns: close, point air-defence weapons of last resort. The Type 21 frigates sported Oerlikon 20mm cannons, and the Landing Ships Logistics (LSL) WW2 vintage 40mm Bofors. Otherwise, air-defence relied on missiles. Sea Dart, a long-range missile designed for operation out at sea, was prone to confusion when its radar reflected off land. Sea Cat, an obsolescent sub-sonic missile guided by its operator over a line-of-sight system suffered no such radar issues. And the 2 Type 22s came with Sea Wolf, a new and promising short-range system, something of an unknown quantity. But the Navy did have Sea Harriers equipped with what would prove to be the devastating, modern AIM-9 Sidewinder missile. The ground forces could add RAPIER, BLOWPIPE and small-arms fire.

On paper the Argentine air force enjoyed a clear advantage, numbering in the region of 240 fast jets. But many were in poor shape as a result of a long-running international arms-embargo. And half of them were deployed to protect against an attack from Chile. Furthermore, to reach the Falklands from their mainland bases the A-4s must conduct an air-to-air refuelling (AAR); with only 2 KC130 tanker aircraft available this significantly limited the number of A-4s that could be put up over the Islands at any one time. The Daggers were not capable of AAR. They must fly in a virtual straight line there and back, giving them a mere ten minutes in the objective area. As for the enemy's Super Etendards, they had eight EXOCET missiles between them. Despite their difficulties, the Argentinians achieved a respectable sortie-rate over the course of the war: approximately 140 for the A-4s and 150 for the Daggers.

Weeks before our arrival, the Argentinians had made the decision to hold back their air power for the landing. On the first day they intended to throw everything in for one overwhelming and decisive air-strike taking on both the amphibious force and the supporting carriers out at sea. But when the moment came they failed to find the carriers. However, they did manage to put forty-five aircraft into the amphibious operating area. Of these they lost ten jets and our Pucara. A number more were damaged by small arms fire. In return they sank *Ardent*, immobilised *Argonaut* and inflicted damage on some of the other escorting warships, including *Antrim*. Significantly, they missed the vital amphibious and logistics ships. In fact, the airstrikes on the vital, first day had not gone well. They had failed to achieve our defeat. And a loss rate of around 20% could not be sustained.

As for enemy ground assault, if there was to be one, to achieve any impact this should have gone in during the opening hours when we had been at our most vulnerable, still coming ashore or otherwise out in the open. Nothing materialised. By late afternoon it was too late. We could discount that threat.

If the enemy had failed in their intention to stop us on Day One, our ground forces were under instructions effectively to stop themselves. And so the scene was set mostly by us, partly by them, for an attritional slugging-match that both sides could probably have done without: we for the lack of a suitably urgent campaign plan, they for failing to hit hard enough soon enough.

It would prove a tough air battle, San Carlos and the carriers sitting at its core, notably hard on the ships' crews close inshore, men at action stations most days for hours, many below decks fearing the worst. Watch officers made frequent 'pipes' to keep those below informed, to help relieve the pressure, making light of things as best they could. Crews more than held their nerve, people finding imaginative ways to ease the tension. One sailor aboard *Antrim* would take cover with a highly inflammable oxyacetylene cylinder and cutter; when eventually asked by his shipmates what the bloody hell he thought he was doing, endangering them with such hazardous equipment, he explained that when they were hit and the ship turned turtle he would cut through the hull to get them all out. They thanked him and asked him in explicit nautical terms to go away, to take it off somewhere else. The ship did get hit. It didn't turn turtle, or sink, the bomb failing to explode. On another occasion as their ship went to action stations to meet an air raid, a member of a damage control team dashed in on his mates frantically shouting a warning.

'Look out, look out!'
'What the f' is it?' they responded, each scrambling for his equipment.
'Down there,' he gasped, eyes rolling, pointing back the way he had come, 'Zulus, thousands of them!'

D+1 started quietly, the enemy gathering themselves after their exertions of the day before. Late afternoon two relatively light raids came in: two Daggers followed shortly after by three A-4s. They entered San Carlos from the south streaking in low past Sussex Mountain, detected by 2 PARA. Within seconds the aircraft were flashing through, one so low as to whip the sea with its jet wash, fine spray left hanging in the light breeze. By then twelve RAPIER were set up. But taken by surprise, they and the ships put up an unexpectedly haphazard resistance. This disturbed us all, Woodward particularly. As RAPIER got up and running, he had planned to thin out his escort ships, passing the greater responsibility for point air-defence of San Carlos to the ground-based air defence forces. But persistent uncertainty surrounding the effectiveness of RAPIER caused him to keep AD warships close inshore. Fortunately, this time the attackers inflicted no damage. The failure of AD radar to detect the raiders' approach and the disappointing performance of RAPIER were ominous indications of our vulnerability.

If our small-arms response had been desultory on that second day, it grew notably brisk over the following days, *Fearless* eventually asking us all to get a grip of it. She occupied a fairly central position out in the bay. Enemy jets were going through level with her upper deck-work. She understood the therapeutic value of firing on enemy aircraft, but was taking too much stray stuff herself from troops holding onto their bursts longer than they might care to admit. I confess that I could have put a burst her way, more mast-height than deck though, as I tracked an A-4 with a magazine of tracer.

Squadron Headquarters continued to search out tasking options, while the troops took the opportunity to sort through kit and otherwise make preparations. We really didn't much like the ease with which the enemy appeared to be flying through our air-defences though. The troops were encouraged to get ashore as often and in any way they could to do a bit of training or participate in the AD effort, simply to stay off the ship during daylight hours.

The Navy too turned minds to reducing risk and improving our defences. Woodward came under pressure from those in San Carlos to bring the carriers in closer to give the Sea Harrier Combat Air Patrols more loiter time around the Amphibious Operating Area. He resisted this strongly, holding firm to his conviction that the loss of a carrier, even now, would probably spell the end. Once we had an operational airstrip ashore, maybe, but not until. Instead he deployed what became known as the '42/22 combination', ships of complementary missile systems: the Type 42 with long range Sea Dart, the Type 22 with closer range Sea Wolf. To start with it involved stationing *Coventry* and *Broadsword* off Pebble Island where they should get clean radar sightings, less cluttered by echoes coming off surrounding land.

Woodward also pressed Clapp and Thompson to speed up their materiel offload, to get vulnerable logistic ships out of the combat area altogether, the unarmed highly visible STUFT in particular. The two 'amphibians' shared Woodward's concerns, but were also determined to achieve a build-up ashore with stockpiles optimised to feed the eventual ground campaign. They had envisaged landing two days of supplies, keeping a further two days on each of the LSLs, bringing one into San Carlos from a holding area well out to the north east of the archipelago as needed to keep things topped up. Now they were under pressure to unload numerous vessels in a sequence and at a volume that disrupted their carefully thought out arrangements and timetable. The logisticians responded manfully to the developing situation and necessary adjustments of plan.

It became difficult to keep track of events and time. There was the day that *Antelope* got hit by two bombs, neither exploding, one of the attackers crashing into her mast. Poor *Antelope* had been with us only a short while. She sank later that day when one of the bombs exploded. Her bows remained visible for a while as if protesting her fate. Could that have been the day I saw the Sea Cat coming off a picket in the entrance to San Carlos Waters? It wobbled clumsily as the operator gathered control to pursue a fast-retiring enemy aircraft. The pilot must have caught sight of it as he passed, for he swung hard wing-over to port, after-burners thundering, to shoot round the headland, out across the Sound, the Sea Cat left bouncing in his wake. That missile was never going to catch him. Could they catch them? A part of me was glad to see the pilot get away with it. We could all see that what the enemy pilots were doing took a lot of guts, and it was difficult not to admire them for it.

Many aircraft never made it home. If they came across the CAP they were almost certainly goners. They were no match for the Sea Harriers and their Sidewinder missiles. On one occasion, an incoming flight of 4 Daggers ran into the CAP. Three were shot down almost immediately. The fourth ditched its bombs and managed to break away. Such was the deterrent effect of the SHAR that the enemy would immediately turn for home if they thought the CAP anywhere near them. This was not funk, but plain common sense, a clear understanding of our technological superiority in the air-to-air part of the battle.

We never saw the CAP. We just knew it was there, hunting around the outside of the San Carlos AD box. The Sea Harriers achieved an extraordinarily high sortie-rate, often fifty or more each day. Not long into the battle the Task Force started to receive more accurate early warning of raids as aircraft launched off Argentina's more southerly air bases, enabling the CAP to pre-position with greater precision. Interception rates improved. Ships and lives were saved.

The day after they sunk *Antelope* the enemy tried a different tactic, concentrating their attacks into a thirty-minute period, most aircraft approaching overland from the south east, rather than from the sea up Falkland Sound or along the north coast of West Falkland. Their intention was to overwhelm our defences by surprise and concentration of effort. Until then they had gone for whatever appeared in front of them. This time they would go after the logistic ships and STUFT, as they should have done from the outset. They had plenty of targets: eleven logistic ships, including the two LPDs, *Fearless* and *Intrepid*, protected by six warships.

As usual, San Carlos Water was bustling, small craft criss-crossing, ferrying back and forth, helicopters too, all on the move, a scene of intense activity. The ships were distributed unevenly, most of them anchored, though generally aligned by the winds channelling down the bay. Over it all, the sound of helicopters set the amphibious area's audio rhythm; Sea Kings with their muted beat, a higher pitch coming in and out as pilots pulled in or let off power as they manoeuvred from ship to ship, ship to shore, shore to ship, appearing never to stop. The smells, too: AVTUR, that pervasive aroma, mixed with brine, an occasional whiff of fuel oil from the damaged ships, all carried on relatively light winds. The weather was calm and bright, as it would remain throughout much of the battle of San Carlos.

On land too a routine had set in. The limited amount of mechanical handling equipment moved constantly from landing-site and jetty to storage-sites, scores of logisticians and others manhandling materiel into stockpiles. On the surrounding hills the troops had gone to ground, most of them out of sight, only occasional movement visible from below. Over the tiny settlements thin wisps of smoke lifted from peat hobs, where brews of tea were constantly on the go for all and any who cared to drop by. Along the foreshore the flotsam of war, much of it from *Antelope*, including sailors' personal effects, left untouched out of respect, seen as a quiet reminder of our fragile individuality amidst the clamour.

Four days into the battle, the first wave came in at 1345 ZULU, again with scant warning, five A-4s going straight for the LSLs. A flight of Daggers had distracted the 42/22 picket. *Sir Galahad*, *Sir Lancelot* and *Sir Bedivere* were each hit, the bombs once more failing to explode. Next came eight Daggers, four of them running into the CAP, failing to get through. *Lancelot* took another un-exploding bomb, this one bouncing off the sea before slamming down her side. *Fearless* was strafed with cannon fire. At 1415 ZULU a final wave of three A-4s roared through, mercifully causing no damage.

Throughout the air raids small boats would continue to ferry back and forth; most helicopters too, some waiting for flight decks to re-open, sitting on the ground somewhere nearby, rotors turning. Even our small-arms fire seemed to become more measured, certainly better disciplined, more careful of friends. The ships, tenders, helicopters, the loggies out in the open stacking their wares, and the hospital over at Ajax Bay, all went on, raid or no raid, the rhythm barely broken, sublimely calm. The noise would pick up as the jets thundered through, after-burners kicking-in with a shattering roar as they completed their bombing runs and made their dash for safety; they felt as much of San Carlos as we, sharing it albeit fleetingly, but at deadly intensity, an indelible part of the whole.

But below the surface calm grew a sense of frustration, perhaps more pronounced within the Army's ranks. It might have been our own NATO, Central Front conditioning taking hold, the institutional 'DNA' of the Army's then principal preoccupation, armoured warfare, with its emphasis on momentum, the constant working of mass times velocity. When we crossed a 'start line', or 'line of departure', we were schooled to get on, not stop. It had been drummed into us: speed and tempo, tempo and speed. Latter day *blitzkreig*. We couldn't fathom the absence of movement. We were told that it was the logistic build up, but couldn't believe it. We knew enough to know that logistics was 'nine tenths'. But did that really mean building the Force Maintenance Area (FMA) to the apparent exclusion of all else, no going forward? We recalled our history and knew to get off a beach, of the importance of pushing 'inland' during the early stages when an enemy may be unbalanced, things in a state of flux.

Instead, it felt to us as though we were drawing attention to our frailty, exposing it: our logistics, the FMA and the support ships. And the enemy appeared to have noticed, accepting the opportunity to go after the LSLs and STUFT free from any distracting developments on land. Sooner than sitting about fixed, taking it on the chin, waiting for some logistical or other catastrophe to overtake us, we soldiers wanted to do something, anything to get the opposition dancing to our tune. We saw a need to be the ones creating the noise and confusion, shielding our vulnerabilities with activity while going after theirs.

Our instinct simply to get on with the war, move away from the beaches, was encouraged by a touching certainty at our level that the 'loggies' would support such a course in any event. We just knew that they delivered. They understood how to cope with mess, expected it. They were accustomed to meeting the more often than not near-unreasonable demands of the 'combat arms'. It was the major feature of a logistician's life, dealing with the naïve demands of the 'F Echelon', providing it with maximum freedom of action, clear of undue administrative concern. They would have expected us to get going and geared themselves to support that while concurrently attending to the deeper mechanics of logistic sustainment. Put another way, we junior 'knife fighters' felt as though we were over-indulging the loggies. We couldn't believe that they themselves would be looking for any such consideration. They must surely expect us to get on, albeit in a way that would enable them to keep up. But to our ingenuous, untutored eyes the deliberate build-up of the FMA, to be completed before taking any offensive action, if that was indeed the intention, was starting to look dangerous, threatening the campaign itself.

At squadron level we saw it all in very simple terms. We should be pressing forward. It had to be wrong to be sitting around. We still couldn't imagine defeat. But we seemed to be inviting some kind of calamity. Well, the Navy and Marines, being the hearts of oak they were, proved better than us at standing 'steady'. We flinched first. We made a move.

14. Mount Kent

It was Mike Rose's idea. He ordered the Squadron forward. We were to get up to Stanley (Map 7). On the face of it the mission was clear enough, recorded as:

> To conduct guerrilla action against
> Arg[entine] Gar[rison] STANLEY area.

But he added a coda:

> Addl [additional] benefit to suck Bde fwd
> [Brigade forward] onto Mt Kent/Challenger.

The second piece resonated 'big time' with us. The land forces must go over to the offensive. Perhaps a move out by the Squadron might serve as an example, encouraging a general, more substantial advance. Certainly worth trying, we all felt. Yet, the addition complicated matters, for me at least. Not so much at the time I received my orders, but later as I got deeper into the business of turning a specific with an aspiration into things for the troops to do. It could have been a matter of knowing too much about the 'commander's intent', or perhaps hopes in this instance. I might have been less conflicted with the first alone, essentially get forward to where we all should be and fight, leaving others to address 'brigade sucking'.

During the orders session, the CO had dwelt on the hoped for spin off. We all knew that hanging around San Carlos wasn't healthy. But he was looking far beyond that. He knew that eventually the battle on land must be won or lost in front of Stanley, and Mount Kent held the key to Stanley. Kent controlled the land approaches into and out of the town and dominated the other features around and about. It constituted 'vital ground' and our enemy appeared to have neglected it! If we could get the Squadron up into the area, even onto Mount Kent, perhaps that might get the Brigade moving to join us, not just triggering the ground campaign, but concurrently securing the key to victory on land: a master-stroke.

I asked the CO that I be allowed to go forward on my own first, to take a look. This might add a day or two. We all understood the need for speed. But it didn't seem altogether wise to drop in at the front of Stanley and start swanning around as we had north of Darwin a few days previously. The enemy had to be patrolling the likely operating areas, or contesting them in some fashion: with artillery and attack helicopters for example. A messy introduction of the Squadron into the area didn't seem to fit well with either aspect of the mission. He agreed.

Afterwards, I settled down to clear my thoughts. It was then that things began to get complicated. The business of Mount Kent and the Brigade came second to the specified task of conducting guerrilla action. But the 'additional benefit' started to take on the greater weight. Raids and such might achieve tactical gains, but the second carried campaign-level significance. Didn't it therefore trump raiding? I allowed my thoughts to roam.

If Mount Kent was vital ground, going begging with us in the area, surely we must take it; wasn't it a dereliction of duty to do otherwise? But how did that square with SAS principles and the direct action task exactly? If it meant taking and holding ground, that would be an unusual thing for the SAS to do; not without precedent, but definitely out of the ordinary. Given the current state of the campaign and the significance of the ground perhaps this was one of those exceptional occasions. There again, we had been tasked to conduct guerrilla action, not seize ground. Mount Kent/Challenger was mentioned as a beneficial side effect to be achieved by the joining Brigade. However, could we achieve both by raiding from Kent? It was a conspicuous feature, a strange place to base a squadron for covert purposes; so possibly not. It seemed to boil down to a straight choice: either cut about making a nuisance of ourselves or do something about Mount Kent. Meandering thoughts weren't getting me far. I returned to first principles.

We had been told to conduct guerrilla operations. That was easy enough to work out. We might deploy as to give each troop a discrete operating area from and within which it would mount and conduct independent attacks. There should be some pre-planned arrangements enabling us to conduct a squadron-level defence should the enemy come out to get us. Alternatively, we might establish a single base area from which we might head out to conduct raids under a tighter, more centralised form of control. This would make it easier to maintain tactical balance for the range of possible eventualities, including defence.

Either way, should the enemy come, we would conduct a mobile, aggressive defence, suggesting that we were the forward part of something much bigger lying not far behind. We must keep moving and avoid being pinned to any one spot, risking defeat in detail.

This brought me back to the mission's second element. Mount Kent/Challenger had been mentioned, but not tied in any hard and fast way to raiding. They had been connected to the hope that others might take a hint and come forward onto them. Presumably, therefore, we were not obliged to locate in and around the mountains. Save that, if the Brigade was to be 'sucked' forward onto the two features, didn't that mean we too should position in their proximity? But might that attract the enemy to the very ground considered vital? Did that in turn mean we should position to secure the ground in readiness for the Brigade?

So it went round and round as I groped for a way that might bring it all together in a single course of action. Perhaps it wasn't possible. But of the two aspects Mount Kent was coming to dominate. So, if we did occupy it and come under attack, how long could we hold out before relief? What would they throw at us? Come to that, would we be relieved, noting that we would have got ourselves into a jam of our own making? I certainly needed to get on the ground for a look.

I went over it all with Danny, explaining that I would take a four-man patrol forward that night. We would drop off to the west of Estancia House to make our way to the area of a saddle not that far below the summit of Mount Kent, on its western flank. I outlined the raiding options, recommending the centralised method. He agreed. I summarised the Kent conundrum—that it seemed the more important part of the mission—and confessed my reluctance to deploy to hold ground per se. If we found the mountain unoccupied, perhaps we could keep it so and raid? It was all rather messy. The recce would attempt to solve the puzzle, before he brought the Squadron in to join us.

As we were about to leave for Mount Kent I heard that H. Jones, commander 2 PARA, wanted to come over to consult us, something to do with a proposed attack or raid by his battle group.[1] Surely no coincidence, it was another sign of movement, of a determination to get on and do something. I was sorry to be missing H. He was always fun, quick, original and faintly irreverent; a soldier through and through. I would have welcomed the opportunity to compare notes. It didn't take much to guess that he wanted our feel for the Argentine garrison down at Goose Green, the location of the nearest sizeable enemy force. H would have had access to the same intelligence as us, but to be certain I arranged for him to have sight of everything we had, should he drop by in my absence. This included G Squadron's surveillance reports. We knew, along with everyone else, that there was a large garrison down there, comprising a battle group and an air wing of Pucaras.

The recce flew in from the sea to reduce the chances of detection by enemy patrols, dropping off midway between Teal Inlet and Estancia

---

[1] 2 PARA attacked Darwin/Goose Green, four or five days later on 28 May defeating a numerically superior Argentine force in prepared positions, effectively achieving moral ascendancy over our enemy throughout the Islands. H died during the battle, winning the Victoria Cross. It was a decisive action. Afterwards the Argentine expulsion from the Falklands took on an air of inevitability, despite further, often severe challenges.

House. Again, there was that momentary disorientation and sense of abandonment as the helicopter departed, almost immediately swallowed up in the darkness. I briefly marvelled once more at the low noise-signature of the Sea King, near perfect for covert operations.

We had no moon, the odd glimpse of stars through thin, low, wispy clouds. Damp, a touch of mist, quiet, a soft breeze that stirred the grass, gently brushing across one's ears. The cold struck to the core. We crouched, each observing his respective arc while Gerry Maltby fixed his NVG head-straps. Quickly done, we moved away from the immediate landing area. After 100 yards or so we stopped again, Gerry to make final adjustments, all four of us settling kit.

Our maps were good, the route straightforward. We knew that the high ground on the horizon to our right ran all the way to Mount Kent. It should be a simple matter of angling up and towards it, avoiding any inlets running in from the sea, climbing gradually to the area of the saddle, our destination. We needed to get there well before first light, to find a lying-up-position from which we might observe the surrounding countryside. I particularly wanted to have a view of Mount Kent and its summit, to be able to observe them during the following day. We all set a bearing and headed off, Gerry leading on NVGs. Impressive, his use of NVGs. I couldn't use them like that, strapped in front of the eyes on the march. They dulled my other senses. I needed everything up and running flat-out, peripheral vision, hearing, smell, all of it coming together to feed sixth sense. NVGs gave me tunnel vision, to the near-exclusion of everything else.

We made good progress. By dawn we were out of the wind and tucked into an unobtrusive rocky outcrop with views up to Mount Kent and south towards Mount Challenger. Mount Kent towered over us, a dark mass of grey rock-runs on its flanks. It looked severe, glowering. The smooth curve of its slopes served to emphasise the impression of forbidding bleakness. There was no escaping its all-seeing presence. And yet it stood unoccupied, not even an observation post as far as we could tell. Our map study showed the slopes to the rear, facing Stanley, falling

241

even more steeply and further than they did on the side we had under observation. To the Argentinians it must surely dominate everything. If it looked as menacing to them as it did to us just then, perhaps it might be possible to move them on from any feeling of vulnerability to something altogether more harmful.

The CO had been right, the place held parallels with Monte Cassino.[2] It dominated the ground, hence defences, in front of Stanley, including all the tracks in and out. From its summit it must be possible to bring down observed artillery and naval gunfire, even air strikes, onto every enemy location up to the town's western boundary, perhaps beyond. Why hadn't their commander seen the danger? We got off a signal calling the Squadron forward to join us, copying to RHQ that it really needed a battalion to take and hold Mount Kent: the place was currently there for the taking, wide open.

As we called for the Squadron, I had yet to commit to a particular course of action. The pure SF hooligan in me favoured guerrilla action from a secure area between Kent and Challenger, while another me gravitated towards deploying the Squadron to secure Mount Kent, denying it to the enemy. Indeed, as I sat observing, my thoughts worked almost exclusively upon taking and holding Kent in a SF acceptable way. An uncomfortable course of action started to emerge. It involved leaving the place alone, not drawing attention to it; more a matter of 'securing' Mount Kent than seizing it. But was that to duck the issue? It did feel mildly evasive, passive even, going somewhat against the grain.

If I had reservations, what of the 'red-meat eaters' about to join me, the 'Merry Men', how might they view it? I drew comfort from a dimly recalled piece of T.E. Lawrence, on the benefits of leaving things some-

---

[2] Monte Cassino dominates one of the principal routes to Rome from the south. In 1944 the Allies had to assault it repeatedly before dislodging its German defenders. Everyone who fought on the Allies' side remarked upon the oppressive, looming, all-seeing presence of the mountain, this bearing heavily upon their state of mind.

times to ensure the enemy continued to act in a way that already served one's interests. I vaguely recalled his attacking the Hejaz railway, not so often as to cause the Turks to cease using it altogether, but at a frequency that would encourage them to continue sending trains down the track, each one a potential target for the Arab guerrilla forces. I could see parallels: if the Argentinians were doing what we wanted, why encourage them to do otherwise? At the moment our foe showed no intention of occupying Mount Kent. Why then draw his attention to it? Why stir him to recognise and make good an error? Of course, should they eventually twig and move to put things right, we must be prepared to try to nip his remedial action in the bud.

As we looked out from the OP a solution along those lines suggested itself. The ground to our front ran relatively easily up to the summit, the remaining sides of the mountain being precipitous and guarded by stone runs. It was the easiest way up. Were we to occupy or otherwise control this access, would that in turn render meaningful influence over the heights? Possibly yes. More certainly, it also sat astride north/south lateral routes on this side of the mountains offering us screened movement out to the flanks for our raids. So, maybe it was possible after all to secure Kent while acting the guerrilla.

Had I known about the mood developing at higher command, the decision would have been easier and quicker to reach: ground, not raids, campaign-level not tactical. Mount Kent was emerging as the thing to go after.

In Britain frustration had been growing at the lack of progress since the landings. At the highest national levels people worried that any more delay might lead to increased pressure in the UN for London to accept a ceasefire. Given our lack of progress on the ground to date, it could be an insistence that proved difficult to resist. We had taken back little more than a number of acres around San Carlos and appeared to be stuck. Eventually, Fieldhouse dealt directly with Thompson. CLFFI was somewhat out of things, still on the end of intermittent communications, on the high seas aboard QE2, making his way to the 'front' as best he could with 5 Brigade. The CinC signalled Thompson to rehearse the political realities as he saw them; he encouraged the brigade commander to get going, move out, build momentum, specifically:

> bring the Darwin/Goose Green operation to a successful conclusion with Union Jack seen to be flying in Darwin. This will enable us to claim possession of Lafonia.[3]

He added:

> ... the reinforcement of the D Squadron base west of the main enemy position [meaning Stanley] will allow us to claim with justification that we now control large areas of East Falkland.[4]

Apparently, aside from Darwin/Goose Green, the CinC and his Land Deputy, Major General Trant,
had in mind the establishment of forward positions by infantry, aligned with that of the Squadron, Mount Kent across to Mount Challenger, from which the enemy in front of Stanley might be threatened with artillery and other offensive fire support, even eliminated. Again, it would appear that Kent held the key. It should be occupied for the concept to work.

This made things awkward for Thompson who had been ordered to wait for CLFFI, his commander, and make no precipitate moves before his arrival. From the occasional conversations he had managed to hold with Moore, he knew that the Land Commander harboured doubts about the wisdom of moving up to Mount Kent before his arrival with 5 Brigade, and before the enemy's air had been further reduced. To make matters even more awkward, the Task Force had just lost its desperately needed heavy-lift helicopters with the sinking of the *Atlantic Conveyer*. This would make any rapid forward deployment most difficult

[3] Lafonia: a vast tract of flat, open grassland lying to the south of the Goose Green peninsula.
[4] Sir Lawrence Freedman, *The Official History of the Falklands Campaign*, vol. II, Abingdon: Routledge, 2005, p. 557.

to achieve and sustain.[5] Nevertheless, Thompson responded by pressing on with 2 PARA's assault of Darwin/Goose Green while starting to develop plans to move 42 Commando and a battery forward to join us. The pace was about to quicken.

* * *

Billy Cormack saw him first; I had sensed Billy stiffen, his weapon coming up slowly. He drew my attention to the man four hundred metres or more to our front. The soldier had emerged as if from nowhere, walking briskly, out in the open, armed with what looked like an M16 or Armalite, wearing a belt-kit, low slung. He had a high-stepping gait, leant-back, and covered the ground fast and positively.

'One of ours,' queried Billy.

Could be, we all agreed, the others having moved to get a better look, all of us taking care not to reveal ourselves. We continued to observe him, intrigued. He appeared to be making his way systematically, progress generally in our direction, moving back and forth, mainly to rock outcrops and any other likely places of concealment. Searching? For us?

'It's Gordon, Gordon Mather,' Gerry stated with conviction. I didn't know Gordon, a member of G Squadron, but accepted Gerry's word for it, although still inclined to caution. What was he doing moving about like that in the open, apparently on his own?

He came closer. Definitely Gordon. We let him come up to us, so as not to break his pattern of movement, before quietly announcing our presence. He didn't break step and continued across, stopping a yard or two short. We remained in cover. He too played his part, gazing nonchalantly into the distance, not facing us as he spoke.

---

[5] By way of an example, it might be noted that it required fifty—sixty Sea King lifts to move a single battery of guns and its ammunition; Chinooks, lost with the *Atlantic Conveyer*, would have reduced the requirement by more than half.

'Good morning,' said Clive Lowther quietly, with the faintest hint of irony. Always polite and calm, was Clive. Gerry joined in, gently teasing Gordon about Standard Operating Procedures (SOPs).

Gordon took the banter well, in the good-natured spirit it was intended, explaining that first he had been told to meet us miles away near Mount Harriet. That had been for the previous night. Then, early that morning he had received instructions to make an RV this coming early evening east of Mount Kent, roughly where we were. He hadn't expected to meet us until after nightfall, when he thought our helicopter due. I was surprised, too, having arranged for G to vacate our operating area, not come into it.

'Gang fuck,' somebody muttered out aloud. An expressive if inelegant phrase with wide utility meaning on this occasion that someone, somewhere, somehow had got their wires crossed, obliging Gordon to make a risky move during daylight hours. Could it have been me? I didn't think so; more likely a change of plan that had yet to come down to us. Actually, it was just as well he had made contact in daylight; at night it could easily have resulted in a 'blue on blue' shoot out, should we have still been unaware of his patrol's presence.

He apologised for any cock-up. We apologised for the cock-up, and for any inconvenience, suggesting as kindly as we could that he should go away as soon as possible, but not before we had taken advantage of the opportunity he had so boldly created to exchange information.

Gordon confirmed the area clear of enemy; over a three weak period he had seen neither hide nor hair of Argentinians up here. They were closer in on Stanley. They appeared utterly uninterested in Mount Kent. I warned him to steer clear of our operating area without going into the detail of our intentions. It then emerged that he had been expecting to go out on the helicopter bringing us in. Everything fell into place; almost certainly a case of crossed wires, the product of cryptically short messaging. We guessed that he was meant to be going out with the helicopters bringing in our main body and advised him, arranging things accordingly. The episode highlighted the difficulty of coordinating tactical detail by signals employing a Second World War method of encryption, transmitted by hand speed Morse over a High Frequency network operating to a system of scheduled calls. Anyway, with things sorted to our mutual benefit and with an exchange of good lucks and take cares he took his leave to re-join his patrol that had in fact been covering his every move and the whole episode undetected by us. He didn't hang around, almost immediately disappearing into a thin mist that had started to roll in from the direction of the sea to the north.

Meeting up with G had given us a lift. The opportunity to go over details face to face was valuable enough, but we also drew from their confidence, their evident ease at being so far forward, behind enemy lines. They made it seem so natural. In particular, Gordon's clarity and assurances with regard to Mount Kent did much to confirm that we were probably on the right track with our nascent plan. Even so, to play safe, we decided to move our location after last light.

Not much happened the rest of that day, save for the enemy patrol up on the lower slopes of Mount Kent! Thank goodness they hadn't turned up during our meeting. There were twelve of them. They had emerged from round the southern flanks of the mountain at around midday, about a kilometre or more from us. They moved at a leisurely pace in single file, a handful of them with rifles slung over their shoulder, all with helmets and their equivalent of our belt-kit. They had one machine-gun between them, an M60 or similar, and a radio operator, the patrol commander to his front heading the file. They seemed relaxed, not expecting trouble; not looking for it either, going through the motions of patrolling. They stopped and sat for a while occasionally glancing our way, taking a break, all of them snacking, a few lighting up cigarettes. After about half an hour they ambled off to complete their stroll, soon disappearing round the northern slopes.

Their entry upon the scene, which came as an unpleasant surprise, put a different complexion on things. The patrol's arrival lay at odds with what G Squadron had told us only a few hours previously. Something had changed. I made a note to warn Gordon. The enemy had altered their pattern of behaviour. Perhaps they had at last cottoned on to their oversight. Maybe they now appreciated the operational significance of the mountain. Conceivably they shared our estimate that the feature dominated the approaches to Stanley. So, what did they intend to do? Something big, such as occupy the place? Or could we expect more roaming patrols? Might they sight observation posts? The options were numerous. But one way or another the situation had moved on, and it felt that a race had begun.

By late afternoon we had received a response to our SITREP sent soon after the departure of the enemy patrol. The Squadron would attempt to join us late the following day, in the early evening, once dark. Good. We hoped nothing irreversible would happen in between times. We settled down to wait, to keep the area under observation for a further twenty-four hours.

The next day, the hours ticked slowly by, nothing untoward, no enemy, the weather perfect until the evening of the insertion when a dense hill fog developed. We knew this spelt trouble and passed a WETREP (weather report) that failed to get through before the helicopters departed San Carlos. The formation arrived absolutely on time, clattering past a few feet above us, unable to see the ground. They must have been inching along. They took a while to pass. We were buffeted by the down-draft as one flew directly overhead, failing to see our shielded torches marking the LZ. It was close enough to reach out and touch, it seemed. Thirty minutes later the weather had cleared, perfect night flying conditions. At least they hadn't hung around. Theirs had been one continuous movement making it difficult for any nearby enemy to determine a particular place of interest along their route. Perhaps our location and intentions would escape notice. To be safe though, we moved off to yet another point of observation, feeling disappointed but not altogether surprised.

The following morning we settled down to keep an eye on the area, still with good views of the mountain, and its surroundings out to Estancia. It should have been a matter of 'hard routine', that is no cooking, and no sleeping in sleeping bags, the four of us kitted and primed ready to spring into immediate action. But the deep, damp, penetrating cold stood to impair our efficiency, encouraging us to ease things a touch.

Some people favoured setting up forward and rear locations, one for rest, the other for observation. But on each move we found ourselves sizeable rock outcrops from which both activities could be conducted. I preferred it that way, having the patrol in all-round defence in one place rather than spread about. It felt tactically more responsive and better balanced. Working in pairs, we maintained 360 degrees of observation, one man of each pair getting rest, the other observing their half of the overall arc; and we had notably long fields of vision, save when mist came down, offering plenty of warning should anyone approach. In every OP we occupied, Billy and I would always take the side nearest Mount Kent.

Aside from what might be in use, everything was packed ready for a swift move. We stayed fully clothed and booted throughout. Weapons were always in hand or to hand. Observers wore their belt kit; a man at rest might take his off to sleep. The 'off watch' man could make a brew during daylight hours, never at night. Food was eaten cold for concern that the smell of cooking might carry. We used no tentage, nor poncho rain-shelters, nothing like that. The recent issue of the odd item of Gore-Tex clothing, including bivy bags, made it possible to get a good, warm sleep on one's turn. Sleeping bags were used for sleep only. Maybe a shade relaxed, the OP nevertheless remained more hive than nest, ready to sting mercilessly if disturbed, exactly as Training Wing had drummed into us those years previously during Selection.

To dispel all and any lingering doubts over what course of action to adopt, when Danny did eventually get in with the others it was to inform me that 42 Commando planned to join us as soon as they could, within a day or two. That had clinched it. We should avoid attracting attention and instead concentrate on *securing* Mount Kent, getting the commando in and up the hill unmolested. The tactical level business of raids and so on could wait.

For lack of available airframes, the Squadron's insertion did not go as we would have wished. Eventually it would be achieved over two successive nights, two troops at a time, the first lift getting in twenty-four hours after the first abortive attempt. Aside from the protracted build up, the frequent toing and froing of helicopters worried me; the enemy must surely notice and react, at the very least patrol to see what was going on. Over the period it felt as though a three way race against time had commenced: to get the Squadron in, before the commando, all before the enemy came at us in strength. I hoped earnestly that we would avoid detection, but resigned myself to having to fight to hold ground until relieved one way or the other.

As they arrived I would quickly brief the troops, to get them moving out to their locations each about a thousand metres or more apart, placing them within machine-gun range of one another. I stressed the importance of mutually supporting fire and the need for concealment. We would engage the enemy preferably on my order, and only if absolutely necessary. With the whole Squadron on the ground, we would eventually spread over two or more grid squares, influencing the better part of four with our firepower. This gave us the room we needed for manoeuvre, to meet and absorb any enemy incursion. If they came in strength, I wanted to confuse the enemy into thinking that we were part of a bigger effort, the screen idea again.

Danny arrived with news from the world outside, offering good and bad. Settling down with him and Geordie into what would be the Squadron headquarters' location I opted for the good news first.

'We're in Darwin Goose Green.'

It came as a surprise. I had forgotten about 'H' and his quest for intelligence, suggesting an attack in that direction. My mind had been so consumed by Mount Kent and its importance that I had completely overlooked the possibility of movement in any direction other than towards us! Myopia, self-absorption, so was it good news then, given that the key to winning appeared to lie up here? Most probably, at the very least we were on the move, with yet another success tipping things in our favour. And the enemy's operational reserve had been poised down there. Presumably 2 PARA had done for it. That must be hugely significant, in both physical and moral terms.

'The bad?'

'I'm afraid your friend 'H' is dead.'

Neither he nor I could have anticipated how hard that would hit: shock at first, stomach wrenching disbelief followed by anger of the deep-down, cold sort. Not directed at anybody, just an overwhelming and sudden feeling that the war had gone on long enough. We were losing too many friends and good people. The helicopter and now this. We had to finish this bloody thing, as quickly as possible, no more hanging around, no more fannying about. We must get on with it.

We fell into silence, me with my thoughts, Danny and Geordie studiously sorting radios before getting off a situation report to RHQ. I had thought it right to warn RHQ of our intentions, the focus on Kent rather than raiding. Now it didn't seem so important. Right then I didn't much care about niceties: H's death had upset my equilibrium. Danny and Geordie could knock out something to send. It didn't need me. I knew what we had to do. Get 42 up that bloody hill. In practical terms nothing else much mattered right then. The message was away with unusual speed thanks to Geordie's skills.

Later, after morning stand-to, having sorted out pressing business and finished our meagre breakfasts, the three of us, Danny, Geordie and I, sat back with a brew to go over things once more, to ensure we were ready for whatever the immediate future might hold. All four troops were deployed, tucked out of sight. Graham back in San Carlos had read the situation for himself. He had ensured the troops had come laden with extra supplies. If it came to a slugging match for Mount Kent, we were not going to go short of 'bullets and beans'. No issues with munitions then; we had Graham to thank for that. The troops covered all approaches to Mount Kent on its western sides, the visible summit and 42's LZ. We were well placed to disrupt any attempt by the enemy to occupy the mountain. Best of all, the Marines were due to be with us before long, possibly at the end of the day. As for the enemy, if they intended to occupy the mountain, they would probably signal this by starting with a site survey. In any event, they were likely to send in recce first, perhaps siting an OP. Of course, we couldn't discount the possibility that they might kick off with a clearance operation in strength, supported by Pucaras and attack helicopters. We didn't like the idea of attack from the air, but we had Stinger and 16 Troop had had time to sort through their initial handling problems. We concluded that the enemy would probably do the thing we hadn't thought of, but that we were as ready as we could be for most eventualities. All would come clear.

The morning was passing peacefully, the weather bright and still, a faint breeze, no movement up on Mount Kent, nothing across the entire area. Danny and I were enjoying a quiet smoke when a large formation of helicopters emerged from behind Mount Kent heading south west: five or six Hueys, two Chinooks, one Puma, flanked by two attack helicopters. Most likely a strong company group.[6] As they were about to disappear, 16 Troop came up on the air asking permission to have a go at them with a Stinger. Far too late, and besides I couldn't see how it could help, downing a helicopter only to stir up a hornet's nest a few hours before 42's arrival. One couldn't fault the enthusiasm, but emphatically, no!

Not long after, as the light started its slow fade to dusk a message came in to inform us that 42 could not join us that day as hoped for;

[6] It was more than likely the enemy reinforcement of Darwin/Goose Green. A company of infantry, held somewhere the far side of Mount Kent from us, perhaps as a reserve or part of a patrol or screen force, was re-deployed to the south of Goose Green by helicopter on the last morning of the battle. Too late to influence events, they were met by a hail of artillery fire directed by 2 PARA. It proved a noble, brave but as it turned out futile effort at retrieving their situation. They might have done better to stay put, to contest our occupation of the mountain's summit: such is hindsight. And such is luck that favoured us on this occasion, 2 PARA's battle directly if unwittingly assisting our efforts up on the vital ground in front of Stanley by drawing off any nearby enemy defenders.

they would make an attempt in a further twenty-four hours. At almost the same instant my VHF set crackled into life. 16 Troop had seen two enemy Huey helicopters drop two patrols of eight men each in front of Bluff Cove Peak, 17 Troop's position. The patrols were heading our way. 17 Troop confirmed that it must be happening in dead ground to them, for they couldn't see.

16 Troop was told to carry on. They were free to manoeuvre, everyone else was to sit tight and not engage unless they positively identified enemy coming onto their position. Clipped messages, no lengthy explanations, we gave little away for a listening enemy to go on, save mention of the helicopters.

Unleashed, 16 Troop burst into life. They decided on an L-shaped ambush. Leaving two GPMGs where they were, ten of the Troop dashed off to position themselves as a killer group, to put flanking fire into the slowly approaching enemy. All the while the light faded. I sensed more than saw the troops dash round to their places. How was it going? The light? Leave them to it. They knew their business.

As they got into position, the ambush set, the light had all but gone. The enemy patrol continued to make its leisurely way up through a stone run, towards the GPMGs. It would be pitch black before they arrived in the preferred killing area. The ambush had little option other than to spring early. Fire crashed out. Instantly the enemy dropped from sight, into the rocks. The fire poured in, tracer arching into the night sky. The flat crump of M203 rifle grenades echoed off the hills. It was about fully dark when the flanking team took casualties, Dick Palmer a round in the buttocks, Carl Rhodes high-velocity splinters in a knee. In all likelihood the hits came from above, from their own troop location. The Troop immediately made the necessary adjustments, maintaining their fire for a while longer. They got nothing back.

'Well, they know we're here now, Cedric,' Danny observed.

'Mmm.'

'What d'you reckon?' he asked, clearly thinking about the next twenty-four hours, and the postponed arrival of the Marines.

'Stay put,' I responded. We didn't seem to have much choice.

No question about it, we were definitely in a race against time now, but after all the uncertainty of recent days it felt good to be committed to a single clear course of action: hold this spot so as to get 42 in and up onto Mount Kent.

We passed word to the Squadron, to hold tight in their defensive positions, to minimise movement overnight. We could have stray enemy about the place. This included 16 Troop who should return to their original positions and not check the ambush site. We could do without prolonging what could become a messy night engagement.

Geordie meanwhile got a message off to RHQ advising them of the situation, warning that if things became too hot, making the LZ untenable, we would try to bring 42 in elsewhere, the location to be notified. We had taken light casualties that might wait to go out with 42, but no longer than that; one way or another we needed a CASEVAC the coming night. That done, we all prepared for what promised to be a busy day to follow, alert for any lost enemy wandering about. The rest of the night passed without further incident.

Shortly after daybreak, John Hamilton, who never slept as far as we could tell, was gazing out at Ted's position over on Bluff Cove Peak when he saw two men moving cautiously out in the open. They looked like enemy. He alerted 17 Troop, asking Chippy to wave or do some such to confirm whether or not the two were his or enemy. Unsurprisingly, Chippy replied that he would rather not. Almost immediately came the crack of a grenade and a short, sharp crash of fire. Then silence. We waited. Time passed. The net remained silent. Eventually, calmly, softly, Danny asked for a SITREP. Chippy responded with equal composure, confirming two enemy dead. The enemy had managed to throw a grenade as they were cut down, wounding Don Masters, not severely, but bad enough to cause worry. He was in discomfort.

Immediately, Geordie started to get off a CASEVAC request, none of us seeing any point in putting this off a moment longer. After this latest contact, the enemy must surely know something was up, and roughly where, and were bound to investigate. There seemed no point in holding onto our casualties. They might slow us up if we had to start manoeuvring hard and fast. In the event it took Geordie all day to get the message away, using hand-cranked Morse over high frequency, given the unfavourable atmospheric conditions. It was a Herculean effort, six to eight hours continuous bashing at the Morse key, relieved only by the occasional brew and biscuit, handed across by Danny. By the time we got our casualties out and back to the medical services in Ajax Bay, two of the injured were barely hanging on, relatively minor wounds having become serious over time in the cold, damp conditions.

At one point Ted came up to ask what he should do about the enemy bodies. It was odd. I guessed that he wanted to share a sense of unease, as much as anything. I advised him to bury them and mark the graves; take and leave ID tags and ensure he got an accurate eight figure grid reference. We wanted to do things properly. I made a mental note to get 16 Troop to check their ambush site too, when the time was right.

The rest of the morning passed uneventfully, each of us glancing at our watches more frequently than needed, urging on the passage of time. I occupied myself for a while, studying map and ground, refining thoughts about our defensive scheme of manoeuvre, developing options. I shared these thoughts with Danny. One of us would be needed to see through what could be a tricky, mobile defence until relieved or forced to withdraw. The enemy must come soon: a couple of hours, possibly three. It would take them that long to mobilise an airmobile reaction force, brief their artillery, rustle up some ground attack air (heaven forbid), then move in on us. Yes, anytime now.

'So let's have one of yours, Cedric.'

I rolled the cigarettes. Still nothing, just Geordie tapping out Morse from among the rocks opposite. The afternoon drew on. The light started to change; slowly, painfully slowly it dimmed. It had been a beautiful, bright day with the faintest breath of wind. The sunlight had sparkled. Now, with the approach of evening the temperature fell, the light taking on a deep, golden glow. And still nothing; no sight nor sound of enemy.

With the CASEVAC request at long last sent successfully, Geordie had rolled back from his radio in relief and a thoroughly deserved sense of satisfaction, another chunk of chocolate and a biscuit tossed his way. The radio came to life again, dot dashing.

'I'll get it', said Danny. He was a pretty accomplished Morse signaller himself. It was RHQ, confirming things were on for that night, asking for a WETREP. Not much longer to wait; still nothing to disturb the quiet. What a lethargic enemy! Surely they must wonder about their missing patrol. In all likelihood the enemy patrol would have managed to radio a contact report. And what of the noise and tracer? At least 16 Troop had not used rocket flares. Good thinking. That would have been visible miles away, clearly sign-posting our whereabouts. Where was the expected enemy reaction?

It came at an inconvenient moment. A five-man enemy patrol dropped off by helicopter down towards Estancia House, immediately making their way towards us. Another recce, but this lot seemed altogether more purposeful than the others. Carrying bergens, they looked and moved much like us. Special Forces? So that was it. Send in the big boys? We calculated that they should be with us on last light, again, about the time the Commando should be arriving. We had to nail this lot. They had the potential to rot up the entire evening. Everyone stood too, silently urging them on, to get to us before the light failed, ahead of 42's ETA.

Eventually they drew near, the light fading to complicate things once more. This time it would be 19 Troop's turn, the enemy coming steadily on towards them. Meanwhile, we deployed troops to secure and mark the LZ. Our casualties were collected for evacuation. They all looked decidedly tired. Must keep them warm. The remaining troops and SHQ kept to their positions, so that the Squadron stayed balanced and each element knew the location of all others. What with a battle-group coming in, a contact probably running concurrently, there would be plenty of scope for blue-on-blue. I told 19 Troop that they should not use flares for fear of dazzling the pilots who would be on NVG. The last thing we needed was for one of the helicopters to go in as a consequence of a pilot losing his bearings near the ground. The troops would have to rely on night-sights and personal NVG.

As dusk moved on to night, John and his team went into contact with a flourish, an enormous weight of automatic fire, and plenty of crumps. Yet again we had been obliged to open up sooner than best, at ranges longer than wanted. The enemy vanished into the rocks amid the deepening dark of the fast-approaching night. One or two fired back, albeit with scant conviction. Resistance crumpled fast as fire poured down, the troops taking full and grateful advantage of the enemies' occasionally offered muzzle flashes. Tracer bounced from the rocks, climbing gracefully into the sky, some cartwheeling with pyrotechnic pizzazz. Most satisfying. 19 Troop had things under control. They were relishing their moment. I guessed they might keep their fire going a little longer than really needed.

I left for the LZ, getting there as 42 arrived, masses of them fanning out into the gathering darkness, instinctively stooping as John's troop continued to blaze away as I thought they would. No point in holding back; John and his people had to suppress the area. We couldn't afford to have enemy on the LZ. It was a vulnerable moment. Mike Rose emerged out of the gloom; sheer luck that I had positioned where his helicopter landed. We exchanged greetings. He didn't ask, taking all in his stride as ever, but I explained the noise. He in turn introduced me to the towering presence of someone called Max Hastings, 'a journalist', he said, who I in turn passed to Danny. For some reason Danny thought him to be Nick Vaux, the Commanding Officer of 42 Commando, and so started to brief him on the situation until halted by an unexpected response, something along the lines:

'That's an unusual gun you have there, what is it?'

Danny in his turn moved him on to one of the troops for safe-keeping, the situation being fluid.

I felt pretty well on top of things, knowing that the ambush was going well, 19 Troop by now probably stretching things out for the pure fun of it. It was pleasurable, the feeling that we had all just managed to get 42 in without mishap, safe and sound, the sense of teamwork. And to top it, no more pussy-footing around for us, for fear of deflecting the enemy from their own errors; we could get stuck in once more—simple.

I sought out 42's command group. They were relieved to hear that we had things in hand, that the area was secure and they need do little more than get up the hill and move into position. Perhaps I may have come across a touch flippant, careless of their concerns, knowing as I did that any enemy in the vicinity were either dead, about to become dead, or otherwise undone. With little or no ceremony, they were soon all on their way up to the summit of Mount Kent, guided by 16 Troop.

42 had asked that we continue to secure the LZ, and generally help with the in-load of the battle group through the rest of the night and into the following morning. We readily agreed to do that, but warned that we ought to be contributing in more usual ways as soon as practicable. I had in mind raiding and such like. We were likely to spot plenty of potential targets from the summit of Mount Kent.

At daybreak some of our artillery came in to set up below us, behind a low ridge, putting them in dead ground to the enemy and any mortar-locating radar. It didn't take them long, the helicopters dropping the 'tubes', heavy equipment and materiel directly into position. Within minutes they were surveyed in, camouflaged, ready for action, but with only a few rounds apiece. The helicopters would return repeatedly, throughout the day, ferrying forward shells and other munitions for guns and marines alike.

I sat for a while on my own, looking across the shallow valley below, taking satisfaction in what we might have helped trigger. My gaze took in the guns. The gunners were going about their business with an air of confidence as though owning the place, in marked contrast to the way we had been creeping about only a few hours previously, avoiding all risk of discovery. At that moment, I envied the conventional troops their way of war, the comfort of operating in numbers, its more overt nature, their ability to move about upright and in daylight, to take possession of ground. It felt so refreshing to be out in the open; and unexpectedly reassuring to see the Royal Artillery going about their rather stylised, crisply executed business. It was as if shelling the approaches to Stanley was something they did every day of the week.

They were equipped with the 105mm Light Gun, capable of firing high explosive, smoke and illumination rounds out to seventeen kilometres on maximum 'charge super'. It meant that in one fell swoop, we had put the entire Argentine force before Stanley under the influence of our guns. In no time the Royal Artillery were responding to fire requests coming in from Mount Kent. It crossed my mind that they probably rendered us redundant: easier to strike tactical, battlefield targets with artillery than engage with one of our painstakingly turned, close quarter raids.

A number of the fire-missions came from 16 Troop deployed within 42's defence perimeter. 18 Troop would be on their way shortly, taking a company of Marines across to Mount Challenger. 17 and 19 Troops were deployed to provide security to the rear of the Commando and the guns, otherwise to act as a reserve. Everything felt right with our world. I thought I would grab a quick nap. It had been a long night.

First, Danny, Geordie and I decided we would have a leisurely breakfast. We might even fry a few slices of bacon grill, a treat after days on hard routine cold rations, relieved by the odd brew.

Before too long bacon grill sizzled cheerily in a mess tin, the smell heavenly, blending perfectly with the comforting whiff of burning hexamine. I had a mug of hot, sweet tea in hand when one of the troops came up on my radio interrupting our reverie. They reported that on clearing their area after first light they had come across an Argentinian wandering about lost, probably from the contact the evening before. I said that they should bring him across to us. We would arrange his evacuation back to the PW (Prisoner of War) cage. Geordie warned off a couple of his signallers to receive and guard the prisoner.

Curious to meet our enemy face to face, after breakfast rather than 'kip' I decided to go with Danny to have a look at our captive. Geordie busied himself with codes and radios and whatnot as usual, staying put. The PW was a big man with Amerindian features, surly, curiously detached, clearly not enjoying his captivity. The signallers were having difficulty with him. He would keep getting up to saunter away. We sat him down only for him to get up almost immediately, to walk off yet again, hands deep in pockets, shoulders hunched, sulking, anything but submissive.

'Sod it! Danny, you speak Spanish.'

He had picked up a smattering about six years earlier, in Buenos Aires as it happened, while he and I had been there training our ambassador's bodyguard.

'Tell him not to do that. Tell him he's a prisoner. He can't just wander off.'

Danny gathered himself, staring at me steadily, quizzically. Then, pulling himself up to his full height, he turned to confront the prisoner. Standing directly in front of him, gazing up, the man towering above, Danny wagged his finger to add weight to his carefully chosen words.

'*Para usted, mi amigo, la Guerra es terminado*,'[7] delivered with a flourish and a final wag of his finger. Danny turned back to me, a huge grin lighting up his face.

'You know, Cedric, not many people get the opportunity to say that.'

Flores, for that was his name, looked blank. Unimpressed, perhaps faintly uncomprehending, he first shook then tossed his head disdainfully before ambling off. Stepping up onto a flat rock he struck a pose. Shoulders squared, back arched, he scanned all about him, taking in the guns, head swinging slowly back and forth, black luxuriant hair swept by the wind. Who did he think he was?

The signallers brought him back. They were tiring of the theatricals, starting to look pissed off, increasingly murderous in a sullen sort of way. Next, with signallers in tow, he made for the rear of our position, hands still deep in pockets, insolent, arrogant, menacing in a machismo

---

[7] 'For you my friend the war is over.'

fashion, kicking carelessly at the diddle-dee, as if about to take his leave of us.

'Bring him over here,' I shouted across to his escort. 'Sit him down.'

They did their best, Flores not sitting, but squatting on his huge, muscular haunches as if to launch himself at us at any moment.

'Fucker,' I said. 'Special Forces?'

'Looks it.'

We rummaged through his bergen and belt kit, checking first that the signallers had searched him for any concealed weapons. They had. He didn't. He had some good stuff, much of it still in its original wrappers, thrown into his bergen in no logical order.

'Left in a hurry,' Danny observed.

We came across a brand new balaclava. I offered it to him. He turned his head away with disdain. Idiot. Fine by me. I kept it. Towards the bottom, of all places, Danny came across his NVG, second generation, a superb optic. Again, brand new; pocketed complete with spare batteries. We turned our attention to his weapon, a massive sports hunting-rifle with a huge telescopic sight to match. Impressive, the sort of thing intended for knocking over elephants. And then we came to the ammunition: hollow point, expanding rounds big enough to tear a gigantic wound in any man, outlawed by the Geneva Conventions! Our surprise and anger showed.

'What the fuck is this?' I growled as best I could, thrusting the thing sharp end forward towards his insolent face.

We needed no Spanish. He knew that he had been caught out. The discovery changed everything. Things dawned on the arrogant bastard. He was in a bad place among very angry people who couldn't care a jot about his well-being any more. He looked less certain, still sulky. He made as if to get up.

'No,' said quietly, with a shake of the head, our cold, still air of menace serving to underscore the trouble he now found himself in. We didn't much like snipers for being snipers, but those with expanding rounds must know that they would be in deep mire if caught. And

Flores did now realise he was in trouble, picking up on our altogether changed mood.

I passed my Armalite to Danny, stood up and chambered one of the 'dum-dums' into the elephant gun. Flores tensed. But I sighted the thing at a patch of lichen on a rock, about twenty yards beyond, to one side of him. It gave an enormous kick, a deafening report. The lichen lived. Not so lucky a patch of diddle-dee. The round powered into the dirt, well off to the right, throwing up a sizeable piece of the Falklands. I wasn't that bad a shot. The thing wasn't even zeroed. I tossed it down in disgust. It clattered on the rocks most satisfactorily. Flores got the point. We held him in contempt: a criminal shit, no better than a gangster, a professional disgrace.

He settled down after that, his animal instinct for survival getting the better of his chauvinism if that was what it had been. As we left, having had enough of him, and taken what we wanted from his kit, his guards asked if they should bind and hood him. Tempting, but that could be interpreted as sensory deprivation and unwarranted physical duress, both in themselves breaches of the conventions. We told them no, but to remove the laces of his boots; and to help themselves to his stuff, but leave him well clothed. On our way back to Geordie and a brew, I remarked to Danny that I hoped we weren't the only side 'playing cricket'.

As we were finishing our brew, about to make our way up to the summit of Mount Kent to see how 16 Troop and 42 were getting on, John Hamilton raced past towards the rear of our position, only to dash back moments later. Seconds after that he sprinted once again to the rear, his legs a blur of cycling motion, followed by one or two of his troop loping. His dashing hither and thither felt at odds with the tranquillity of the morning, warm in the sun when sheltered from the faint, chill breeze.

'Is he always like that before breakfast,' I asked with forbearance, reflecting on his early morning energy, not looking for an answer, being at ease with life, just then contemplating when we might tuck into our two of the four miniature bottles of Argentine whisky we had found among Flores' rations. The other two had gone to the signallers.

'There's another enemy patrol coming our way,' growled Geordie in explanation, taking a call on the VHF set.

'He's got it covered.'

Broad daylight this time. We should have this one dead to rights. I decided to observe.

There were five of them, in all probability another Special Forces patrol, wandering along right out in the open and making no attempt at using the ground to mask their progress. They looked rather sorry, harmless. In fact they constituted a real threat, coming up on the rear of the gun line. Perhaps worse, they had strayed close to the helicopters' low-flying route into and out of the Mount Kent LZ. John must nail them quickly, before the helicopters returned.

Just as the enemy neared the Troop's rapidly set ambush, the patrol began to drift off to the south. The Troop let rip, two GPMGs among them, an overwhelming weight of fire, a potent mix of single aimed shots from the rifles and short bursts of carefully directed automatic fire from the guns. The enemy dived behind a large rock, all of them scrambling, with not enough room, the odd leg appearing then disappearing, only to reappear then disappear. They were a fair distance from us, not far short of the range that tracer burns out. Rounds hammered into the rock and ground all about. Tracer ricocheted skywards or swirled round the heather. It must have been hellish down there.

Before long a rifle butt emerged, waved back and forth from behind the rock, then a shred of white cloth. John stopped immediately. Good. Then he and his troop jumped to their feet to dash forward. Not quite so good. Not the best way to take a surrender, if that was what they had in mind. What *did* they have in mind? I picked myself up and ran to catch them. I need not have worried. By the time I arrived at the rock the patrol medics were already squabbling good naturedly among themselves over how best to administer the first aid, three of the enemy having relatively minor injuries to their limbs. I left them to it, advising John to drop his prisoners off at SHQ, to join Flores for evacuation to the rear.

That had been the fourth enemy patrol in about 48 hours, each stopped in its tracks with losses inflicted. We could account for two dead and six captured of whom three were wounded. That left a further eighteen others scattered or lying somewhere dead or injured. If this was an enemy patrol programme with the purpose of contesting our approaches to his main defences we had surely rotted it up, if not utterly defeated it in this area.[8]

However, we noted that the gunners had taken the odd, fairly accurate salvo of counter-battery fire, heavy 155mm stuff, the shells airbursting over the crest lying a few hundred metres to the front of the gun-line. This suggested that the enemy might be directing their fire employing artillery-detecting radar from behind their forwardmost positions or an OP out front, perhaps both. The troops were instructed to conduct clearance patrols and otherwise keep the surrounding countryside under constant observation. We found nothing, no OP, no more remnants from previous contacts nor any other enemy patrols.

After all the distractions, I eventually made it up onto Mount Kent to find that 16 Troop and 42 had a grandstand view right into Stanley. The enemy positions were laid out before us. In time, it should be possible to pinpoint very nearly each and every individual position. It truly was the Falklands' very own Monte Cassino. The guns didn't have much ammunition to spare, but 16 Troop had had a go at targets that presented themselves. I could see another, about three or four kilometres distant, a long line of troops standing patiently in the open, queuing for a meal most likely. What could be more dispiriting than coming under fire while lining up for one's grub? A fair number of things, but it seemed a worthwhile target: a concentration of enemy out in the open. We asked for the guns and promptly got a 'tube' for ranging purposes. The round passed

[8] The Argentinians deployed a patrol screen in front of Stanley to destroy our reconnaissance forces and otherwise disrupt the advance from San Carlos. Of the 170 men available for the mission, fifty were deployed of whom thirty-two were killed, wounded or otherwise lost, the Squadron accounting for a significant proportion.

overhead. We saw no fall of shot. The enemy continued to queue. Another round. All of us watched intently this time. Nothing.

'That's the problem,' said someone from behind. 'It's a small shell and, they splat into the peat. Not a lot to see.'

'Smoke?'

'Not much apparently, I think they are holding it back.'

Not wishing to waste ammunition, and thinking that this sort of thing was probably best left to the battle group, we stood the guns down, thanking them. The Argentinians got on with their meal, we with our observation and easy-going chatter.

Not long after, over to our left, a Harrier shot into view, launching through the gap between Mount Estancia and Mount Vernet. All hell broke out, the noise carrying across to us, a huge, angry weight of small-arms fire. No harm done. He had rocketed through, presumably taking the enemy by surprise. Unbelievably, the plane re-emerged a few moments later, from behind some far hills, to line up for a second run on exactly the same bearing. What for? What target could be so important as to justify breaking 'Fighter Ground-Attack Rules 1 and 2' concurrently: never go round twice, and never, never, ever on the same track. Madness. Sure enough, he was hit. I had witnessed exactly this kind of thing before, a Strike Master in Dhofar hit when going round a second time on an identical attack profile. The Harrier rocked, pulled hard, clawed for height, wobbling, before disappearing out towards the sea and its 'mother'.

If that was bad, what unfolded next was almost too difficult to watch: a slow unfolding horror show. A Sea King with an under-slung load, probably ammunition for the guns, clattered overhead then down the slope to our front. It flew steadily out to the enemy at no great speed, in a perfectly straight line, about sixty feet above the ground. One could sense the uncertainty in the cab as they worked to match terrain to map, the loadmaster in the back scanning for a landing-zone and ground party. They had to know that we were no further forward than Mount Kent, surely, only enemy beyond. How could they fly right over the biggest mountain in the area and fail to recognise it? And how could they miss Stanley coming up on the nose, a mere nine miles distant, glimmering in the sunlight? And there were the enemy troops, out in the open, about a mile or two ahead, still queuing patiently for their lunch, or was it breakfast? On they flew. At any moment the enemy must notice. Perhaps they had, but scoff had trumped war. Otherwise, and if the Harrier episode was anything to go by, it would be over quickly. We all gazed in horror, mesmerised, silently imploring the crew to turn back.

A shade north of Two Sisters the penny dropped. Slowly, painfully slowly, the pilot made a gentle, flat turn so as to keep his load from oscillating. Then, with every bit as much care as he had gone in he flew nonchalantly back out, maintaining his deliberate, unhurried pace. Most men would have ditched the load and made a dash for it; not these ones. Their navigation may have been suspect. They may simply have been badly briefed. But these were steady, dedicated Royal Navy airmen on a mission to deliver a load. And they were going to do exactly that, deliver all of it, in one piece.

We silently urged them on. I wanted to avert my eyes, but gazed on helplessly. What was the enemy waiting for? They must have seen them. Perhaps the Argentinians couldn't find it in themselves to strike down a crew of such serene, unthreatening calm; or possibly they couldn't believe it to be one of ours that far forward. Then there he was, almost home, the helicopter climbing little by little back up the steep eastern slopes of Mount Kent. At last, it passed overhead at no more than a fast walking-pace. We waved at them, as much in relief as to welcome them back, our affection for the Navy rising another notch. They flew by, the loadmaster in the door clearly untroubled, casually raising a thumb in salute.

Late afternoon, over at Estancia House, three or four miles distant, we saw hundreds of troops, trailing in from the direction of Teal Inlet, many milling around the settlement and its buildings, others fanning out, yet more moving deliberately on towards Stanley. We alerted the guns, enemy in the open, lots of them. But something gave us pause.

These troops seemed different, their movement slow, albeit steady, as if burdened by the weight of equipment. And darker than the enemy we had seen to date, whose drab olive uniforms had blended well into the grassland. These troops stood out more, almost black against the dun tones of their surroundings. And was that the odd splash of red? Realisation burst upon us. Maroon! Paras! They must be ours. It turned out to be 3 PARA, walking in from San Carlos, a distance of about fifty miles. We stood down the guns, feeling rather sheepish, another artillery close shave! I was starting to distrust myself with guns.

We had not known of 3 PARA's move, let alone anticipated time of arrival, which was probably my error. We had established liaison with 42, but obviously not close enough. Clearly, things couldn't continue as they were, with us acting independently in and among 3 Commando Brigade's battle-space. If we were to avoid accidents we should come under the Brigade's tactical control, be coordinated into the battle just as any other brigade asset. I had no doctrinal hang-ups with that as such, providing the tasking justified it. And there was the rub. I couldn't see what we might do that one of the Brigade's own couldn't do just as well, if not better given that we were not practised at the brigade level. Of course, it would be one thing to join the Brigade, quite another to get back out again should we want or need to for higher level work. The Brigade would grow accustomed to having us, and correspondingly reluctant to release us. I had come across this before in another operational theatre. Thus, rather than subordinate to the Brigade, it seemed preferable to get out of the way. We had done all that could be reasonably expected of us in the Mount Kent area. I liked to think that we had made a signal contribution, having helped get the ground campaign underway and conventional forces up onto vital ground, to the right place on the map for what must surely be the approaching climax. We should move on and attempt to find employment of comparable impact, preferably in depth and in our own battle space. RHQ agreed. We left soon after.

15. To the West

We arrived in San Carlos to find *Intrepid* had returned to sea, 5 Brigade all over the place, accommodation tight. Yet, against what must have been near insurmountable odds Graham had secured us space on *Fearless*, moving his tons of equipment and materiel yet again. It would have to do for the time being, until we could find a place better suited to our needs: less crowded, less likely to sail off, less liable to get sunk. Somewhere ashore would have been good, but our base communications needed power. We had no suitable generator. And any space in and among the settlements had long since been snaffled.

If anything San Carlos looked busier than ever, the Force Maintenance Area a scene of unceasing industry, small boats and helicopters coming and going, all intent on pumping supplies forwards to the troops up at Stanley. We were at the very beating heart of our enterprise, the cross-over point where the 8,000-mile supply line fed into the battles and engagements and with that the nation's hopes and expectations. Were this place to fall the land campaign should fail, certainly as currently crafted. But the tireless energy of San Carlos, its determined rhythm, increased our confidence. We knew that the battalions could do it. We had seen for ourselves their resolve and quiet, professional conviction. Here was evidence that they would get the stuff necessary with which to do it. Who could ever doubt the determining power of logistics?

Shortly after we embarked, an air raid was launched. We kept out of the way, hoping for the best, *Fearless* being an obvious and prized target. A couple of A4s shot through, no harm done to either side. HQ 3 Commando Brigade had disembarked some time previously, to set up on the beach, as much for safety as for reasons of space. We really should try to do likewise. Mike Rose drew our attention to *Sir Lancelot*, an unloaded logistic ship that had been bombed, now awaiting repairs. She sat at the end of the bay. He reckoned that she must be an unlikely target for enemy air, having been obviously hit before. Besides, she was well tucked away behind a shallow hill and to the side of the enemy's customary bombing run, notably difficult to get at. Why not take a look?

I went across myself, taking a small recce party that included Geordie, to check that the ship could support our communications. As we came aboard, making our way down a stairwell, the ship went to 'Air Raid Warning Red', the alert piped over the address system in drawled, lugubrious, faintly bored sounding tones. To inject an air of calm we assumed. Instantly, pandemonium broke out, this serving to confirm our assumption. As if from nowhere, a surprisingly large number of animated Chinese men dashed into view, the ship's laundrymen.[1] One of them tried to push past us, to get top-side, presumably to his action station. Improbably, he wore a Second World War vintage steel helmet and round horn-rimmed glasses—truly!

He implored me to get out of the way, bouncing frantically from one foot to the other, this way then that, he tried with increasing desperation to get past me, up the narrow steps. I tried with equal vigour to do as he implored, urgently trying to make myself scarce, moving from side to side in unintended, synchronised opposition.

From above came a dull *pom, pom, pom*, the ship gently reverberating as she fired her Second World War vintage Bofors gun at some Argentinian. My involuntary dance companion redoubled his efforts to squeeze through, shooting past. I turned to Geordie, pressing hard against the bulkhead to remain out of the way as others dashed past.

'I like this place. What you think?' I asked with the Bofors gun very much in mind. What better action station, even if simply to serve as an additional look-out?

---

[1] It was the custom at the time to engage men from Hong Kong to serve on HM ships and RFAs as laundrymen. They had been offered the opportunity to leave the ships at Gibraltar or Ascension. Almost all of them elected to remain with their ships.

'It'll do,' he growled, in that Geordie way of his. But I could tell that he too was already much taken with *Lancelot*.

The Captain and his First Lieutenant bade us welcome. The ship became our home for the rest of the war. She had bags of room, plenty of food, a flight-deck and a huge hole marking the passage of the un-exploding bomb that had shot through her. She had power and could move, but had been declared un-seaworthy. We were soon settled in, having the ship more or less to ourselves. The troops spent time ashore or otherwise training and making preparations while the Squadron's leadership turned its collective mind to 'what next?'

Things had been moving steadily against the Argentinians for a while. The Task Force put the enemy's air-losses at about eighty aircraft, and understood the remaining air-frames to be experiencing severe maintenance problems, including damage to engines through salt spray ingestion.[2] Many of their best pilots had been lost, this also taking the edge off their attacks. Their navy had been driven from the sea, the army attracting mounting criticism for its passive performance to date. The air force felt particularly sore, seeing that their heroic efforts had not been reciprocated, perhaps even squandered. Not healthy at the best of times, Argentine inter-service cooperation was beginning to break down.

At the senior levels any optimism ebbed away; few enemy commanders had faith anymore in being able to maintain an effective resistance. Instead, thoughts turned from a successful defence of the Falklands to securing a passable if not wholly respectable bargaining position. This encouraged some to consider reinforcing West Falkland, possibly by sea, perhaps by parachute. Operationally, this should enable them to

[2] According to reliable Argentine sources, between 1 May and 7 June their aircraft losses stood at 45 aircraft: 2 Mirage III, 11 Mirage V, 16 A4, 1 Canberra bomber, 14 Pucara, and 1 C130. The figures should include the Skyvan and 4 Beechcraft Mentor reconnaissance aircraft destroyed at Pebble Island, the Squadron therefore accounting for a significant percentage of Argentina's in-theatre tactical aircraft losses at that time.

threaten our rear, and it could be expected to improve Argentina's political prospects in the event of a negotiated settlement.

Before the landings they had employed parachute re-supply as part of an air-bridge between Argentina and the Islands, making drops at Port Howard and Goose Green. Intelligence assessed that up to five further attempts had been made since the landings, mainly in the West, all failing probably due to weather rather than our air-defences. With a mere half dozen C130s and ten Fokker Friendships though, the enemy could achieve only so much using this insertion method; that is to say, not a lot.

However, Argentinian press reports began talking of a force of 1,500 fully-equipped men taking up position in West Falkland in order to open up a second front, to catch us in some pincer movement. Fanciful perhaps, but a strengthened garrison in the West might well improve the enemy's strategic posture. The prospect had to be taken seriously. At the very least it could enhance their ability to mount raids into our rear, including San Carlos, standing to cause considerable disruption and hurt. The unwelcome possibility of a re-invigorated enemy in unhindered possession of West Falkland had seized the attention of the Commander-in-Chief in Northwood.

The issue had caught our attention too, the sort of thing we should be on the look out for. Emotionally, we would have preferred to contribute more directly to the offensive culminating in front of Stanley. But other-wise, with a significant threat possibly emerging in depth to our rear we should probably do something to help fend it off, leaving our conventional forces free to get on, clear of all and any distraction behind them. RHQ agreed and encouraged us to do just that: switch to what looked a lot like strategic/operational-level defence.

We gathered the Squadron command group, Danny, Geordie and Graham, to do a quick estimate of the situation. We didn't have much to go on. G Squadron had recovered their patrols from the West the week previously, well before the enemy's thinking had become appar-ent, and as the Task Force focused almost wholly on Stanley. After more than a month in the field on continuous hard routine, in the wet and cold, without benefit of the modern, weather-proof clothing that had only recently come down from Hereford, it had made much sense to bring in patrols from wherever it seemed possible; those up and around Stanley stayed put to the very end. Accordingly short of 'eyes on' intelligence, as a matter of urgency we should re-insert patrols to cover the enemy's main locations of Port Howard and Fox Bay.

Aside from re-establishing the intelligence effort, we would need to hold elements of the Squadron at readiness to exploit any arising opportunities. However, responsiveness was going to be a problem. All helicopters were busy feeding troops, materiel and other necessities up to the front; we could find ourselves on the hind tit. Unless the target clearly carried campaign-level significance we might struggle to get more than the odd frame. Perhaps we should adopt a more deliberate, programmed approach, effectively booking helicopters in advance for a pre-determined attack or two. A series of raids would show the enemy that they had not been forgotten, that we had influence over their affairs, that reinforcement of the West was hazardous, if not unviable. Clearly, if 'int' came up with anything specific, we should still act opportunistically. But, whatever method we adopted, one way or another the West must be contested. It had to feel as dangerous to the enemy as any other part of the Islands.

Later, we gathered the Squadron's wider leadership to run over things once more, to check that our initial assessment made sense, that nothing had been overlooked. These meetings could become time-consuming affairs, but mostly they achieved a thorough examination of any situation, often throwing up imaginative and unexpected ideas. People got to have a say. This helped to achieve 'buy-in' to the eventually adopted plan. On this occasion we talked our way back round to where we started, confirming a course of action recorded in our 'war diary' as:

Deny enemy respite & prevent reinforcement.

the intention being to keep the enemy in the West as they were: out of things.

I went over the allocation of 'troops to tasks' with Danny. As Ted's Boat Troop had done the recces for South Georgia and Pebble Island, it was probably time to give others a crack. Besides, we should probably try to hold them back against the possibility of boat work emerging from the recce/int effort. Similarly as Air Troop had the Stinger they should be kept ready to respond to contact intelligence concerning enemy transport aircraft. That left the re-constituted Mountain Troop and Mobility Troop with which to lead off.

Responsibility for reconnoitring Port Howard and Fox Bay fell to John Hamilton's troop. There were already sizeable Argentinian garrisons at both locations making them the most likely enemy positions for reinforcement, natural targets then for us. John was briefed that 'stand-off' attack must be our preferred option, employing the ship's guns or airstrike. But as ever, more covert options at up to squadron strength would be considered for any high pay-off targets that might benefit from such intimate treatment. In short, his were offensive action, trigger ops, not surveillance patrols. We were looking for things to hit and a recommended method of attack. He understood perfectly, electing to observe Port Howard himself, Billy Ratcliffe, his troop staff sergeant, taking Fox Bay.

The Navy strongly suspected the presence of an enemy OP in the vicinity of Mount Rosalie reporting ship movements; a target of operational significance. We should destroy the patrol or at least drive it back into Port Howard. Either would do, offering a most useful early win. The task fell to Pete Sutherby's Mobility Troop. Sensibly, they decided to insert a recce before committing to any particular method of attack.

Shortly after our initial planning-session, intelligence identified the Rat Castle Shanty area as a likely drop zone for parachute delivered reinforcements. It didn't seem altogether a very likely location, but 'intelligence' was reasonably confident. We felt obliged to cover it. Air Troop took the task. They were to put in an OP to keep the area under observation, deploying with Stingers to take advantage of any fleeting target; otherwise, we would attempt to reinforce them should the intelligence firm up in any way.

The various patrols were soon successfully inserted, the remainder of the Squadron prepared to respond. A day or two later we discovered that the enemy were going down the Warrah Road by vehicle, driving from Port Howard towards Fox Bay. Either that or we guessed officers were popping out from time to time for some out of season fishing on the Warrah river, famous for its sea trout. Boat Troop was tasked to destroy the officers' fishing trip, if that was what it was, at a point distant from the settlement.

If we could do for the Mount Rosalie OP and hit the anglers, the Argentinians at Port Howard in particular should start to feel rather beleaguered. Add some form of attack onto one or other of the settlements, the enemy's main locations, or a success with the Stinger, and it could be job done, the enemy feeling well and truly hemmed in, reluctant to venture into the surrounding hinterland.

With four possibilities underway and most of the remaining troops ashore training during daylight hours, there followed a relatively tranquil spell for SHQ, the serenity disturbed briefly on most days as the Chinese and other crew dashed off to their action-stations on 'Air Raid Warning Red'. The doleful pipes once memorably advising:

'Whoever it was who tied up alongside, can now find his tender 600 feet astern.'

Lancelot, bearing her injuries well, was a ship at ease with her lot; literally in the front line, if slightly to one side. While awaiting repairs she fought on as best she could with her Bofors gun claiming a number of hits. Her gunners simply laid the weapon as before, and the many times before that, firing off a clip of ammunition ahead of the poor Argentinian airmen who, having only the one entry-point at that end of the bay, must adopt a similar run-in on each occasion.

It was at this time that the CO, Mike Rose, initiated a stratagem of campaign-level impact. He always had many bright ideas, so many in fact that they could feel exhausting to those on the receiving end. The trick for dealing with them was two-pronged, and wholly necessary to apply if one wanted to keep work-load to manageable levels. First, try to minimise face-to-face exposure, for his thoughts were liable to come tumbling out once in conversation; and second, adopt only the ideas one liked, or those that got a second mention, for he would move rapidly on, forgetting most of them in his surging drive through life. This one was a 'repeater'.

He had set up his headquarters alongside 3 Commando Brigade in one of the settlement buildings in San Carlos, sharing accommodation with the owners. Mike, the household and one or two of his small staff were gathered round the kitchen table enjoying a brew, his brain moving restlessly, making connections.

Our current circumstances put him in mind of a CT hostage/barricade situation, albeit on a far greater scale: an Argentine army hemmed into Stanley holding our people against their will. Even so, its fundamentals were not that dissimilar from the Princess Gate siege. There would be principles common to both situations. For instance, under such conditions it was highly desirable to establish communication in an attempt to achieve a negotiated settlement in preference to the always unpredictable and dangerous use of force. The Metropolitan police had achieved such a link at Princess Gate, contributing materially to the eventual success.

Of course there was more to it than simply opening a communications link. It required the skilful execution of a well-crafted negotiating strategy. Mike had been working on this with a Costa Rican born Royal Marine, Captain Rob Bell. Bell spoke fluent and idiomatic Latin American Spanish and had helped with the surrender at Darwin/Goose Green. The two of them consulted a senior Argentine officer, a prisoner-of-war aboard *Fearless*. He advised them on suitable themes, and pitfalls to be avoided, suggesting that they start up a conversation as early as possible. They must work out their own message specifics. He wouldn't help with those, saying that their approach would require careful timing. Simply put, the worse the enemy's prospects, the more susceptible he should become to a sympathetic approach. This was likely to occur as the enemy's defences in front of Stanley started to collapse, when any prospect of relief had faded. Rose and Bell knew enough to appeal to the Argentinian's decency and humanity, and to help them maintain some sense of dignity. They had briefed CLFFI. Moore was content, allowing the two of them to run with the matter, essentially leaving them to develop our approach to the enemy's surrender in the Falklands. But there remained the issue of a communications link.

Somehow, apparently, the conversation round the table had turned to medical matters. The Falkland Islanders mentioned their system of 'doctor's rounds', a daily facility conducted over radio when the GP in the hospital in Stanley would hold a surgery. It would happen most mornings. Ailing people out in the Camp could send in their symptoms over a radio link. The doctor at the other end instructed treatment, often involving the prescription of drugs from a pack provided by the hospital for retention by the settlements' managers. Privacy, when needed, should be achieved by doctor and patient switching to another channel reserved for more private use; of course, most people moved with the switch to keep abreast, particularly when it involved cases of interest. Fortunately San Carlos had a telephone connection thereby getting round the issue of medical confidentiality. It seemed the service was still up and running, the Argentine occupation forces having left it open for humanitarian reasons.

Mike sparked immediately.[3] Could this be the link they were looking for? Was this the means? His brain raced at the prospects; a direct line to the enemy commander himself perhaps. Could they bring psychological pressure to bear? Might they moderate the conflict? They should try to develop mutual respect, possibly more? That must help when it came to discussing the principles and modalities of surrender, surely?

He thought he should give it a go, make a call there and then. The hospital came up almost immediately. Mike responded that he had

[3] The idea of operational level negotiation was probably first seeded during a conversation between Mike Rose and Chris Keeble, acting CO 2 PARA, the day after the battle of Darwin/Goose Green. The battle was closed by talks conducted through a captured Argentinian officer aided by Captain Rob Bell RM and the Battalion's padre, David Cooper.

rarely felt better before explaining who he was and that he should like to speak with an Argentinian officer. The nurse at the other end, an Islander, offered that it shouldn't be difficult to find one, getting him onto the line another matter. Give her time to find someone suitable.

Mike dashed off to find Rob Bell. They made their first contact on 5 June, not long after we all returned from Mount Kent, shortly after the morning brew. They got through to a Captain Barry Melbourne Hussey of the Argentine Navy, the chief administrative officer on Menendez's staff. He explained that he had no authority to discuss surrender; but they all agreed that it made sense to open a link between the two sides and their respective headquarters. He would listen in each day at 1300 local. Bell assured Hussey that the line at our end would be manned twenty-four hours a day.

From the outset, the tenor was civilised and wholly reasonable. Perhaps the gracious tone helped keep the conflict within bounds, eventually getting us through the notably precarious closing hours of the conflict with decency. At one point the importance of protecting the civilian population had been raised. The enemy was quick to assure Mike that they understood their responsibilities and that all precautions were being taken. It proved to be a brilliant initiative, a signal contribution, the product of well-informed opportunism. It underscored the value of having the courage to push responsibility down through an organisation, of encouraging subordinates to pick up, if not actually seek out responsibility and think for themselves.

Aboard *Lancelot*, unaware of the CO's work on the surrender strategy, we were discovering that the ship had pretty well everything that we could reasonably wish for. There was plenty of well-prepared food. Most people had a bed, or plenty of deck-space upon which to set up a basha. At first, communication had been a challenge, but Geordie soon had us fully up and running, connected back to the UK, never once losing communication with the patrols ashore. He even managed a direct link to RHQ out in the San Carlos settlement. I wasn't much impressed by that though, preferring a workable connection to higher headquarters, nothing too cosy. We even found a padre who put on a service or two, to address our spiritual needs. These were always well attended, even by the most hard-bitten of our number. Congregating like that, sharing a softer, more spiritual moment away from the war, strengthened one, not in any jingoistic way, but quietly. Among all the excitements and harshness, it helped to be reminded of our shared humanity.

Geordie first alerted us to trouble when the signallers picked up our Port Howard recce's intra-patrol VHF communications. It was early morning. One of the call signs was attempting to alert another to the presence of a strong enemy force about to come down on them. It was stomach-wrenching. On receiving the news I felt physically sick. It was a nightmare coming true: compromise deep behind enemy lines. Throughout the war I had been dreading this moment, knowing that it must come. I instinctively and stupidly glanced at my watch, to calculate the time remaining until last light. There were hours to go before the cover of darkness.

I prayed that the patrol would escape detection. This was unlikely. Apparently the call-sign had sounded desperate, almost imploring a response from the other end; the enemy had to be very close for they were transmitting in whispers. I knew that John, if discovered, would probably attempt to fight his way out. It would be the in-built, instinctive reaction, his holding to the principle that SAS positions were hives, not nests. The odds must be heavily stacked against success. A four-man patrol was designed for escaping detection and evading, rather than taking on and defeating a numerically superior enemy. The prospects were grim. On the face of it, there appeared little or nothing to do. But we couldn't just sit it out. Perhaps we could get there in time to help turn the tables. Or, maybe we could intercept the enemy on their way back into base, defeat them, release any captives. It might be simply a matter of going to the patrol's Emergency RV, to recover any escapees. It was all rather despairing, abject stuff. But we couldn't just sit on our hands. We alerted our Quick Reaction Force (QRF).

However, getting our hands on a helicopter to carry us across Falkland Sound into the objective area proved difficult. Although anticipated, under the circumstances this came as a bewildering shock. John's patrol faced what we feared most. We couldn't understand how others couldn't see or share our dismay. Perhaps they saw only occupational hazard to be accepted as part of one's lot. This was war, and given its scale what of a four-man patrol? Maybe somewhat emotionally, I believed we deserved better; the objective reality of the situation brought me up hard.

John Hamilton and his team had taken two days to get into a position of observation, two men forward looking onto the objective area, the second pair a few hundred metres or so to the rear. The locations were sited to enable one to support the other with fire if need be. Keen to get things going, John went forward with Roy Fonseka that first morning on target. He hoped to find something of consequence, a communications node or a headquarters would be good.

It was wintry cold, bitter, a thin dusting of snow on the rocks and grass. A biting, damp wind cut to the marrow. Roy shivered as he bit down on his rock-like chocolate bar; a poor breakfast, but such is hard routine. The open grassland looked peaceful enough. Dark, rocky outcrops and craggy hilltops lifted from the grass and heather, adding to a sense of sparse severity. Distant views of steel grey sea offered little relief. Sheep-farming country they called it, not that one saw many sheep, for they were scattered across a vast area. Port Howard was one of the larger settlements on the West, more ranch than farm, the livestock near-wild, bolting at the barest glimpse of man.

Roy watched the snow settle on his clothes, melting here and there. He brushed it off. He felt uneasy. Something was not right. His sixth sense had triggered. Then he got it, his gut lurching at the comprehension. There, at his feet, lodged between two rocks lay a sliver of paper, a sweet-wrapper. Someone had been there before. And if they had been once, they might return. The patrol must get away from this place; but it was only just after first light. They would have to get through the rest of the day, wait until dark before making their move. Eight or more long, anxious hours stretched ahead. He looked across to where John sat gazing out towards the settlement. He tried to attract his attention, to tell him what he had discovered. He gently tossed a bit of grit. John glanced back, acknowledged, then signalled that he was going to relieve himself. Seconds later he flew back round the corner,

'Bloody hell, Fonz, we're surrounded!'

Almost in the same instant Roy heard the grenade's metallic clatter as it bounced off the rocks, dropping into their position. No time to get up and run. They both dived to the ground, the noise shattering. It made their ears ring, otherwise, incredibly, not a scratch.

'About ten of them,' John replied to Roy's shouted question: bad, but not hopeless.

The two of them were well-armed, both with rapid-firing assault rifles, ideal for a close-quarter fight, and plenty of ammunition. They were in a strong position, bullet proof, with reasonable fields of fire. Furthermore, the position to the rear should be able to bring down fire, putting the enemy in an awkward situation. It might even be possible to turn the tables on them, to defeat the enemy patrol, let alone escape. Roy couldn't understand why cross-fire hadn't come down already, nor for that matter how the enemy had been able to come in on them from behind without warning. He picked up the radio, to make contact and explain their intention to take on the enemy. Nothing but squelch. There was part of the answer: 'comms failure'. Why did communications always fail at critical moments? No point in wasting time. They had to act and fast.

Unfortunately, the Argentinians had indeed come in from the direction of the rear position, right through it. As dawn broke the LUP discovered the enemy, lots of them, feet away. The two patrol members were right in and among the opposition, with little or no prospect of opening up on the radio without being heard. They would first have to crawl out to one side, to get out of earshot, before warning John and Roy. It took an age during which time, unknown to them, a number of the enemy had moved further down the hill in the direction of the OP. The two eventually found a place from where they might try to transmit, still with Argentinians close by. But they had lost line of sight to the OP, and with it communications. With increasing desperation, they attempted to raise John and Roy. Failing to make contact, they made to move to a position from where they might give supporting fire if needed. It was then that they heard the grenade followed almost immediately by small arms fire. Events had accelerated beyond any prospect of their being able to influence them.

After the grenade, down in the forward position John and Roy had no time for deliberation. They responded instinctively. They would fight their way out. No point in moving away from the enemy. That would funnel them towards the sea, eventually have them pinned to the shoreline. They must go back up the hill, into and through the enemy, to reach the land beyond, perhaps pick up the LUP party on their way through. Roy broke cover, to take up the first bound. John gave covering fire. Turn about, one firing aimed shots, the other dashing, they hoped to rock the enemy back with the sheer violence and audacity of their onslaught. Incredibly, Roy thrilled to the challenge, senses racing, heart pounding. On hearing John's fire from behind he had sprinted into the open, launching a grenade from his M203. It sailed harmlessly over the heads of the enemy to his front. A member of the Argentinian patrol later reported that, 'A very bold, aggressive dark man came out with guns blazing.'

For an instant, it seemed to work. The closest enemy recoiled, taken aback by the speed and ferocity of the counter attack, its intensity and volume of fire. The Argentinians threw themselves into cover. For fleeting seconds escape beckoned. But, the enemy were too numerous; they quickly overcame their surprise. They gathered themselves, their fire increasing in volume and accuracy, having never fully stopped. The end came quickly, with a terrible inevitability.

It would be difficult to say who got hit first. By then both Roy and John were skirmishing out in the open, taking the enemy head on. It came like a sledge-hammer blow for Roy, grazing his arm, rifle sent flying. He dropped to the ground, jacket riddled with holes, otherwise unscathed. He reached about for his weapon. John had also stopped firing, mortally wounded in the back. Roy tried one last throw of the dice. He shouted out an order instructing the enemy to cease. Incredibly they did, coming forward cautiously, weapons levelled to take him captive. They immediately administered first aid to John but were unable to save his life. The contact had lasted no time at all.

Back in San Carlos we eventually got the helicopters. Having failed to get them ourselves, we had turned to RHQ for help. Mike Rose had gone straight to the top, to COMAW, Commodore Clapp. There had followed a heated exchange as COMAW held to the force level agreement on the use of our insufficient number of helicopters: getting the battle groups and their munitions forward. It was a moment of high drama and some emotion. Clapp recognised the urgency together with the morale implications of our request for the use of two helicopters. He had forces prone to capture himself, his own pilots. But he stuck courageously and determinedly to the agreed priorities until Brigadier Waters, the Land Forces' Deputy intervened. Waters could see both sides clearly, offering that the logistic flow might withstand the loss of a couple of frames for a short period. He indicated that Land Forces had no objection. The QRF might be flown, an exception made this once.

With that assurance, and with good grace, Commodore Clapp released two Sea Kings from the logistic out load, accepting that it had been a highly charged moment, one of those instances when things can get said that preferably shouldn't be said, when rationality and logic can get trumped as they sometimes shall, but perhaps shouldn't, by considerations not of the head, but of the heart.

We were quickly on our way. As we crossed the Sound in broad daylight with the enemy coast coming up on the nose, I noticed the pilots shrinking into their seats. They weren't enjoying it. I couldn't see the problem. One would have to be seriously unlucky to run into any enemy fighter aircraft out here hunting for helicopters. I suppose there was a chance we might come across an enemy fighter bomber making good its escape from San Carlos. Odds must be against. And one would have to be right out of luck to run into ground forces, beyond the patrol we had already located, that we were hoping to meet and take on in any event.

As the helicopters departed the drop-off point and we shook out into formation for what could amount to an advance to contact, I noticed that I was still wearing my jungle boots, footwear I reserved for the warm comfort of the ships. Big mistake. We had left in a rush. This was going to be uncomfortable.

Aside from my freezing cold feet, the deployment proved fairly unremarkable. We were far too late to intervene. Giving up all thoughts of intercepting the enemy or turning the situation to our advantage, we instead made our way to the patrol's Emergency RV in the hope of picking up the two survivors. Moving across the open grassland, I caught sight of movement at the very edge of my peripheral vision, off to the right. Turning, I saw two Sea Harriers feet above the ground, racing in towards us. Too late, brace, take it on the chin. They flashed past having either recognised us as friendlies or having been briefed on our presence or simply too busy, on their way to something else. It was a salutary experience. The battle space was filling with a large number of diverse force elements butting up against one another. It demanded careful coordination. With all the distraction of the helicopters, I had not personally attended to this aspect of the rescue operation, relying instead on others to manage our introduction onto the ground beyond the amphibious operating area. I needed to be more careful in future.

We pressed on to find our two missing on the wrong side of a stretch of water. They swam across, relieved to be recovered to comparative safety, but then bitterly cold. After reviewing the situation, we became convinced that there was nothing more to do other than return to base.

On our way back, 18 Troop brought in an enemy they had found holed up in Burro Shanty, a pitiful specimen. He had been found with no weapon, but pots and pans, filthy sleeping bags and other detritus lying around the shack, evidence of occupation by up to six others. We couldn't work out how he fitted in. Perhaps the enemy used the shanty as a patrol base and he was the cook, either that or he was a deserter. We didn't have time to investigate.

Surrounded by inquisitive, glaring, face-blackened cutthroats talking in tongues, demons from what must have felt like his worst nightmares, he shook uncontrollably, eyes rolling. I offered him one of my roll-ups. He immediately pissed his pants and defecated. I knew my cigarettes were not well rolled, but this was a bit rum. After all, I made them out of liquorice paper and Old Holborn, a sweet, mellow tobacco. I didn't have very many and I had simply been trying to cheer him up.

'Boss, he probably thinks it's to be his last one,' advised someone better attuned than me, handing the poor fellow a more reassuring cube of chocolate instead. Hernando was taken back to *Fearless* to be cleaned up. Just in case he was a deserter, we persuaded the ship to take him on as a spare hand for a spell, to keep him separate from other prisoners. As and when the PW population started to grow again perhaps they could slip him in with a better chance of his going unnoticed. This may have contravened a Geneva protocol, but thereafter, for a while he could be found washing dishes in the galley, perfectly content with a broad grin on his face most of the time, clean, well-fed and in appreciative company.

In Port Howard, Roy had been found in possession of one or two items of Argentinian military kit, lifted from the skirmishes on Mount Kent. It didn't go down well with some of his captors. His interrogator, an intelligence officer with indifferent English, began foaming at the mouth in indignation, putting a pistol to Roy's head. At exactly the right moment the Royal Navy intervened. A ship had sailed across from San Carlos that evening to put a few rounds down, across the enemy's 'bows'.

As the shells burst, everyone scattered. Roy was thrown back into a dank hole below the sheep-shearing shed where he remained for much of his captivity, coming out for a bit more interrogation and an occasional break and exercise. The Navy mounted several gunnery raids over the coming nights to maintain pressure on the enemy's West Falkland garrisons, those on Port Howard helping to keep Roy's spirits up, perhaps his captors straight.

On the whole, the mouth foaming incident aside, the enemy behaved properly, displaying genuine admiration for Roy and John. They recognised their courage, burying John with military honours in the Port Howard cemetery. Upon the cessation of hostilities they congratulated Roy on his resolute behaviour and exemplary conduct after capture. Emerging from his hole for the last time, his captors had gathered to applaud him, an officer presenting one of their Special Forces' berets as a token of their esteem.

After Roy's capture the enemy at Port Howard had stopped patrolling up to the Warrah river, whether or not as a result of finding John Hamilton's patrol in such close proximity it would be difficult to say. But it had to be the prudent thing: to cease all non-essential movement beyond their defensive perimeter, treating the surrounding area as contested. After several days we re-called the 17 Troop ambush.

Down at Fox Bay East, Billy Ratcliffe and his patrol were finding it difficult to get into the likely target areas. The settlement and its surroundings had been ringed with minefields. There were lanes through, but well guarded. To compound matters, the gently undulating grassland may have offered good fields of view, but the settlement and main enemy localities lay out of sight down by the shoreline. It was much the same over at Fox Bay West. Billy proposed to keep plugging away at it.

The 18 Troop recce in the area of Mount Rosalie located enemy inserting by helicopter. As the Troop prepared to reinforce to take them on, the enemy helicopter returned to feed in even more troops. It seemed the recce itself may have been detected, the tables turned. If so, having lost surprise and being now up against a numerically stronger force, I decided to withdraw the patrol. The Troop was bitterly disappointed. They had been looking forward to a 'punch up'. But if we were to discourage the enemy from venturing out, we must beat them soundly whenever we met them. After John's loss, we needed a categorically clear, emphatic win. The Troop could go back in when the situation improved.

For a while things seemed more auspicious, with 16 Troop ambushing the enemy's possible parachute entry point. So much so that we reinforced them with members of B Squadron then starting to arrive in theatre, moving the strengthened force to a newly assessed enemy DZ. Once more the intelligence people displayed high confidence. Nothing came of it.

We had been operating in the West for the better part of a week. Over that time the likelihood of the enemy attempting anything of significance on or from West Falkland had receded. It couldn't be discounted altogether. The Task Force must continue to keep an eye on things. But as the campaign reached its climax, it felt increasingly that the Squadron's main, offensive capacities should be switched once more onto Stanley. From the CO down, none of us felt able to leave the big battalions to make the final efforts on their own. It simply didn't feel right to concentrate on what had become an outside possibility in the rear, when there was a racing certainty of need up at 'the front'. This war had to stop. It must be brought to a close as soon as possible, ending in our victory. Everything available should be brought to bear 'to make that so', including us!

16. On to Stanley

The battalion battle groups were being brought to battle in front of Stanley not so much in line with a plan of exhaustively predetermined operational design, rather one that had emerged in response to developments, reflecting among other things opportunism, expediency, some prior thought and even an amount of egoism. It largely reflected conditions within the land forces' higher chain of command.

By the time Major General Moore arrived in theatre after what must have felt like self-imposed exile, on land the dice had been cast by others responding to events, the Squadron included. He could have got to us earlier to impose his will more directly, but had turned down the opportunity to parachute into the TEZ, seeing this as unduly flamboyant and so hostage to media hyperbole. Moreover, with only the one brigade on the ground at that time, the force level and situation didn't appear to require his early presence.

During his absence much had happened. Goose Green had been captured and despite his concerns 42 Commando flown up to Mount Kent with the rest of 3 Commando Brigade following hard on their heels. The moves had been triggered by the C-in-C's wish to get us out of San Carlos and on to take ground, the operation having stalled in part as a result of CLFFI's own instructions to Thompson prior to 3 Commando Brigade's landing. As such, Moore was the architect of his own initial loss of control of the land campaign—in more ways than one.

Neither CLFFI nor his small headquarters ever became that operationally apparent to us, not in any keenly felt way; not in the way that we had felt, and continued to feel, Admiral Woodward's presence. We understood Moore to be a thoroughly decent, evidently sensitive man who wore a strange, nondescript hat so as to avoid offending by any display of preference for his own marine tribe over others. As if we cared. Professional performance was all that mattered to us older lags at least, those who had been in theatre from the start; and anyway, the various tribes appeared to be getting on just fine.

We knew Thompson though. He had the advantage of being 'The Brigade Commander', of the much admired, highly visible 3 Commando Brigade. We had grown accustomed to him being 'The' land commander. He had been there through the seminal period, first planning then conducting the landings. We had learnt to trust him. He had our full confidence. Even the PARAs accepted him. The pause after the landings had been unexpected, odd and most unwelcome. But our censure never attached to him. He got the benefit of any doubt. He came across as knowing his business, and he looked the part, boxer's nose included. If we thought about it at all, we just expected him to be the one, the man who would lead all of us through. Even when it became known that he wasn't the overall land commander, in a way we all continued to see him as the leader; well, certainly those of us that had landed with him that day in San Carlos.

As for Brigadier Wilson of 5 Brigade, I recall looking forward to the arrival of more Army after first hearing of the possibility around the time of the San Carlos pause. There was an admirable, solid, utterly dependable quality to the Marines. We expected an Army formation to start going about things in ways more familiar, possibly with a lot less patience. Arriving with CLFFI, Wilson did indeed bring a certain thrusting drive. Perhaps unsurprisingly, it felt at odds with the singularity that had been building across the Force. Efforts to find a distinctive place for a second brigade seemed to detract from an operation already nicely underway, that might have been reinforced rather than modified to accommodate a newcomer.

The addition of a second brigade introduced the option of an advance out of the beachhead up to Stanley from the south via Fitzroy as well as the one underway in the north through Teal Inlet. Moore favoured the two-axes option, arguing that it could be employed to confuse or distract the enemy who would have to look in two directions at once, making it difficult for our foe to choose where best to concentrate to meet us. Wilson had spent much time assiduously going over such thoughts with Moore while on board QE2, as they made passage to theatre together. Wilson forcibly promoted the two-axes idea. It would give 5 Brigade its own, discrete avenue of advance up the southern route, 3 Commando Brigade already well down the northern axis and in possession of Mount Kent. Two-axes may have looked good as a divisional scheme of manoeuvre when viewed on a map back on QE2; it was less compelling on the ground.

First, it was questionable that the enemy would find the two-axes ploy that confusing since both routes met just outside Stanley, not that far apart, albeit either side of Mount Kent/Challenger, ground marking our forward line of troops, so already covered off by the enemy. And from the area of approximate convergence the lie of the land continued to funnel attackers into what was effectively an amphitheatre of mutually supporting defensive positions. The Argentinians should be able to cope with most two-pronged eventualities without much need, if any, of shuffling troops from one side to another. Their artillery could switch fire to wherever needed without having to move gun-lines and of course their air and aviation could similarly shift effortlessly from side to side, back and forth.

Second, we didn't have sufficient numbers of helicopters and vehicles to get a divisional-sized force down one axis without strain, let alone two. It would be more efficient to ripple men and materiel down one reasonably well-serviced route, to arrive at the other end as formed battle groups, than to trickle them down two inadequately resourced routes to arrive piecemeal before their enemy.

Third, the northern route offered better security than the southern. The carrier group manoeuvred off the north coast, placing the northern axis comfortably within its air defence envelope, optimising the capabilities of both the Sea Harrier CAP and missile ships. Even more significant, now that we were on Mount Kent, the enemy must experience difficulty in maintaining surveillance over the northern approaches; whereas, the southern axis lay under Argentine observation for much of its length. Thus, ships and smaller craft might support sea movement in the north with a degree of safety not achievable in the south.

Moore issued his orders for the advance on 1 June, two days before we came back from Mount Kent. Despite the strong operational and logistical arguments against, it was to be an advance on two axes, 3 Commando Brigade on the northern via Teal Inlet, 5 Infantry Brigade the southern via Fitzroy/Bluff Cove, both coming together in the area of Mount Kent/ Mount Challenger. In some ways, this merely formalised the existing situation. 3 Commando were well down their axis with two battle-groups already in and around Mount Kent; 5 Brigade at the start of theirs with the re-subordinated 2 PARA down at Darwin/ Goose Green.

With 3 Commando Brigade already closing on the Mount Kent area, perhaps the idea had always been to drive in from the north, on the left, 5 Brigade serving to follow through upon their eventual arrival south of Mount challenger. But then 2 PARA did something that stood to bring 5 Brigade more prominently into the frame.

The battle-hardened 2 PARA battle group may have been in need of rest and an amount of re-constitution, but that was not something wholly recognised by the battalion itself. Responding to their near-atavistic urge to get on, they pushed up to Swan Inlet to find the telephone line from there to Fitzroy intact. A quick call confirmed Fitzroy Settlement, twenty miles to the east, clear of enemy. Commandeering the one surviving RAF Chinook helicopter in theatre, the battalion's centre of mass was soon forward, in and around the Fitzroy/Bluff Cove area, pretty well aligning with 3 Commando's lead elements over at Mount Kent. This put Wilson more certainly back in the hunt. If only, and only if, he could get the rest of his formation up to join 2 PARA the two brigades should be in a position of close-operational parity for the finale.

At this juncture the fragility of the southern axis started to become apparent. It was longer than the northern route. The Welsh Guards attempted to join 2 PARA on foot, walking out from San Carlos. After a short distance they turned back, their rate of progress, less than one mile in the hour, making a route-march impractical. Any all-terrain vehicles and most of the helicopters were taken up in servicing the northern route. And so eventually, with deep misgivings and after much urging the Navy agreed to help move 5 Brigade's units forward by ship. This was a highly risky undertaking. The loss of a capital ship such as *Fearless* or *Intrepid* with hundreds of troops on board might shake national resolve, cause a loss of public support. Operationally, such loss stood to reduce our combat-power on land to below levels needed to win. Hence, no major naval units were to be used.

The LSLs had been employed before to move troops and materiel down the northern axis from San Carlos to Teal Inlet. It was hoped to repeat the success in the south. And so it was that on 8 June the Argentinians found the two LSLs *Sir Tristram* and *Sir Galahad*, loaded with troops, anchored in Bluff Cove, in view of their forward OPs. The enemy lost no time in mustering an air strike of ten fast jets, resulting in the death of forty-nine soldiers and sailors, the injury of 115 others, the loss of one LSL and severe damage to the other. It was a terrible blow.

Even as the two Brigades closed in on Stanley, there remained the matter of how to deal with its defenders. Most of us assumed there would be a gradual, careful unpicking of the enemy's positions, some of them perhaps concurrently, the more difficult ones in sequence, the predictability of the process to be relieved by imaginative tactics at the unit level, in particular the skilled application of all-arms cooperation and local surprise.

Wilson put forward an alternative. He advocated a concentrated strike to drive in from his southern axis, to punch a gap in the enemy's outer perimeter in the area of Mount Harriet. Through this the battle groups would pour, his leading, to hit the defended localities beyond. The idea may have reflected the Army's then institutional focus on the physics of armoured warfare part of which envisaged formations breaking through an enemy's defences to tear into their vulnerable rear areas.

Whether it did or not, the proposal appeared at odds with the circumstances. Before us lay a crucible of war comprising a network of rock strewn hills prepared for mutually supporting defence. The slopes, stone runs and numerous minefields afforded little room or scope for rapid manoeuvre. Our troops would be on foot, weighed down by equipment, vulnerable to every type of enemy plunging and interlocking fire. The 'cascading torrent' of armoured warfare envisages near continuous movement, virtually nonstop action, fresh echelons passing through exhausted forces, to be replaced in their turn until decision. But our lines of communication back to San Carlos couldn't cope with the continuous depletion of resources at intense combat rates. We would need pauses between events to feed men and materiel forward, particularly artillery ammunition. We simply didn't have the helicopters and other vehicles necessary to sustain such a concept. And even if somehow we did overcome all to break through and tear ahead, we would come upon Stanley, a 'rear area' not so much vulnerable as severely complicated, populated by our own people and still held by the enemy, with by-passed forces to our rear presumably, still able to intervene. The idea never gained much traction. It dropped from sight after the Bluff Cove/Fitzroy tragedy.

On the other side of the hill things were going from bad to worse. An air of desperation began to take hold of our enemy. At one point, in anguish the Argentinian High Command yet again considered an attack from West Falkland coordinated with one out of Stanley. It was pure fantasy. Eventually, sober counsel prevailed. Their only course lay in reinforcing the already-prepared defences as best they could and wait for us to come onto them, hoping that further setbacks such as the one at Bluff Cove might dent our offensive capabilities and spirit sufficiently to enable them to stop our progress and achieve a stalemate, if not something better. And so Menendez was instructed to hold his ground, to fight and not surrender.

Moore's confirmatory orders for the attack were issued on the 9 June. 3 Commando Brigade, including 3 PARA, would drive in the enemy's northern perimeter on the first night. 5 Brigade would follow this up taking two to three days to defeat the remaining, outer positions. If necessary, with the outlying mountains thus cleared, the Commando Brigade would then push into Stanley.

Forward of Mount Kent, around the fringes of Stanley elements of G Squadron and the SBS had remained on the ground, some patrols having started on their second continuous month in the field behind enemy lines. As our forces closed in on Stanley the patrols switched from information reporting to offensive action, directing air, artillery and naval gunfire and occasionally air strikes. It proved a major contribution, bringing much needed precision to the joint fires effort, inflicting considerable physical and psychological harm on the enemy. We hoped to add to their unheralded achievements.

RHQ determined the immediate, additional contribution we were to make up at Stanley. It came in two parts, both aimed at degrading the enemy's morale as well as causing physical damage. The first in sequence would be executed by the Navy, the second by the Squadron. Each displayed in full the hallmarks of Mike Rose's restless imagination. I wished that we had come up with the first, and from the outset harboured reservations about the other.

The initial operation displayed a certain unadorned elegance. Over a period, it had come to the attention of RHQ's tiny intelligence cell that the Argentine commander would chair a regular conference of his principals in the Council offices on Ross Road, on Stanley's waterfront and in plain view of the hills to the north. The CO saw the potential immediately, persuading CLFFI and the Navy that they should attempt to hit it, thereby decapitating the Argentinian operational command-structure in one fell stroke. This might complicate eventual negotiations, but the loss of their top commanders at such a critical juncture could well precipitate the occupier's collapse. Worth a try, the attack received the go-ahead.

The target, a particular room, in a specific building, at a given time, had to be struck with utmost accuracy. Naval gunfire could be discounted for being too imprecise, requiring a number of ranging shots, not to mention the complications associated with positioning a ship and a fire direction party at the right time. Artillery was out of range and a laser designated bomb delivered by Harrier too destructive, likely to cause civilian casualties. The weapon of choice proved to be the AS12 missile launched from a helicopter. With the destructive power of a 5-inch shell, placed accurately inside the room it should upset the meeting without causing undue damage to buildings and people in the surrounding area.

A WILCO Wessex V crew was found. The mission called for daring for although the AS12 had a range of 7,000 metres, the ground dictated that the helicopter go well forward, coming within range of Stanley's air defences that included the fearsome, rapid-firing Rheinmetal anti-aircraft guns. The SACLOS (Semi Automatic Command to Line of Sight) missile could take as long as thirty seconds to fly to its target, a whole minute or more of exposure if both available missiles were fired. This demanded nerves of steel, pilot and weapon operator literally having to hold steady in probably strong, blustery winds, all the while under intense enemy fire.

On the morning of 11 June, with calculated abandon, the helicopter dashed down on Stanley before pausing in the hover about a mile or more from his target. In sight of the enemy, two missiles were launched. The first grazed past the Council offices at precisely the right moment, hitting the police station to the rear with a fearful crash. The second splashed into the harbour to the front of the target. Even though the officers attending the meeting and all others survived physical injury, including those in the police station at the time, the attack caused much consternation. In the ensuing confusion the enemy managed to shoot down one of their own helicopters. It was an enterprising, gutsy effort, the Wessex receiving a great deal of attention from the moment it engaged until making good its escape. The whole thing took three or four minutes, a long time in which to hold not just steady, but perfectly still, under fire.

Later that day, during the night of 11/12 June, Thompson and his battle-groups went at the enemy's outer defences in a sequence difficult to obscure: Mount Longdon, Two Sisters and Mount Harriet. A shortage of readily available Naval and artillery gun ammunition only added to their difficulties. But if we were easy for the enemy to read at brigade-level, commanding officers of the battle groups ensured we came over cryptic at theirs. Each attack was meticulously planned, each tactically distinct.

It wasn't easy. The enemy had prepared their positions thoroughly employing the range of devices including artfully sited minefields, machine guns on fixed lines and skilfully pre-registered artillery defensive fire. They would fight hard. But although the defences of each hill had been sited to support another, in the event mutually supporting fire never materialised as it should. The positions fell piecemeal.

3 PARA taking on Mount Longdon chose to conduct a 'silent attack', seeking to repeat the success of their recce patrols of the preceding nights by creeping up onto the enemy, saving their sparse allocation of artillery and naval gunfire for on-call tasks as required. Things had gone well up to the point a paratrooper set off a mine during the final approach. The alerted enemy fought well until overwhelmed by the Paras' professional skill, drive and sheer grit.

In the centre 45 Commando's assault on the twin peaks of Two Sisters also started silently, going 'noisy' as the Marines tore into enemy defences based on a series of heavy and medium machine-gun nests. It was another stiff fight, the Marines taking well-directed enemy mortar and artillery fire. Again success was secured through the skilful counter-use of mortars, light artillery and naval gunfire combined with relentless infantry engagement. Afterwards, 45 reported that 'although some enemy stand and fight bravely, the majority of them will run when confronted by aggressive and determined troops'.

Our old friends 42 Commando took on Mount Harriet. They had used their time on Mount Kent astutely, developing a refined feel for the enemy's positions and routine and the ground to their front. Employing this knowledge, they were able to get in behind their foe. In addition, they employed artillery as a diversion onto the opposition's forward positions, a courageous and well-calculated use of their limited allocation of fire support. The combination proved devastating. They achieved near total tactical surprise. Heavy casualties were inflicted on the enemy for the relatively light losses of three killed and thirteen wounded.

It was now 5 Brigade's turn. The reduction of the enemy's outer defences was to be completed with the seizure of Tumbledown, Mount William and Sapper Hill over successive nights and days by respectively the Scots Guards, 1/7 Gurkha Rifles and the Welsh Guards. The plan was amended with the re-subordination of 2 PARA to 3 Brigade for an attack onto Wireless Ridge to be mounted concurrent with that on Tumbledown. With that done, 3 Commando Brigade would be free and positioned to go into town, should that unwelcome necessity arise.

The Regiment's inclusion into the arrangements, Special Forces' second contribution to the final push, involved the Squadron mounting operations forward of the battle groups, into the rear areas of Stanley with the purpose of distracting the enemy; drawing off their fire; tying down their reserves; and otherwise increasing the physical and psychological pressures on a hemmed in foe under attack from all sides. We would have to get a wiggle on if we were to make it in time. We had already missed 3 Commando's initial attacks.

We all liked the idea of helping 2 PARA in particular. The Regiment and the Parachute Regiment had close ties and more than passing empathy. In this instance there was a heightened sense of kinship. They were Falkland veterans with the already celebrated battle for Darwin/Goose Green behind them; we were seasoned too, albeit in a less intense fashion, having started in South Georgia an age ago it then seemed. It struck us as being wholly right and proper to be in at the finish supporting our friends, the Parachute Regiment particularly. But I remained uneasy about certain practical aspects of our proposed input.

A cursory map study confirmed that there wasn't a lot of ground remaining forward of the battle groups, little manoeuvre space to the

Stanley area period. We were going to be hedged in by the sea and funnelled by terrain. To get in and among the enemy, at any chosen place
in their rear, we would have to cross water.

And what room there was looked pretty congested, occupied and
under the influence of both the enemy and our own forces. It could all
get close and personal, yet we were neither familiar nor practised in the
tactics of the all-arms battle, let alone honed in the complexities of
coordinating ourselves into such a crowded, joint battle space. We were
by nature geared to being 'out there' more or less on our own. There
had been no opportunity to get with the Brigades or their units to go
over the necessary control measures. The risk of fratricide had to be
high. And if that wasn't enough, nor had we discussed directly with
them how exactly we were to fit into their battle.

Therein lay another problem: our strength and its relation to time.
We habitually operated at a numerical disadvantage, this colouring virtually everything we did. Movement required stealth, any offensive
actions surprise and precision. If we were to get the utmost out of our
small numbers, customarily an SAS attack would be preceded by some
form of recce to find the covered routes in, the ways out, to determine
precisely how and where to strike. Of course it could be much the same
for the battle-groups, the difference a matter of degree. Our needs
were highly exacting. We must proceed with due caution, strike hard
and fast before withdrawing; they might fight to get in and stay to wear
down an enemy through continuous action. They needed surprise sufficient to keep them ahead of any enemy reaction; we needed surprise
to ensure we met no reaction. We might need days rather than hours to
prepare and mount our attacks.

However, at this stage in the conflict our own battle procedures were
slick, based upon frequent practice under severe conditions. We could
take on complex special operations with little or no fuss, referring back
to previous actions, modifying a practice here, a tactic there. In our own
terms, we were quick and agile, able to operate at high tempo, switching
from one thing to another without having to put much thought into its

mechanics; instead, we could concentrate on what to do, rather than how to do it. We knew what was important, what might be abbreviated or even left out, and under what circumstances. Observers may have discerned a distinctive D Squadron style. The reality was more prosaic. We were simply experienced, attuned to our war.

And so despite being aware of the difficulties and differences, I was encouraged to think we could make it all work. It very nearly didn't.

Our part in the final Battle for Stanley as ordered by RHQ, and recorded in our war diary, was for the Squadron to get forward to:

Occupy Murrell and conduct ops in rear area Stanley.

That was it, as broad as that, no specific mention of 2 PARA (Map 8).

As usual, I had made a quick assessment, going over the mission with Danny, Geordie and Graham. We read the occupation of the Murrell Heights as a task in itself, to enable us thereafter to conduct offensive operations over an indefinite period into the enemy's rear. So clearing Murrell and its surroundings should come first. We didn't see this taking long, a day maybe; nor did we expect to meet anything sizeable, the odd enemy patrol perhaps. We were uncertain about the consequences of coming across anything larger; we might go after it, seeing it as part of the 'rear area [of] Stanley'. But would that help the battle groups? We might have to refer back to RHQ.

Likewise, the nature and frequency of our attacks had not been pinned down. They could range from directing joint fires through sabotage attacks to large scale, squadron-sized raids. It had not seemed necessary to discuss this in any way with Mike Rose before our departure. Neither of us felt inclined to prescribe the options. We were of one mind, get forward as soon as possible and help the battle groups in whatever way that fit, presented itself. That said, 2 PARA's attack onto Wireless Ridge had been mentioned; we should support it if we could.

The four of us moved rapidly on. There seemed not much more to it than get the Squadron in, secure Murrell, and then exploit opportunities for some direct action. We would apply our tried and tested methods, recce being a *sine qua non*. I did surmise that we might have only the one opportunity to mount an attack at squadron strength. Given the compactness of the area, interlaced by water obstacles, it could prove near impossible to achieve full tactical surprise a second time round— astonishment perhaps. We all saw the airfield behind Stanley as an enticing prospect, a successful raid offering potential for operational-level impact. Otherwise, it looked like stand off attacks employing guns or air or our own longer-range weapons; raiding by such fire in precisely applied concentrations could prove notably effective. We could see how working progressively through a select target list might cause our enemy intense consternation and hurt. Of course, any method of attack must move things along for our big battalions, but the less need for tactical coordination—us with them, them with us—the better.

As it turned out our thinking was not precisely aligned with that of RHQ: emphatically my fault. And Danny was always telling me that: 'assumption is the mother of fuck up, Cedric'. The CO saw us opening our efforts at maximum strength with a diversionary attack in support of 2 PARA. We would be carried in by three Royal Marine rigid raiding craft to assault Cortley Hill about two miles along from Wireless Ridge, the battle group's objective. I viewed things similarly save that for RHQ this was a definite appointment. I had come to see it as something we should do if we could. And 'should' somehow morphed into 'unlikely', given the press of time. It was truly a tall order: to mount a tactical diversion of numerous working parts within hours of getting onto the ground. So my mind had moved onto other options in an easier to manage time-frame. Things might have turned out badly, but for the skill of the troops.

As we prepared to deploy from San Carlos our weakened state became evident. Carrying on with four troops after the loss of the helicopter had foxed me if not the rest of the Squadron with its appearance of normality. We should maintain operations on West Falkland, those involving 18 and 19 Troops. That left only 16 and 17 Troops for Stanley, both depleted by casualties sustained on Mount Kent. Unhesitatingly, G

Squadron stepped forward, their 23 Troop making up our numbers. They came with enthusiasm. After weeks of careful surveillance patrolling they were ready to throw their weight around. The Squadron shared their willing if not their fervour. We would deploy forward from San Carlos by helicopter, the three Rigid Raiders and their coxswains by coaster dropping off near Berkley Sound to make their way to Cochon Island, there to await call forward.

The moves went to plan, the Squadron dropping into Estancia to wait for cover of darkness before continuing on. The place was busy, a small, advanced logistic node. Helicopters came and went, momentarily disturbing the tranquillity. Some islanders with a battered Land Rover and tractor had pitched in, helping to organise materiel into orderly stacks. Somebody had a grip of the place, a seasoned 'B Echelon' commander we guessed, a Para most likely for there were one or two of them about. No fuss, the whole thing unhurriedly business-like.

So here too were the reassuring signs of people in the swing of things. The Task Force looked and felt unstoppable. But then, most of us up at the front had no inkling that the ships and aircraft were becoming frayed, in desperate need of deep maintenance. And not many of us knew that the guns, naval and artillery, were running low on ammunition, our supply chain straining to keep up with the demand. Even if we had, I suspect we would not have been unduly bothered. We were going to win.

17. The Last Night

Landing at night into the Murrell, in dead ground to Stanley, we were received by an SBS patrol that came under our tactical control. They gave us a quick situation report, sounding sparky and very much on the ball. They believed the immediate area clear of enemy, but could not vouch for the hills a little further to the east overlooking Berkley Sound. We all knew that the Argentinians had half-expected the Task Force to come in that way. The enemy might still have forces in positions of observation overlooking the seaward approaches. I thanked the SBS for their report and asked that they join Ted's Boat Troop. The SITREP matched our previous assessment, confirming that we should clear through what was in effect our immediate rear the following morning, in a few hours' time.

Operating in daylight would be something of a departure but the risks sat comfortably with our understanding of things, our instincts, and with what the SBS had reported. The sweep would be conducted in strength, distant from and largely out of sight of the enemy in Stanley. We thought that smaller enemy units were unlikely to fight with determination. If we ran into anything aggressive and sizeable, beyond our immediate capacity to handle, we might conduct a fighting withdrawal towards 3 PARA then in the area of Mount Longdon, drawing the enemy onto their probable destruction. That would be a sporting exercise, tactically tricky, but something I knew the Squadron could handle, the Paras likewise. One way or another we should be spending our time productively.

The sweep through Twelve O'Clock Mountain and beyond proved the area clear of enemy, save for an eight-man patrol that made off into the distance. 16 Troop attempted to cut them off, but the Argentinians had a head start and could move at pace, knowing the ground and what lay before them. They didn't appear to pose much of a threat. We abandoned our necessarily careful pursuit for lack of time, the light fading as the evening drew in. Possibly this was a mistake, for the patrol may have had a hand in one or two of our later difficulties.

Back on Beagle Ridge, a short conversation over the TACSAT with the CO established that the rigid raiding-craft had made it to Cochon Island undetected, ready to be called forward for a squadron-size diversionary attack in support of 2 PARA's assault of Wireless Ridge that very evening, in a few hours time! How was it going? Fine!

This pulled me up. It shouldn't have. But I had been holding to the idea that we would be doing things in our proven way, to our timings. We had been observing Stanley during the day through optics, but had come up with nothing suitable as a squadron target. The SBS patrol couldn't help and they had been in the area a while. I had intended to push patrols out that night to take a fresh look through the coming day from different angles. I was particularly keen to get some eyes on the area of the airport and harbour, Port William and Blanco Bay. But now here we were about to lunge off into the largely unknown in no time flat, most probably using up our one and only large-scale shot.

We might have honed our skills, cut our teeth on a range of things in the past weeks, but could we pull this off: in a couple of hours, from a cold start, without supporting intelligence, conduct an attack against an unknown target, almost certainly defended by an alert, numerically superior, and more heavily armed enemy in prepared positions, protected by mines and wire, behind a water obstacle to be crossed using unfamiliar motor-boats, driven by people we had never worked with before. There was only one way to find out.

Danny passed me one of his roll-ups, Geordie a brew. Neither said much, both sensing my dark mood, one of deep foreboding, tinged with irritation, not to mention guilt at succumbing so stupidly to wishful thinking. I disliked the feeling of not being in full control of our actions, but settled down with a map, pencil and paper to knock out a set of orders for something about as enticing as a 'forlorn hope.'[1] I kicked myself for not making different use of our day. But reflecting on it, how might we have made better use of the time? There had been no opportunity to push recces out the night of our insertion and fatuous to recce for possible targets in broad daylight, moving on forward slopes in full view of Stanley. I jerked myself out of it. This bordered on mental whinging, unlikely to get us anywhere. Besides, sometimes you have to do things that don't appear to square well within the immediate horizon, but nevertheless add up in the overall scheme of things. 'Time to get on John.'

Of necessity, the plan of attack would have to be simple, if not downright rudimentary. Stick to something broadly generic in design—or how I imagined such a boating expedition to look. This was to be extemporisation in its most extreme form, only made possible by the slickness of our drills and the WILCO of the troops; made palatable because it was in aid of our mates in 2 PARA. We had no immediately obvious high-value target to go for, no target save for enemy to our front. Nor was there precision, nothing to be precise about. We didn't even have proven ways in and out. As for surprise: possibly yes, but most likely in the 'they must be kidding sense', rather than the paralysing way we needed. That left speed and aggression: get in by stealth, when it went noisy hit hard and fast and leave 'toot sweet'.

The 'team' gathered for orders, more the explanation of a scheme of manoeuvre with a few coordinating points thrown in than detailed instructions in the conventional sense. I explained our purpose as being to help 2 PARA's attack onto Wireless Ridge in a few hours' time by drawing attention to ourselves. If it worked we might tie down any enemy reserve for a crucial period. More likely, we should bring artillery defensive fire down on ourselves, away from the battle group.

---

[1] 'Forlorn hope': those chosen to take the lead, where the chances of survival are low such as the storming of a breach in an enemy's defences. In the British Army the term is particularly associated with the Napoleonic period, when the duty might be sought after, survivors often generously rewarded.

Nobody liked the sound of that, noting that we had no body armour, not even a single steel helmet between the lot of us! I didn't need to mention the morale aspect. We all saw that the enemy must be nearing collapse. We liked to think that our confidence to tear into his rear and flanks, contrasting with his growing sense of doom, could be the sort of thing that might hasten his collapse, if not trigger it.

Desperately out of time, the operation's essential architecture had to come straight off my map: the holding and assembly areas, boat pick-up point, drop off point, routes in, routes out, landing area, objective area, fire-support positions, RVs, rally-points, communication-nodes. There was no actual target though. All salient aspects had been determined without benefit of direct observation, going untested by reconnaissance. It had been a matter of dropping a template solution onto the map and calling it a plan. D Squadron people accepted it without demur, recognising that at times needs must. G Squadron and the SBS clearly expected more, while taking their lead from 'D'. This was not my finest moment, but there was no quibbling. All was received in near silence. It might not have been the best of plans, but we could all see that the thing had simplicity going for it. Everyone understood its shape and form. Each could see his part. It might work.

As everyone dispersed to make their preparations in the limited time remaining, Ted stayed back. His was a central role. He and his troop, including the SBS, would go across Hernden Water to Cortley Hill by rigid raiding-craft to hit whatever they could find in front of them and then come back out, no hanging around. The rest of the Squadron would support as best they could with fire from the 'home bank'. Ted expressed concern at the lack of a target, beyond 'enemy to your front, carry on'. I sympathised. I agreed that he could make for the old oil storage tanks clearly shown on the map. I didn't think he would get that far, nowhere near. I don't think he did either. But if it helped him to have 'an aiming mark', something to go for, he should have it. On reflection it hadn't been a clever choice. The oil, if any existed, might have been needed for humanitarian use after our increasingly likely victory. But mistakes get made in war. And this one was made when the needs of my troops trumped virtually all other considerations. I simply wasn't thinking much beyond the immediate moment and its tactical demands.

I knew Ted and his people were probably in for bit of a rough night. They knew it. We all knew it. I told Danny that I would go across with them and that therefore he would have to control the 'home bank'. I felt a strong need to share the danger. He regarded me steadily before taking me off to one side. Firmly, quietly, gently even, he explained why that was unnecessary, in fact a bad idea. He conceded that Ted was going to get into a jam. He was the man best suited to command his troop. It didn't need me there to complicate his job further. I would be needed where I could control the whole thing, connecting upwards, directing downwards, helping Ted get in and out by employing the remainder of the Squadron's resources and calling for supporting fire from above if necessary.

Danny would be happy to take on the home bank and all that that entailed of course, but it was really for me to do. He was right. Despite my better judgement and resolve, I had let the 'noise' of sentiment creep in. I had strayed from strict objectivity. It had been unprofessional. Ted and the Squadron didn't need me to make some emotional point with an unnecessary gesture. This was not the moment for posturing. We all had to be at the right places, operating at peak effectiveness. It had taken Danny to remind me of my proper station, to get me back on track. The moment passed, and he and I got down to the business of checking over the details of SHQ's part one last time. Then, a quick 'scoff' of cold steak and kidney pudding washed down with another of Geordie's brews and we were off.

There wasn't much to see: a dark, still night, quiet; much quieter than I had expected. Distant noises drifted in on the gentle breeze, some shell-fire and small arms, not loud, sporadic, presumably 2 PARA's attack. An occasional illumination round cast an orange glow off to our right. I had expected more to it than that. Then again I had not been that close before to a full-scale, battle-group attack on a live enemy by night. Perhaps it hadn't gone well? Maybe 2 PARA's attack had stalled? I thought it highly unlikely that it had been defeated.

Danny, Geordie and I had found a shallow hollow with views across Hernden Water, about a mile north of the oil storage tanks as an albatross might fly. Most of the remainder of the 'home bank' force lay to our right. This would put the three of us close to the centre of the Squadron, with Ted's water-borne assault due to go in 500 metres or thereabouts over to our left. It became a matter of waiting. Not long I hoped, if that was indeed 2 PARA over there, the noise and light having increased. If we were going to help we needed to get stuck in pronto.

Was that a motor? Could it be the Rigid Raiders? Perhaps I imagined it. It could have been the wind gently blowing across the diddle-dee?

Moments later the peace was shattered by a ferocious crash of small-arms fire of every possible type: assault-rifles, machine-guns, heavy machine-guns, the crump of grenades. It was difficult to tell exactly whose was what, what was whose. Except the heavy machine-guns had to be theirs, we didn't have any. My radio crackled into life. It was Ted. He had landed. Got stuck. Couldn't get forward. Still on the beach. Couldn't move, not at all. About to take hits. He would have to come back. Now. Immediately. Not sure if he could get back out!

Fuck, fuck, fuck! The brain raced, clouded. What to do? What were the options? First things first. Steady! Get fire down. It hardly needed me to tell them, but I radioed nevertheless, urging the 'home bank' to give what covering fire they could, to keep it off the beach for fear of hitting our own, placing as much as possible onto the hill above, and any muzzle flashes. They did, and with that things got really bad. From the hillside to our front, across the narrow stretch of water, enemy fire poured into us, anti-aircraft guns, machine-guns, heavy machine-guns, kitchen sink too as far as I could tell. The whole bloody hill lighted up, ablaze with muzzle flashes. A whirlwind of stuff, theirs not ours, the tracer starting slowly as discernible, individual moving points of light on the far side of the water, streaking in as solid flashes, smacking and cracking, fizzing and swirling, the din deafening, the ground churning around us.

One of the basic, tactical battle-drills is to 'win the fire-fight'. I could recall Sergeant Dougie Worsfall, Grenadier Guards, drumming this into his new charges the junior cadets of Gaza Company, Intake 41, Royal Military Academy Sandhurst, fourteen years previously. No winning this one Dougie, I thought to myself wistfully: funny how the mind works in moments of crisis.

Must regain a semblance of control. I tried to raise Ted on the radio, but failed to get onto the net for the excited chatter of G's 23 Troop, unfamiliar with our terse radio procedures. Furious, I eventually broke in, asking them impolitely to do what they could without talking about it. We needed an uncluttered net. They cleared the air and tried to get on with it. But there really was no winning this fight. Our fire gradually slackened as the enemy imposed their superiority. Next it could be their will over ours. I thought I would give it a go myself, a more personal shot at winning the fire fight, to encourage the others to increase their fire.

I shot off a magazine at the hill above where I reckoned Ted and his troop to be, in the direction of the airport, where a few moments earlier I had heard a C130 land. Perhaps my overs would reach that far. Horror! In all the excitement I had forgotten my practice of loading a few rounds of tracer at the bottom of the magazine, to signal the imminent need for a magazine change. The tracer sped away, a blazing unmissable stream of intermittent light leading back to my exact fold in the ground; well, the shallow depression at that moment shared with Danny and Geordie. Instantly, the ground around us churned over and over, great dense clods of earth flying, thrashed by the anti-aircraft gun opposite and a lot else besides. The din was crushing. Head spinning, ears ringing, eyes rolling, momentarily at sixes and sevens, I apologised to my companions. I promised to stop mucking around and to concentrate on breaking contact, getting us out of the sodding mess we found ourselves in. We had certainly created noise, if not a thorough going diversion, the Argentinians appeared to be having a whale of a time.

Ted was still not sure he could get out the way he had gone in. I warned our liaison officer at Brigade to advise 2 PARA that the Troop might have to fight its way out, eventually coming in on their forward positions. Unfortunately, this was somehow misconstrued as a request for help. At no point did we do that; a ridiculous notion, to expect a major change of the brigade plan, simply to come to our rescue. Besides, 2 PARA had more than enough on their plate. This was our problem, for us to sort out. I just didn't want Ted shot up by the battle group, if we had to exercise that option, if he ever got that far. That was all.

The 'home bank' fire had become measured, save for that of one not particularly clever clown a short distance over to our left who would fire long, somewhat erratic bursts from his GPMG at tiresome frequency in Ted's direction. Each time his tracer would attract a deluge of anti-aircraft fire in return from the hill immediately opposite, across the water. One had to admire his determination, but it didn't seem to be achieving much: getting uncomfortably close to Ted and the boaters, while bringing serious weight of fire down on himself and us. It must surely end in tears before too long. I tried a few times, shouting across for him to take more bloody care, aimed bursts at the anti-aircraft guns perhaps, not towards Ted. I couldn't get through to him. I got Danny to try. No joy. Nothing would induce the man to cease his erratic ways. I muttered to myself, something about G Squadron, first radio discipline, now fire discipline. Which was unfair, for actually the rest of the home bank troops, more than half of them G, were putting up a notably skilled and brave resistance, taking careful, well aimed, well considered shots at identifiable enemy locations across the water. And they were no longer chatting about it on the net!

Similarly, over on the far bank Ted and his team were beginning to get a handle on their part of the engagement. They realised that the enemy couldn't bring fire to bear on the beach itself, including a short twenty yard stretch of water. To do so they must leave the protection of their trenches; at the moment the enemy showed no interest in doing that, either to improve their marksmanship, or to mount a counter-attack. Of course, the longer Ted left it, the more likely it was that the enemy would overcome their reservations, or perhaps bring indirect, mortar fire to bear. Ted had to act soon. He warned me that he intended to re-embark and make a dash for safety, relying on the Rigid Raiders' impressive speed and manoeuvrability. If he got his timings right, perhaps he could get out into the darkness of Blanco Bay before the enemy reacted with effective, well-aimed fire. Once he broke contact, he would make his way round to the pre-planned drop off point. I told him to crack on. We would do what we could, putting down covering fire— just give us the word.

I warned the home bank to give it all they could on my word, to cover Ted's withdrawal. We all picked our target, the net dead, silent, only matey putting out the odd burst of GPMG. He really was trying. Ted embarked his troops. The boats pushed carefully back from the beach to prowl quietly, slowly, to and fro, keeping to the calm, still water, hoping not to alert the enemy with the noise of their idling engines, watching the fire-churned sea beyond, alert for any pause or easing of the enemy's barrage. The troops did what they could to make themselves small, balled, peering over the gunwales, praying the enemy might stop, their attention shift at least. Ted warned us that they were ready. Back and forth his boats cruised, alert, fully primed, ready to seize their moment, but nothing, no let up. Then we put down our covering fire, only to get a devastating broadside in return, a wall of sheeting, cracking, banging and spitting hot metal. It felt cataclysmic. Whether any of it had lifted from Ted and his beach it would be difficult to say. But the boats made their move, taking advantage of the din and turmoil all about. The coxswains gunned their engines, in near unison throwing the Rigid Raiders hard over, turning on a sixpence. The boats leapt forward with a roar, charging at the wall of enemy fire, towards the beckoning safety of the darkness beyond. Momentarily losing all sense of direction, they simply powered through the boiling water. The noise across our entire front was near bewildering, tracer flashes blinding. Little of it came from us. Once more the home bank effort had been promptly supressed, reduced to the occasional carefully considered shot, the sheer weight and fury of the enemy's anti-aircraft and machine guns otherwise incontestable.

Ted and his team were soon running out across the Bay, the coxswains skilfully bringing their craft up onto the plane to maximise their speed. It was exhilarating. They found themselves tearing through a steady procession of small craft ferrying injured Argentinians to a hospital ship, lights ablaze further out in the harbour. The raiders swerved their way through before veering off towards the drop-off point. As they cleared the medical tenders the hospital ship trained one of its searchlights. The Rigid Raiders frantically weaved to break free of the treacherous beam. They started to attract fire. A G Squadron call-sign sparked up on the net, urgently informing us of the situation, seeking permission to snipe out the hospital ship's light with a MILAN missile. I hesitated.

The ship was in the wrong, abusing its status under the Conventions of War. It was putting the lives of my soldiers at severe risk. An ignorant conscript might be operating the searchlight, but the ship's actions had served to bring down fire onto my troops. It was my duty to protect my troops. We had a right to self-defence. At any moment this might end very badly for one or more of the raiding craft, involving the loss of the crew and all passengers for nobody would survive long in the ice-cold water, wounded or otherwise, not loaded with kit. Sod amateurs: war should be left to professionals. The bastard Flores flashed through my mind. We could well be the only ones playing cricket. *No*, I responded, repeating myself for good measure, *no*! A few more seconds and the raiders should be in the clear. I prayed so.

Ted and his people did make it, having to leave the empty boats on the foreshore, soon destroyed by enemy fire, putting paid to anymore cross water ventures. It had been really good of the G Squadron people to ask about firing on the hospital ship though. Funny how the squadrons differed; only in small ways perhaps, yet it mounted to each with its own distinct character. I was warming to 23 Troop. I made a mental note to thank and commend them when and if I got the chance but forgot, being overtaken by events.

'Let's go, Danny,' I said, informing him that Ted had made it off the beach, by then well out into Blanco Bay.

'Tell that numpty with the GPMG to fall in behind us.'

As we all got up to withdraw Danny shouted across only to get another burst of fire, this time directed inaccurately at us. An Argentinian, it had to be an Argentinian! I experienced a short, sharp pang of guilt for thinking that it could have been one of us, one of G Squadron unfamiliar with our ways. How could I have thought that? All along we had been shouting across at an enemy position, possibly a member of that patrol we had failed to nail earlier in the day. How come we hadn't twigged before now? Time to go. Time to draw a line under the night, before something went wrong! We slipped away, crouching low, scurrying off to one side, fast.

As we neared the rallying point, a large pond selected off the map, there came the unmistakeable swish of heavy artillery rounds shuffling close-by overhead; lots of them, a whole battery's worth, moaning, droning, dropping down. It had to be 155mm. They were seriously big bangs. The pond and the surrounding area erupted, churned, perhaps a mere 100 yards in front of the leading troops. The soft ground absorbed much of the energy. The shock waves powered through us, then came a shower of detritus, bits of rock, metal, water and plenty of muddy turf and a confetti of shredded vegetation.

'How the hell did they manage that?' I asked, of nobody in particular, not expecting an answer.

We veered away, quick check, no hits. The artillery kept coming, but not following, not yet. I guessed it could be a good map appreciation. Or it could be a piece of smart surveillance kit: radar, NVGs. We were forward-sloped to Cortley Hill. Perhaps a sharp enemy artillery OP was tracking our withdrawal. Could it be that patrol again, the one we missed? However it had been done, our respect for Argentine artillery increased. Remaining alert to all possibilities, we pressed on fast, to get out of surveillance range preferably, into dead ground certainly. The artillery continued a while, falling behind us.

In the Squadron RV we took stock, putting out a protective screen. The 'home bank' troops were all back in, no casualties; miraculous, not a scratch. I couldn't quite believe we had got away with it. So far, so good. We waited for Ted's people. Their last report had indicated that they had made it across Blanco Bay, still taking fire as they landed, the Rigid Raiders a write-off.

We didn't have long to wait. Shadowy figures slipped in to take their place on the Squadron's defensive perimeter. I didn't want to linger, being keen to get back to the security of our positions of the afternoon before, well-sited for defence. I was now definitely worried about that possible enemy patrol. It could yet cause harm. We should have nailed it when we had the outside chance the previous afternoon.

Somebody came across to report that the shadows were indeed Ted's people, all accounted for, including the Rigid Raider coxswains. We had two casualties, both walking wounded. My Mount Kent patrol companion, Clive Lowther had been hit somewhere in the shoulder as the boats made their dash out into the bay and (Our) Brummie Stokes had taken a hit high in the thigh, a mortar splinter, as the boats beached on the home bank, at the very moment of reaching relative safety. I went across to see for myself. Old D Squadron hands, I had a soft spot for them both. They had managed to walk out, effectively conducting their own CASEVAC. Clive sat leaning up against his pack, Carl Rhodes about to check his field dressing. Clive sounded strong and in good shape all things considered. He had even managed to carry his bergen despite his injuries; typical of Clive, quietly self-sufficient, never complaining. I asked him how he felt.

'Fine. Rarely better, Boss,' he responded, 'nothing too bad—feels numb—some difficulty breathing, otherwise okay.'

I asked Carl if I could take a quick look. Shining my shielded torch where he pointed, on seeing more blood and mess than expected I involuntarily blurted out loud and clear.

'Oh, fucking hell!'

Clive promptly passed out. Carl gave me an ear full. I turned my attention to Brummie, reminding myself about warmth and reassurance and a nice, hot cup of tea. I didn't examine Brummie. He didn't seem keen, assuring me that he was 'Okay, Boss, okay', waving me off weakly.

Unexpectedly, as we were about to move, a Gazelle helicopter turned up, called forward by Geordie who had anticipated the need. Our casualties were soon on their way. I didn't give the matter much thought. It was how we were by then, people aware, thinking and doing for themselves, knowing that their actions would be supported whether right or wrong, provided they acted in good faith. And this initiative had been spot on, made by Geordie while I had been preoccupied by our security, the mechanics of withdrawal and rendering Clive unconscious.

Dawn broke with us back on Murrell Ridge in a strong defensive position. We were tired, somewhat drained. A certain fuzzy apathy had descended upon us. It was often like that after a stiff contact. The calm had an unreal, strangely intense, quality. Senses were heightened and yet mushy; but then my ears were still not right, still ringing from when Danny had fired a burst a few inches from my right ear—or I had got within a few inches of Danny's muzzle in the thick of last night's fire fight? Either way, I felt cocooned in 'white noise'. Little was quite as it should be. My hearing never fully really recovered. It was probably the body coming down unevenly after its prolonged adrenalin-fuelled excitement, a little at odds with itself. Time would bring everything back into equilibrium, but I savoured the calm, the tranquillity, the contrasts, the raised awareness, re-establishing normality.

We had got off lightly. Clive and Brummie were in Ajax Bay, the Field Hospital back at San Carlos; we knew that the Field Surgical Team had yet to lose a single casualty making it that far. And 2 PARA had triumphed. I liked to think we had helped.[2] That left Stanley. We would start to think about that after breakfast.

[2] Our raid that night came in for criticism. It was not executed as we would have wished. But beyond dispute, we drew the enemy's fire upon ourselves for quite a while, during 2 PARA's assault. It included a lot of heavy artillery. How much it added to the psychological pressure on the enemy we might never know. But 2 PARA's forward positions reported the enemy withdrawing from the direction of Cortley Hill not long after the raid, streaming past them to get into Stanley.

I breakfasted on two oatmeal blocks, mashed into warmed water to make a passable porridge, followed by beans and a bar of chocolate: two days rations. I felt like pushing the boat out. Tomorrow's breakfast? Tomorrow's problem. Perhaps we would get a resupply by then. I took my brew across to join Danny and Geordie, both sitting with their backs to a large rock, finding a little warmth from the sun low on the northern horizon. For once Geordie was off the radio, leaving that to one of his entirely capable signallers. Nothing was coming in. All was peaceful. We chatted softly, not a lot, spasmodically, as we came down off our high of the night before, feeling strangely secure, the immediate area cleared and the Squadron deployed for defence as well as conceal-ment. It crossed my mind to do something about that Argentinian patrol still out there presumably. Use 23 Troop? Keep the Squadron's troops back to recce for potential targets the coming night? I still rather fan-cied the airport. I recalled the C130 from the previous night; perhaps a stand-off Stinger attack if we had the range, noting that we could be short of firing point options, having lost the boats. But a successful strike with a man-portable air defence weapon could help shut down their air-bridge, and certainly get some response. I made a mental note to coordinate anything like that with higher formation, to keep our helicopters and air out of the way. As I drew up a list of things to address, I rolled a shoddy cigarette, passing it to Danny who tucked it behind his ear, still working on his brew. I rolled another for myself. Geordie didn't use them.

'Boss, come and take a look at this,' our moment of quiet was broken by the excited urging of one of the signallers. I put my cigarette away, to crawl across to join him. We peered carefully over the ridge, down towards Stanley. I accepted the use of his proffered binoculars.

'There', he whispered 'not sure what they're doing. And there.'

Sure enough, three or four miles from us, plainly visible through our optics, there were many hundreds of enemy troops out in the open. Perhaps thousands. They moved slowly, drifting away from where our battle groups must be. A dark oozing mass flowed into Stanley, around

Stanley, some even making their way out towards the airport. And over it all, silence. The guns had stopped. Nothing, just the sound of the wind. So, this was what a broken army looked like, for we knew what it meant, what we were gazing upon. Even from that distance, we could see that they were done: a vast mass of spent men slowly departing.

No formal word came down to us, not until a few hours later, but we knew it was over.[3] No cheering, no back-slapping, no hand-shakes, no 'man-hugs', none of that, little talk even. We simply stood up in silence mainly, hushed, half-whispered conversations. Perhaps we too were emotionally spent; certainly tired from the night before. In broad day-light we stood on the sky-line taking simple pleasure in that itself: standing upright, peering down on Stanley and enjoying the weak, faintly-warming sunlight.

We had come a long way and we shared our moment of victory quietly, together, each deep in his own thoughts. I remembered my cigarette, lit it, Danny his too, half expecting Lawrence to join us, offering one of his Rolos.

[3] The CO confirmed 'ENDEX', as some wag coined it (END of EXercise, a word used to inform all participants that a training exercise had concluded), when he dropped in by Gazelle helicopter on his way to Stanley to help nego-tiate the surrender. We gave him a Union Jack to fly over Government House, his destination. This held an elegant symmetry for it was a D Squadron Union Jack raised first at King Edward Point, South Georgia's administrative cen-tre at the start, and a D Squadron Union Jack raised first over the principal symbol of our sovereignty in the Falklands at the end.

Epilogue

So It Was Done

Port Howard cemetery lies a mile or more outside the settlement. Sheltered from the wind by the surrounding hills and the thick gorse hedges nearby, it sits on a small promontory with views down a narrow inlet. The sea lies a short distance away, behind a small headland, through a narrow passage. The cemetery is approached down an open, grassed track, running across fields cropped short by sheep. In summer the yellow-blossomed gorse gives off the gentle smell of warmed butter, host to nesting song birds.

Not now. It was mid-winter, and nothing much stirred. There was no sound, not even a gull; only the occasional soft brush of a breeze. But the light sparkled, pure, soft winter sunlight casting long shadows. The water in the bay below rippled from time to time.

John had been buried in the corner, nestled up against the bright, white picket fencing in a grave marked by a simple cross bearing his rank and name: Captain John Hamilton. The Argentinians had put him there with care and respect, recognising his valour. Now we came to say our goodbyes, to John and our other lost friends and comrades, all but John with no grave.

We weren't many. There had been only the one helicopter available to lift us across from San Carlos. The Commanding Officer had joined us, and one or two others, but mainly we comprised members of the two squadrons. All those remaining of his troop had come. They were few, their number sorely depleted, lost at sea as we had crossed that time from HMS *Hermes* the Flag Ship over to HMS *Intrepid* in preparation for the landings. Was it really only four weeks previously when so many of our company had perished, given up to the sea? Was it truly only a hundred days or so since we set off from Hereford, young, eager, our spirits so high?

RFA *Lancelot* had found us a padre. We gathered with him around the grave, with our thoughts, our memories, and our prayers. The CO asked whether we were to fire a volley in salute. We said no. We didn't want to disturb John's peace in that way, or that of the others, or the serenity of this place. We were done with all that, for now, until perhaps called upon again. We remembered. Then we left.

Appendix

Arms and Equipment

Equipment and its carriage had long been an issue in the Regiment, the view being we carried too much kit. We knew it, but seemed unable to do anything about it. One of my earliest regimental memories was of Peter de la Billière, my first SAS Commanding Officer, exhorting us to carry less; that had been back in 1973. It made not the slightest difference, in part because we were all able to carry prodigious loads. Selection ensured the Regiment was manned by those able to carry weight, night and day for extended periods, over considerable distances, across and through all manner of terrain. Even in the jungle we would carry a full bergen as well as belt-kit around our waist. None of us ever wanted to be found short. We were trained to go out front, far from any base, where re-supply could not be assured.

We might trim our food stocks, but never ammunition. We were determined not to run out of that. Ironically the solution lay with the bergen itself, the very thing that seemed to be causing the problem. We would carry a fighting load on the belt, principally ammunition, plus a few necessities for survival, water, food, medicine and such like: everything else went in the bergen. The bergen could be dropped in the event of contact with the enemy, or cached before an anticipated contact, this conferring a degree of agility. Nonetheless, we remained overloaded—but at least in those days we were spared the need to wear body armour!

During the Falkland conflict, I don't recall ever specifying the weapon-mix to be carried at troop-level, leaving this to commanders and their teams to judge, dependent upon their task. Most of us preferred 5.56 mm ammunition. Very much lighter than 7.62 mm, it might have less range, be less hard-hitting, but out to 300–400 metres it was good enough. One could carry a lot of 5.56 mm, and it went with the AR15/M16, a handy assault-rifle capable of automatic fire and notably accurate out to its battle-range. Generally we rated volume of fire over single-shot accuracy—not that the Army's standard issue 7.62 Self-Loading Rifle (SLR), with its single-shot function, was any more accurate out to 300 metres than our 5.56 assault weapons. It was simply that much heavier, and harder-hitting at the sharp end than its 5.56 counterpart. We did like the 7.62 General Purpose Machine Gun (GPMG or Jimpy), though. No full troop would venture out without two GPMGs as a minimum, valued for their weight of fire, hard-hitting and long range. Otherwise, grenades, pistols, bayonets, big knives were a matter of personal choice. I never bothered with a second weapon or grenades, preferring to carry extra chocolate.

Contrary to popular belief, we had few specialist weapons to draw upon. There was some 'demolition kit'—plastic explosive, time-pencils, fuses and detonators, not dissimilar to the stuff used by our founders back in the 1940s, or parachuted into the French resistance. Shortly before departing Hereford we had managed to get our hands on a few of the then thoroughly up-to-date MILAN anti-tank missiles. There were also the trusty 81 mm mortars, and later a few 60 mm mortars from our US Special Forces friends. The one exotic item, again coming later from the USA, was the Stinger anti-aircraft missile: eight of them. We enjoyed limited success, being unpractised in their use.

Certainly towards the end we must have appeared disorderly and ragged, many of us clothed in the cotton shirts and trousers we had used in Kenya, supplemented with items purchased in Hereford's farmers' shops and outdoor outlets: nylon fleeces, that kind of thing, most of it not altogether appropriate for maritime use, given its poor fire-retarding properties. Perhaps the sailors had picked up on this, for I noticed that a fair few of the Squadron had managed to get themselves one of those dashing white polo-neck sweaters, worn by the likes of Jack Hawkins in *The Cruel Sea*, WW2 submariners and survivors. It was not the sole, attractive item in the Navy's survivor-pack that 'Jack' had been handing out to the Squadron, the blue cotton shirt being another much-sought-after item, trousers too. After *Sheffield*, I asked Lawrence to get a grip of this mild form of 'proffing'. The Navy was likely to need their survivor packs for survivors and others in desperate need; we had more than enough white sweaters by then. Over top of all this we would wear the ample SAS smock, cotton, merely shower-proof, but nevertheless effective at cutting out the wind, particularly when the cloth became damp.

Across the Squadron there was a mix of footwear. Mountain Troop tended to have the best, their own purchased, then state-of-the-art boots. The rest of us made do with the Army's standard DMS (Directly Moulded Sole), rubber-soled boot, or, as in my case, the Northern Ireland patrol boot. Most of the Northern Ireland boots gave out under the damp, intensely-cold conditions, including mine that split across the bottom. As for the DMS boots, they would soak up water, the cheap leather serving as a sponge. Some of us got round the problem by wearing NBC galoshes, simple rubberised over-boots, probably the first and only time the item was appreciated and sought after.

Trench foot became an issue among the battalions. We fared better, enjoying the advantage of being based on the ships, where we could escape the weather from time to time, and feed up on four square navy meals.

Later in the war, new boots and an amount of Gore-Tex clothing turned up, including much sought-after quilted jackets. Bronco back in Hereford had managed to buy up Cotswold Camping's entire UK stock of olive-green, hollow-fill fibre jackets. Even then, we didn't have enough to go round. Graham issued them solely to those most likely to go ashore. If we had looked assorted before the Gore-Tex distribution, we must have looked positively composite afterwards. Our dress may have grated on some, but not on the Navy, who simply accepted us for what we were.

Tidy minds must have been in near melt-down as the conflict progressed, for once we all got ashore soldiers and marines alike became increasingly dishevelled, while more and more business-like in appearance and behaviour, the superfluous and all other flannel stripped away. It put me in mind of one of Training Wing's maxims, posted by the legendary 'Wing' Sergeant Major, Geordie Lillico, MM:

'Judge not a fighting dog by its coat, but by its teeth.'
Chinese proverb

Index

INDEX

INDEX